MW01013913

Unruly Masses

International Studies in Social History
General Editor: Marcel van der Linden,
International Institute of Social History, Amsterdam

UNRULY MASSES
The Other Side of Fin-de-Siècle Vienna

**Wolfgang Maderthaner
and Lutz Musner**

Berghahn Books
NEW YORK • OXFORD

Published in 2008 by
Berghahn Books
www.berghahnbooks.com

First published in Germany as *Anarchie der Vorstadt*, Campus Verlag
©1999 Campus Verlag

English Language translation ©Wolfgang Maderthaner and Lutz Musner
Translated into English by David Fernbach and Michael Huffmaster
The English translation has been made possible by financial contributions
from MA 7 – Kulturabteilung der Stadt Wien and
BMWF – Bundesministerium für Wissenschaft und Forschung

Library of Congress Cataloging-in-Publication Data
Maderthaner, Wolfgang.
Unruly masses : the other side of fin-de-siècle Vienna / Wolfgang
Maderthaner and Lutz Musner. -- 1st ed.
    p. cm. -- (International studies in social history ; v. 13)
Includes bibliographical references and index.
ISBN 978-1-84545-345-9 (hardback : alk. paper) -- ISBN 978-1-84545-
446-3 (pbk. : alk. paper)
    1. Vienna (Austria)--Social conditions--19th century. 2. Mass society. 3.
Social structure--Austria--Vienna--History--19th century. 4. City and town
life--Austria--Vienna--History--19th century. I. Musner, Lutz. II. Title.

DB854.M24 2008
943.6'130441--dc22

2008014701

British Library Cataloguing in Publication Data
A catalogue record for this book is available from the British Library

Printed in the United States on acid-free paper.

ISBN: 978-1-84545-345-9 (hardback)

CONTENTS

LIST OF FIGURES

ACKNOWLEDGEMENTS

This book is indebted to a number of well-known cultural scholars for their valuable criticism, references, suggestions, and proposals. We would particularly like to mention here Helmut Gruber (New York Polytechnic) and Anson Rabinbach (Princeton University), who read the first drafts and contributed greatly to the final version by their suggestions and critical indications. The same goes for Dan Diner (Universities of Leipzig and Tel Aviv) and David Frisby (University of Glasgow), as well as Rolf Lindner and Horst Wenzel (both of the Humboldt University, Berlin), who were kind enough to read through the manuscript during their stay as guest scholars at the International Research Center for Cultural Sciences (IFK) in Vienna. Carl E. Schorske and Gotthart Wunberg, doyens of cultural-historical and literary-historical research into Viennese modernism, they helped the authors, with great empathy and constructive criticism, to recognize certain weaknesses in their work and to assess it in the context of international modernism research. We must similarly thank Peter Feldbauer (University of Vienna) and Ferdinand Opll (Vienna State and Provincial Archive), Aleida Assmann (University of Constance), and Christina Lutter (University of Vienna), who supported and facilitated our efforts by their constructive criticism.

The present cultural-historical study of the Viennese suburbs around 1900 is part of a wider research project into Viennese modernism, supported by the Federal Ministry for Science and Communications and conducted by the Association for the History of the Workers' Movement (VGA), in which Roman Horak and Siegried Mattl (both of the University of Vienna), Michaela Maier (Association for the History of the Workers' Movement), Gerhard Meißl (Vienna City and Provincial Archive), and Alfred Pfoser (Vienna City Library) are all involved. We thank them all not only for a congenial atmosphere of critical debate and for discussion going beyond departmental divisions, but above all for their deep friendship, which helped us successfully overcome difficult phases in our work. Nicole Dietrich decisively broadened the empirical basis of these essays by her archival and research work, and we are grateful to Claudia Mazanek for an extremely diligent and competent proofreading of the manuscript.

All the above gave us help and support in numerous ways. We remain solely responsible if not all of their suggestions have been heeded to the same extent in the final version.

Vienna, February 1999

CHAPTER 1

INTRODUCTION

Initially it was nothing more than a vague discontent, nothing more specific than that, really. Gradually, though, it found more pronounced expression in a countless number of debates, arguments, and controversies—and not just in the sober spaces of the academy, but in late-night discussions in cafés and suburban bars as well. The discontent was with a particular practice in the discourse on Viennese modernism, and with the way it had established itself in the mid 1980s and since become the dominant trend, serving to promote academic careers in its elite version while in its popularized version forming a basis for city marketing and tourism strategies. It started with Carl E. Schorske's masterpiece on turn-of-the-century Vienna's elite culture published in the early 1980s.[1] But instead of qualifying and supplementing Schorske's approach, which admitted the possibility of an "other" modernity, it became the tendency to ontologize the *fin de siècle* as the sum of its intellectual and artistic achievements and thus to stylize it as a treasure chest of the most precious objects of high culture. The world of the suburbs, the lives of immigrants, proletarians, and urban pariahs, remained virtually out of sight, similar to the way the literature of high Viennese modernism ignores them. Their particular connection with the center, a combination of economic integration and social and cultural exclusion, was never discussed in the scholarly literature on the period. If the suburbs were mentioned at all, it was either as a place of deviance, disorder, poverty, and immorality, or as the terrain where the Red Vienna movement of the inter-war years had its utopian beginnings (as the suburbs were indeed to provide the broad social basis for the movement's municipal and political achievements).

At the same time, the suburbs were always present as a topic of popular discourse on Vienna and the Viennese "essence." They were present in classical Viennese song and especially in a canon of legends and myths that were largely orally transmitted. These spoke of the great hunger revolts; of an uninhibited zest for life governed by the pleasure principle, even in a context of extreme poverty; of gangs of youth that were both feared and admired; of major gangsters and petty crooks who posed as social rebels and who found considerable support among the suburban population; of laundress balls and rag balls; of so-called "broken-glass dances" in sordid dives and bars; and of territories of insubordination that turned the order of the center into chaos and that could not be brought to heel by any government of any political stripe.

Seeking the traces of these popular myths on the ground, the authors took an extended walk in August of 1997 through the Neulerchenfeld quarter of Ottakring, still a proletarian district today as it was at the turn of the century, and also still an area of immigration and unrestricted rack-renting. Though we ourselves moved to Vienna from the Austrian provinces and are familiar with various aspects of suburban life, one thing that first became clear to us on that hot summer day when the city seemed quite deserted was that social misery here has always been concealed behind a façade of impressive beauty evidently designed to suggest a homogeneous urban landscape modeled on the classicizing architecture of the Ringstraße. The tenement blocks of Ottakringerstraße, Thaliastraße, Koppstraße, and Herbststraße judged from their outward appearance are really splendid buildings, in many cases hardly inferior to the celebrated mansions of the Ringstraße. In their outward appearance they present not so much a contrast to the center as its symbolic continuation, and thus they disguise the division of social space that is so characteristic of the city. For Vienna's topography follows a concentric model in which inner and outer suburbs are grouped around the center in a social gradient. The boundaries, however, are established less by architectural and aesthetic differences than by the social marking of urban terrain. It is not simply the material form of the city that localizes the different social groupings and classes, but rather forms of cultural practice that establish both the different perceptions and uses of the urban terrain and the degree of communication or separation. The external illusion of a homogeneous urban landscape, however, merely serves to highlight the politics of identity and social differentiation throughout the city.

With these considerations in mind, it seemed appropriate to approach the topic of "Vienna around 1900" from its margins and to ask whether the city could be read in this sense as a social text.

Robert Musil begins *The Man Without Qualities* in a surprising way. A detailed meteorological description of a fine day in August 1913 in the capital of Kakania situates Central Europe in a political and atmospheric metaphor between the Atlantic and Tsarist climatic zones. This "meteorological" perspective implicitly thematizes the revolutionary technological leap of World War I, echoing its innovations in aircraft and telecommunications, thus making these into descriptive parameters of the city via a screen of stereoscopic three-dimensionality. From this general perspective Musil jumps directly to a depiction of urban life that makes Vienna the object of a new form of urban textuality.[2] Automobiles race through narrow streets; their movements condense into linear patterns, which then dissolve again in other spaces. Sounds combine into profiles of noise that articulate the city's melody,

from which in turn clear notes break forth and fly off like fragments of stone.
And the entire mix of acceleration and inertia, of noises, sounds, and sound
sequence, combines into a pattern that allegedly makes it easy for the observer
to recognize the "Royal and Imperial" capital, even "after years of absence
[and] with closed eyes."

What Musil undertakes here is evidently an attempt not just to make the
physiognomy of a *fin de siècle* metropolis an object of literature, but rather to
decipher urban life in its entirety as emblematic of modernity. Mobility and
acceleration express for him a city's "total" identity, by which it is more clearly
recognizable than by any one particular characteristic, no matter how
significant.

For many of Musil's contemporaries, the city had become the favored
metaphor for modernity. Yet it was Musil who first transcribed the city as a
social text, suggesting an approach that proves useful for our present
investigation. As the following quotation illustrates, such an approach
involves the conflation of symbolic sphere and material urban form, the
linearities and contingencies of the social, the acceleration and stagnation of
forms of life, and the reification of social relations and social references into
specific forms of urbanity:

> Like all big cities it was made up of irregularity, change, forward spurts, failures to
> keep step, collisions of objects and interests, punctuated by unfathomable silences;
> made up of pathways and untrodden ways, of one great rhythmic beat as well as the
> chronic discord and mutual displacement of all its contending rhythms. All in all,
> it was like a boiling bubble inside a pot made of the durable stuff of buildings, laws,
> regulations, and historical traditions.[3]

What enabled Musil to choose this approach and analytical perspective? What
new signatures had modernity inscribed on the body of the city? How had
human perceptions and values changed so that the metropolis could appear as
a social, that is, socially legible, text?

One might assume that the perception of the city as social text was the
consequence of a new form of hegemony that established the primacy of
writing over the inherited oral cultures of pre-modern urbanism. We aim to
demonstrate, however, that the causes and interactions are considerably more
complex than this.

We shall argue, based on the Viennese example, that discourses and texts
as a project of the symbolic representation of the city are constitutive of the
liberal, bourgeois era. This project creates not only a dynamic and fluctuating
relationship of center and periphery, placing elite culture in tension with the
popular cultures of the suburbs; it simultaneously creates new forms of social,
cultural, and economic inequality and division that segment the city while also
amalgamating it into broken relations of exchange characterized by
domination. The tense and conflict-laden interaction between division and
homogenization introduces a social dynamic that is characteristic of the
formation of early forms of mass culture. For the distance between the
popular and the elite that is transmitted via the historical memory of the

1. The Favoriten Street car line around 1900. Source: Historisches Museum der Stadt Wien.

lower classes, the attendant oppositional nature of suburban life, and the continuing existence and metamorphosis of contemporary subcultures perforate the politics of order articulated by the bourgeois representation of the city. They produce countermovements. They evade the comprehensive establishment of the center's hegemony. The subcultures as the "other" of the bourgeois representation of the city remain present, in their contingency and diffuseness, as dissonant voices in the public space. It is their ambiguity, their apparently undisciplined and "savage" nature, their existence as the antithesis of progress and civilization, that make them appear in the bourgeois view as raw, crude, and indeed amorphous. This view allows them neither a noteworthy origin nor a rational future; they are therefore without history. Yet this lack of history does not mean merely impotence and unconditional subjugation, but rather also represents a barrier that continually removes from them their entire symbolic subordination and "inner colonial" domination. They can be decoded as a puzzle of modernity and of the modern city—in other words as a modernity that leaves no trace.

Although this "other" is described in elite discourse as formless and amorphous and is marginalized by being attributed threatening "facts" arousing both political and sexual anxiety, it continues to exist as social difference. It manifests itself in everyday culture, in the beer halls and bars, in places of popular entertainment such as the Prater and the Neulerchenfeld in Ottakring, and in the music halls and vaudeville shows. It is also expressed in the urban no man's land of petty crime, youth gangs, and prostitution—a no man's land that cannot be simply described in terms of social and cultural deviance, but that is also part of a wider spectrum of the world of the suburb. This spectrum combines wretched living conditions with strategies of material and moral survival; it includes industrially disciplined work as well as episodic everyday escape, petty criminality dressed up as social rebellion, and politically articulated insubordination.

The segmentation of the urban terrain by the social thus symbolically determines the difference of domination and dependence, and in many respects also the topographic difference of center and periphery. The suburb takes shape first of all in the mind before it is realized as a material configuration. Such a dynamic concept of the suburb defines things differently according to context and analytical perspective—actual places with different histories (old and new suburbs), zones of social and cultural segregation, areas marginalized in relation to the center, and imagined territories of the Other. In Georg Simmel's words, therefore, we understand the limits that separate urban territories from one another not as "a spatial fact with sociological effects," but as "a sociological reality that takes spatial form."[4] The tensions between high and popular culture, between hegemony and social difference, between the prescribed identity of the "masses" and their "anarchic" insubordination—tensions that are inscribed in the city as a whole—are the key themes of this work. It is an attempt to read the city as the text of a social reality.

On September 17, 1911, the proletarian quarter of Ottakring rose up in a hunger revolt. What was at issue, however, was not simply malnutrition and lack of food; rather, the revolt represented the first broad rebellion of the marginalized suburban masses. These were composed not only of those urban lower classes that had "always been there"; they were above all the large number of recently arrived immigrants whose desires for a better life in the city were threatened by the new realities of work, consumption, and reproduction. They had left behind their cultures of origin, which were generally oral and informal and mostly rural and pre-modern, to develop new perspectives of life in the metropolis. They sought both a specific place and a new home in an urban topography that was increasingly given a new configuration, linear and fragmented, by technology, science, and rational planning. Forced onto the margins, they were unable to establish a new home territory, but found themselves in a state of subjective impoverishment and both individual and collective alienation. Their displacement into the industrial planned grids of modernity not only inscribed a perceptible panorama of misery onto their bodies, but also prescribed and abstracted their existence as the dark, dangerous, amorphous, and "other" side of the urban order. Their existence, symbolically marked by difference and trauma, allowed no more than a minimum of freedom and self-recognition. It developed along vectors of power, impotence, and dissent; of adaptation, indifference, and deviance; and of lethargy, rebellion, and emerging mass politics.

In what follows we seek to broaden, qualify, and correct the image of Vienna at the turn of the century that has previously been portrayed in studies of modernism, principally one of high culture and the elites. The point is to understand the suburbs not simply as an annex but rather as something internal to modernity. We take them as a field in which popular culture is articulated on the one hand as a medium of exchange and of the negotiation of narratives of progress and rationalization, and on the other as sociocultural strategies of survival and self-assertion. They thus decisively contribute to determining the so-called leading cultures of the center. We consequently reject the assumption of a monocausal relation of determination between center and periphery, and instead highlight how the two reciprocally limit, influence, and constitute each another, leading to changes in their characteristics and symptoms. In this perspective, the historical texture of Vienna at the turn of the century is not structured and determined simply by a clearly defined center. This texture should be seen rather as a patchwork in which power and impotence, politics and culture, the popular and the elite, are woven into a pattern that lends *fin de siècle* Vienna its specificity and singularity.

CHAPTER 2

ANARCHY IN OTTAKRING

For the first time since that October day of 1848 when Windischgrätz's troops reconquered the imperial capital, the army fired on the people of Vienna. Something that had not happened even during the most violent storms of the struggle for universal suffrage, occurred in Vienna on September 17. There were whole quarters of the city where not a house, not a window, not a lamppost remained unscathed. In the proletarian quarter of Ottakring, school buildings and streetcars were set ablaze. Barricades were constructed, the troops fired on the people, and behind the frenzied crowd the lumpenproletariat plundered shops.

This is how Otto Bauer—secretary of the Social Democrats in Parliament, outstanding representative of the young Austro-Marxist theoreticians who haunted the Café Central, and later first lieutenant in the royal and imperial army decorated several times for bravery[5]—opened his comprehensive critique of the events of September 17, 1911, which was published in the theoretical organ of the German Social Democrats.[6] It was the "global calamity" of inflation, intensified in Austria by a series of particular circumstances, that had driven the mass of Viennese working people to "desperation" and inflamed an "ordinary street demonstration" into the (apparently) "aimless revolt" of the suburbs.

Otto Bauer explained this uprising of Vienna's suburban proletariat, which ran counter to the political strategy and intention of the Social Democratic elites of the time in every respect, in terms of a wide-ranging theoretical assessment of social development under the late Habsburg monarchy. The superficial economic prosperity of the years around 1910 had done nothing to change the fact that in relation to the industrialized countries of Western and Central Europe, there was a lower wage level in Austria but a higher level of prices. The entire national economy suffered as much from the most recent phenomena of capitalist organization (trusts and syndicates) as it did from a general backwardness. Guild legislation had long held back the expansion of industry and wholesale trade while limiting the market in more or less every branch of production to a small number of enterprises combined in cartels and thus deliberately promoting the formation of private monopolies. At the same time, qualification tests and compulsory trade associations permitted even smaller companies to fix prices as they saw fit. Agriculture and animal husbandry stagnated. Though nearly half the population was still employed in this sector, the greater part of foodstuff needs had to be met by imports from other countries, such as the German Empire, where only 30 percent of the population still worked in agriculture and forestry. Neither the Alpine provinces nor the eastern territories of Austria were in a position to guarantee the food supply needed by the cities and industrial zones, while Hungarian agriculture (the main "natural" resource import) suffered from the same dramatic failures as did Galician.

The establishment of the dual monarchy in 1867 had created a single economic zone, but the territory was ruled by two states, two governments, and two parliaments; all economic legislation was thus dependent on interstate treaties and subject to international law. The contradiction that Austria and Hungary were legally sovereign states, but economically and militarily a common state and a common market, turned disputes over economic policy into legal battles over the interpretation of international treaties. The Hungarian government, as the executive of the great Magyar landlords, had put through, in combination with the Austrian landed proprietors, a complex system of agricultural protection and import restrictions. This system found new legal expression in the customs tariff of 1906, a compromise between industrial and finance capital, on the one hand, and landed property and the large agriculturalists, on the other.

At a point in time when the structural and technological backwardness of Austrian and Hungarian agriculture meant that foodstuffs had increasingly to be imported from abroad, the rising world market prices were driven further upwards by import duties and quotas. In this context, the entire urban population felt the effects of inflation on living standards, despite a relatively favorable economic conjuncture in the first decade of the new century. The *Arbeiter-Zeitung* summed up the situation as follows:

> Inflation has cut the purchasing power of money by at least one-third. The worker feels simply cheated on his payday ... Previously he was just about able to rent for his family one room and a kitchen; today he has to share this cramped accommodation with two lodgers. Previously he could eat a piece of beef three times a week; today he can only afford this luxury once a week. Previously he had a few pence left over for a Sunday excursion, a glass of beer, and some cigarettes; now he has to give up all this if he is to feed his children adequately.[7]

In a rare instance of agreement, an editorial in the *Neue Freie Presse* showed how much the persistent inflation had become a problem for more than just one social class:

> The widest sections of the population suffer from the horrific inflation. The middle class groans under the continuing general upward movement of prices no less severely than the working class. Most families find their budget in disarray, as they

have to pay high prices for the most indispensable provisions, such as meat, flour, milk, eggs, and oil, and have nothing left over for the unreasonably high costs of rent. The social question was once defined as a knife-and-fork question, and the inflation that is now hitting Austria harder than any other country is the most serious social problem the state currently faces ... Not the least reason for the economic hardship the population is suffering is that Austria has forgotten to pursue a generous consumption policy.[8]

In Vienna, the problem of inflated food prices was further sharpened by a dramatic development in the housing market. Bad housing conditions, high rents, and a pressing shortage of accommodation were the result of speculation in land and building, even in building materials. On top of this, government and local taxes (the Vienna municipality drew some two-thirds of its general income from the tax on housing) led to a near cessation of construction on housing for workers. As early as 1907, while the economic conjuncture was still favorable, a serious downward trend in the construction industry had already been noted. By 1910 the annual increase in housing had fallen to its lowest level since the early 1890s, while in the outlying districts new building was down by as much as a quarter from its previous peak. Linked with this, the number of empty dwellings in the workers' districts rose to a spectacular degree. Hernals, Ottakring, Fünfhaus, Rudolfsheim, and Simmering had only minimal housing reserves by 1910, Meidling and Favoriten virtually none at all.[9]

In these circumstances, rents could often be dictated almost independently of market mechanisms, and an ever greater number of suburban residents had to be satisfied with dwellings of the worst quality at massively overvalued prices. "To keep a tenancy in this situation, it was necessary at times to vegetate even below the subsistence minimum."[10] The small apartments that were urgently needed, but that came onto the market only in small numbers and at exorbitant rents in the outlying districts, were often unobtainable. Otto Bauer sums up the situation concisely: "We have worse popular housing, higher rents, and an acuter housing shortage than any other European metropolis. Thousands of people in Vienna can no longer find accommodation."[11] This statement, however, bears the mark of its origin in political agitation; for, even in the Habsburg Empire, it is clear from the evidence available that the living standards and housing situation of the broad urban masses in Prague and Budapest were significantly below the Viennese level.[12] Yet Bauer's propagandist assertion certainly reflected the state of mind of the suburban population of Vienna at the time.

The tense situation in the housing market, coupled with rampant inflation in food prices, created by summer 1911 symptoms of extraordinary unrest among the suburban population. The food market at Simmering, for example, could continue in business only under the protection of a large police contingent, while the tenement quarters saw regular spontaneous demonstrations against landlords or their agents. On the evening of September 9, as on the two preceding days, several hundred persons gathered outside a tenement block in Meidling to protest against the rise in rents and the agents entrusted with collecting these. With effective support from neighboring blocks, the crowd grew rapidly in a short space of time and attacked intervening policemen with showers of stones, going on to break a number of windowpanes and street lamps. A patrol of three policemen arrested a young stone-thrower, leading to an angry exchange of blows with some of the demonstrators who tried to free the prisoner, in the course of which one of the policemen suffered serious knife injuries. Since, in the words of the police report, the patrol's situation had become "very threatened," one of the policemen fired several warning shots as a way of summoning support from the nearby station, and by about ten o'clock it was possible "finally to disperse the mob on the street." His Imperial Majesty was moved to pencil in the following comment regarding these incidents on his daily report: "It is about time to put an end to these repeated street excesses."[13]

By this time, however, it was already the common experience of large sections of the Viennese working class that organized protest and demonstrations had an effect on political life. When the feudal-clerical government of Count Taaffee lost its majority in 1893 with the growth of petit-bourgeois nationalist radicalism, and the parliament of the privileged classes could no longer guarantee a viable government majority, Count Badeni introduced an electoral reform designed to introduce a fifth curia with universal male suffrage. This was based on the subtle calculation that the fear of proletarian representation in parliament would lead to a unification of the German and Czech middle classes. To the working masses, however, the extension of the franchise inevitably appeared to be a direct result of their street demonstrations. A similar chain of events followed in 1905, in the wake of major debates over the introduction of universal male suffrage. In order to intimidate the rebellious Hungarian magnates, the crown announced a program of universal suffrage in Hungary, while news of the outbreak of revolution in Russia together with the great demonstration of the Viennese workers on the Ringstraße lent new weight to the arguments of the street, leading to the electoral reform of 1906. On October 2, 1910, another large demonstration raised the demand for meat to be released to the open market. And indeed, after withdrawing from its trade agreement with Serbia as punishment for the country's stubbornness in the annexation crisis, and with the collapse in the supply of Romanian cattle on account of the customs war, the government decided on the import of cheap meat from Argentina. Once again, a street demonstration had shown a direct, positive result, and sections of the organized working class began to display a vague belief in the omnipotence of public demonstrations.

The government, however, had to renege on its promise a few months later, following pressure from Hungarian landowners and Austrian farmers, and reimpose the barrier on Argentine meat. Voices were immediately raised calling for more major demonstrations; it was the masses themselves, according to Otto Bauer, who were accomplishing their will in the Social Democratic rank-and-file organizations.[14] A further factor here was that the Social Democrats were in no position to fulfill the overly optimistic expectations that were placed on their presence and work in the "people's parliament." The traditional division of labor between economic and political forms of struggle stagnated, and the reciprocal paralysis of the ruling forces prevented the formation of any alliances to implement its main political, social, and economic demands. The Social Democrats were left to their own devices, resorting to defending collective agreements that had been achieved, to struggles against the wave of housing evictions or to compromises to maintain the viability of the parliament. Stagnation and defensiveness made them resort to their traditional instrument of street politics.

In the context of a series of protest meetings, the Vienna Social Democrats organized a street demonstration for September 17, 1911. The mood in the city was extremely tense, and the tone of the speeches unusually sharp. The parliamentary reperesentative Franz Schuhmeier, for example, declared that the prime minister could hear the windows rattle and the cries of desperation from the street if only he cared to do so. For Max Winter, city reporter for the *Arbeiter-Zeitung*, it was high time to let the street speak once again and proclaim the will of the people. In such desperate circumstances, party secretary Leopold Winarsky noted, the people had no one to rely on, and the women's affairs representative Gabriele Profit proclaimed that those who "starved the people" would soon hear their cry of distress, the cries of mothers in despair.[15] The incidents that followed a popular meeting in Favoriten provided a foretaste of the events of September 17. After the meeting adjourned, some 4,000 participants returned through the streets of the district "amidst demonstrative shouts and song," reaching the workers' quarters around eight in the evening. As larger groups took their way home toward the outskirts of town through Laxenburgerstraße, new demonstrations broke out on the Arthaberplatz, which were then joined by the "mob and street rabble." The windows of two bakers' shops and an inn were broken, the bakeries plundered, and a police detachment stoned. The police "were forced to disperse the growing crowd of 2,000 persons by firing blanks," and were finally only able "to restore order" after a quarter of an hour.[16]

Although this remained an isolated incident, the recently appointed governor and former Prime Minister Baron von Bienerth felt compelled to make comprehensive security provisions, particularly in light of the fact that the Social Democratic party leadership, contrary to its usual practice, had failed to hire security forces for September 17 and neglected to lay down any obligatory route for the march. The whole inner city, along with key points in its surroundings, was occupied by the military. In the early hours of the morning the police authorities had summoned all their officials, doctors, agents, and guards, as well as special security forces, in addition to which there was a military force of six battalions and sixteen squadrons. Key points in the inner city were manned by nine squadrons, together with 2,000 foot and 240 mounted guards, 135 police officers, and a corresponding number of temporary personnel with the aim of safeguarding the court, the ministries, and other threatened public targets. The security forces were positioned in such a way that "appropriately strong contingents and reserves were deployed at threatened points. Thus 600 foot and 120 mounted agents were posted at the station on Landhausgasse and on Michaelerplatz, in order to prevent any demonstration in front of the Hofburg, the ministerial council, or the governor's office; other points in the inner city and the outer districts were occupied in a similar way."[17]

In the course of the morning, moreover, a division of uhlans, hussars, and dragoons, several battalions of Hungarian infantry, a battalion of Bosnian infantry, and Deutschmeister guards were posted in the inner city and along the Ring. And, though the cavalry were initially cheered by the crowd, and there were scenes of open fraternization with the Deutschmeister,[18] the massive contingent of Bosnian and Hungarian infantry was increasingly taken as a symbolic provocation. The *Arbeiter-Zeitung* spoke of a "counter-demonstration of all the terror the state had at its disposal" and a "symbolic demonstration of war by the ruling powers":[19]

> The first soldiers' helmets were seen at the Maria Theresia monument, and the hussars were met with a cry of furious indignation. The next encampment was established on the Schmerlingplatz, and further ahead in the side streets near the Hofburg the war colors of dragoons and hussars could be seen. Between the military and the demonstrators was a chain of foot and mounted police. Almost every officer was accompanied by a police agent as well as several plainclothes men with their bicycles, who did messenger service. The parliament building was guarded only by policemen, who stood shoulder to shoulder from one end of the ramp to the other.[20]

Starting in the early morning, a crowd of 100,000 had paraded from their assembly points in the outlying districts to the Rathausplatz and to the front of the parliament, including tramway workers and post and telegraph employees in their uniforms. At five different places, each of the Social Democratic parliamentary representatives for Vienna addressed the demonstrators. Red flags, signs, and banners with slogans such as "Down with meat speculators" and "Open the borders" were hung from lampposts around the Rathaus and elsewhere. Toward eleven o'clock, the demonstration was over, and the bulk of the demonstrators began their march back to the suburbs.

The local groups from Landstraße and Simmering attempted to penetrate the inner city. Through Teinfaltstraße, which had been left open by the police, a dense crowd made its way toward the Freyung, "singing and shouting passionately." At the entry to the Heidenschuss they found themselves

2. The September upheavals of 1911. Source: Verein für Geschichte der Arbeiterbewegung Wien.

confronting a double police cordon, behind which cavalry had taken up position at the Ministry of War. By a magical magnetism, the crowd moved toward the police line; they came to a halt, "shouting and swinging their sticks in frightening fashion," and then "the incited elements stormed the cordon." The police then hastily improvised a tribune from which various Social Democratic representatives called on the crowd to desist, but "with only partial success." Time and again the demonstrators pressed against the police barricade, until the Social Democratic national party secretary Julius Deutsch prevailed on the commander to withdraw his troops. At this moment the tension noticeably relaxed, almost immediately calm set in, and the bulk of demonstrators left the Freyung in a surprisingly short time while the police pressed the rest back down Tiefer Graben without significant resistance.[21]

At this point, around midday, there were still a few thousand demonstrators on the Rathausplatz, "a tremendous crowd with no aim or plan moving back and forth between the many police and military barriers" composed overwhelmingly of "those irresponsible youth who do not obey any instruction and who form a body of hangers-on at every demonstration, unwilling to leave partly out of curiosity, partly out of overenthusiasm."[22] A police report came to the conclusion that these young demonstrators consisted of a disproportionate number of adolescents from Ottakring, and that this district was evidently the "breeding ground of excess."[23] Toward midday, the police, who had thus far exercised great self-control and tactical sense, began to clear the Rathausplatz. The crowd of 4,000 to 5,000, simultaneously restrained and incited by the demonstrative and ostentatious intervention of the military, suffered the first attacks and manhunts, which went as far as the Kärntnerring.

3. September 1911. Disturbances in the Rathaus quarter. Source: Verein für Geschichte der Arbeiterbewegung Wien.

A chance event unleashed the crowd's anger, which could no longer be kept in check; an outbreak of rage led to outright street battles. Somewhere in the crowd a youth fired a revolver into the air, and several firecrackers were also exploded. From a sizable group who were jeering in the Lichtenfelsgasse in front of the mayor's residence, the first stone was hurled against the Rathaus,[24] and this gave the signal for an all-out bombardment. Not a window remained unbroken on the first floor of the Rathaus. The police commissioner for the inner city then had the Lichtenfelsgasse evacuated by armed guards and summoned the military mounted detachment that was situated on Maria Theresien-Platz. The intervening force was met with a volley of beer mugs, stones, plates, and chairs hurled from a neighboring bar, sticks were thrown under horses' hooves, and benches were taken from the open space behind the Rathaus and laid across the street. While this was going on, the demonstrators who had been pushed into Rathausstraße began to break windows on the back side of the building. At the same time, the crowd that had been pressed back across the Ring and the Schmerlingplatz started bombarding the Justice Department buildings with stones, and the Kraft restaurant and the Café Bellaria were devastated.[25] When the Social Democratic representative Anton David hurried to the assistance of a police commissioner who was caught in a crowd, he himself was attacked by the enraged demonstrators. Another section of the crowd supported David, and a fierce exchange of blows followed.[26]

Although the police and military managed to clear the streets without resistance, the dispersed "leaderless and unrestrained bands" continued to regroup. After being pursued, they poured back again from the side streets, re-formed, and recommenced their action: "The cavalry then combed the streets of the Rathaus quarter, in file and by squadron, driving the crowd before them. But the crowd was stubborn. They retreated from one place only to gather again at another. It happened repeatedly that as soon as the military had moved on, the cordon of security police was again broken."[27] Only after exhausting confrontations did the forces of order manage "to disperse the compact mass of troublemakers" and force them back to the districts of Neubau and Josefstadt.[28]

The storm now began to move out through Lerchenfelderstraße and Burggasse. Several dispersed groups joined up, breaking windows in businesses and shops and smashing gas lamps. They devastated the Café Brillantengrund, attacked the municipal office of the Eighth District and the buildings of the Royal Hungarian Guard, and they tried to storm the police station on Schottenfeldgasse, letting loose a hail of stones against the enraged policemen. Streetcars were attacked on Neubaugasse and Westbahnstraße. Not a single street lamp was unscathed along the whole of Lerchenfelderstraße, right up to the Gürtel, while shop display windows also fell victim to the seemingly pointless rage of the crowd so intensely incited by the continuing police attacks.[29] Looting soon began. The Hena Issaksohn glass shop and that of the Agentor works, both on Kaiserstraße, were stormed, with lamps, lighters, silverware, cigar boxes, and cutlery sets being stolen.[30]

By this time at the latest, the demonstrators had been joined by the "street mob," the "lumpenproletariat," the "disaffected youth of Ottakring," described by the *Arbeiter-Zeitung* as "those quite young and irresponsible people whom no one knew and no one had summoned,"[31] or, as the *Neue Freie Presse* put it, "those elements that join in every tumult," the "familiar flotsam of any metropolis."[32] They stormed ahead of the demonstrators proper, destroying street lamps and windows wherever they could. A dozen or so lads fourteen or fifteen years old suddenly appeared on Wimbergergasse coming from the Gürtel (in the opposite direction of the march), calmly breaking windows in about half of the buildings on the street as far up as the third story, "as if they were taking care of their daily business." As soon as the demonstrators approached, they vanished as quickly as they had appeared.

Burggasse and Lerchenfeldstraße served as safety valves, but the continued actions of the armed forces, together with the groups of demonstrators, who merged together again and attacked, escalated into a regular street rebellion. The battlefield was the grid-plan district known as "New Ottakring," which had been created in the 1890s following the latest American model of town planning. This quarter was bordered on its longer sides by Gablenzgasse, on the one hand, and Grundsteingasse and Friedrich Kaisergasse, on the other (a length of about 1.3 kilometers), and on its shorter sides by the Lerchenfelder Gürtel and the suburban railroad (about half a kilometer). Gablenzgasse defined the boundary as far as the Schmelz, an urban no man's land that formed the reservoir "from which the crowd of troublemakers drew its reserves."[33] At the intersection of the suburban railroad with Thaliastraße there was a tobacco factory, on Gablenzsgasse there were barracks, and around Hofferplatz and Habsburgplatz (now called Schuhmeierplatz) there were a number of school buildings.

As quickly as possible the police precinct in Ottakring dispatched all its available manpower, securing strategic targets such as the municipal district office and the tax office, the tobacco factory, the suburban railroad station and goods yard, the railroad works, etc. On the Gürtel and on Panikengasse, streetcars were overturned and set on fire, while at the crossroads of Thaliastraße and Lerchenfelder Gürtel the first barricade was constructed from the fencing of a road works project and other available materials. Along the whole of Thaliastraße, barbed wire was hung from one street lamp to the next, while street benches and gas pipes were made into additional barricades. The demolition of street lamps continued uninterrupted.

The impressive military backup that arrived occupied the tobacco factory first of all, fearing an attack on it; subsequently the main roads were blockaded. Wherever the military were seen, they were met with deafening cries, "stones and bits of metal were hurled at them, and they were attacked with sticks."[34] Attempts to clear the streets by firing blanks brought little success, as the demonstrators withdrew immediately only to form up again at other points, using their superior knowledge of the local terrain, while the commanding officers were completely ignorant of this part of the city, and each division of troops had to be accompanied by mounted police who knew the area.[35]

According to the Vienna police authorities, it was impossible to prevent the demolition of buildings and even arson, "since whole groups of troublemakers appeared first at one place, then another, all across the district, committing acts of violence everywhere and scattering again as soon as they caught sight of the police and military." On account of the leaderless and undisciplined masses and the danger this implied, "it was necessary to call up all available military forces in Vienna." Even so, it took "several hours" to put down the disturbances, due to the fact that "the criminal elements were effectively supported by sections of the local population in their violent resistance to state power, and were incited to continue their atrocities."[36] Stones, pieces of metal, beer glasses, and other objects rained down on the police and military from the tenement windows. The royal and imperial police chief Emil Frömmel, who had already led the intervention at the Freyung, was hit on the head by a flatiron and seriously injured.

The events aroused the entire district. The youthful rioters were joined by crowds of curious onlookers. Bunches of people hung out of windows, bars and coffeehouses were full to bursting, and the agitated people discussed the same theme over and over in countless variations. If "lumpenproletariat" and adolescents exploited a situation in which the police had lost control, the uprising was also marked by moments of passion in which "mass anger inflamed to the point of ecstasy" became the incitement to action:

> Just consider, a forest of bayonets pointing at the crowd, threatening at any moment a hail of deadly bullets. They were aware of this, they knew the fate they would meet if things really turned serious. They did not doubt that their bodies would cover the ground, they had to know that it was deadly serious to go up against the military. But their anger was boiling and driving them onward. In

4. Social protest on the brief day of anarchy.
Source: Verein für Geschichte der Arbeiterbewegung Wien.

contempt of danger and even of death, it pressed them forward with irresistible force, right into the forest of bayonets, though they knew that it was pointless, since an unarmed crowd can never prevail against armed force. A fabulous ecstatic courage forced them into the orbit of this unequal struggle. And this courage became a hard test for the soldiers themselves, since—we must admit—they would do anything to avoid being covered with the blood of unarmed people. Shots rang out. The first salvo echoed, and one might have expected this to have a sobering effect. Even in battle, a salvo at point-blank range has a remarkable effect on an attacking force. But, after only a few steps back, the crowd turned around and pressed forward again with irresistible force until another volley, again sadly taking its toll, forced them once more to retreat, but not to flee. Only a few paces away the crowd still confronted the military, not moving from the spot, hedged in by soldiers and officers.[37]

Around three in the afternoon the southwestern district, bordered by Thaliastraße, Kreitnergasse, and the Schmelz, was occupied by the military. Koppstraße was sealed off by Bosnians at Kreitnergasse and Klausgasse, who were showered with a hail of stones from the demonstrators, which had regrouped on the open square in front of the Heiliger-Geist church, at that time in the course of construction. The Bosnians advanced with bayonets drawn, the crowd "raged and shouted like crazy, unsparing with their stones,"[38] retreating to a wide undeveloped space on the western side of Klausgasse, close to the workers' quarters, where they regrouped again. When a first volley was heard from Koppstraße, fired over the heads of the demonstrators, the crowd broke out into "fearful shrieks and cries" and started once more to bombard the military with stones. The soldiers managed to arrest one stone-thrower, whom the officer Ernst Hofmann led away under the protection of four mounted police. In an angry struggle, the prisoner was freed by the demonstrators. When the crowd demanded that the policeman, already seriously injured by sticks and stones, be handed over to them, the commander of the Bosnian infantry company gave the order to fire.[39] Once again shots were fired over the heads of the crowd, and bullets struck the scaffolding around a building site up to a height of three stories. Three demonstrators were so seriously injured by ricochets that they subsequently died from their wounds; twenty-year-old Franz Joachimsthaler was hit in the stomach and died on the way to hospital. Meanwhile the military commenced a bayonet charge, and nineteen-year-old Otto Brötzenberger, who just happened to be passing by and tried to take refuge in the workers' quarters, was struck in the breast.

Although, as the police report noted, news of the use of weapons had spread rapidly through the district, "the troublemakers did not refrain from further damage."[40] At the Schmelz, the district heating plant and the Manner chocolate factory had already been attacked. The security authorities had not taken into account, however, that "schools would be a welcome target of devastation for the mob."[41] The daily press all agreed in speaking of a "boys' revolution," a "kids' battle," a "revolt of the Ottakring youth." The attacks were directed at the secondary school on Habsburgplatz, the vaccine facility in Possingerstraße, and the elementary schools on Hofferplatz and in

Koppstraße. It was the "children of the stone-strewn Schmelz," chiefly twelve-to fourteen-year-olds, together with a few older youths aged seventeen to eighteen, who rose up in a brief frenzy of destruction. Part of it was the thrill of a drama, a production with something new, big, and destructive about it, where they could be both the actors and the spectators. Alongside the street youth came women and mothers, who, as the *Arbeiter-Zeitung* complained, "found it hard to explain what was happening," and who, when "they should have been thinking clearly and responsibly," let themselves be carried away by the game of destruction and brought the lads stones in their skirts[42]—those lads who suddenly populated all the side streets and squares as if they had simply appeared out of nowhere,[43] and who, as soon as the military retreated, vanished as if on command. A school employee reported that he had several times heard slang[44] expressions such as "It's hotting up!"[45] Only on the Habsburgplatz did a battle between military and street youth rage until dark.

The school there had already been the target of constant attacks in the afternoon. A ripped-out bench served as a battering ram against the school gate. Catalogs, books, volumes, everything made of paper was destroyed, thrown into the street, and burned; finally the school building itself was set on fire, and the arriving fire brigade was obstructed in every way possible. Children's playthings were not spared, and some dumbbells from the gymnasium later found a new use as weapons.

The same picture of raging destruction presented itself on all sides—destruction of the monuments of a modernity experienced by the rebels almost exclusively as an instance of discipline and control. The elementary school buildings on Hofferplatz were stormed, the massive iron railings torn away, and hundreds of bars ripped off. They served both as weapons and as tools, and the bricks torn from the foundation were used as missiles. Here again, books, catalogs, forms, and notebooks were removed, torn into pieces, and thrown onto the street. A bonfire of paper was built and lit, "with the hellish noise of a gruesome concert." At the secondary school on Thalhaimergasse the chemistry lab and everything in it was completely destroyed and set on fire, as was the vaccination facility next to the secondary school on Possingergasse.

Not until around ten o'clock, when Ottakring lay entirely in darkness, were the police and military able to bring the situation under control:

> The headquarters of the armed force was set up on Hofferplatz. There were infantrymen, rifles heaped into pyramids, and a large number of cavalry. The intention was to build up a regular armed camp there under cover of darkness. Messengers hurried back and forth, mounted and foot patrols went out and returned, military commands resounded, and weapons clinked threateningly. Anyone going up Thaliastraße would come up against strong military cordons blocking the street at several points ... By side streets, which like Thaliastraße itself were veiled in darkness, it was still possible to reach the outer limits of the district ... Only a few groups of people could be seen, made up of curious bystanders. They were discussing the evening's events ... The military were now in complete control of the terrain.[46]

Thus the hot breath of anarchy abruptly came to an end on that long September day in 1911. The hunger revolt offers a ready example of how the accumulation of crises in the living situation of the suburban proletariat, together with the unfulfilled expectations of the Social Democrats—whose presence in the parliament since 1907 had apparently become irrelevant—could lead to an explosive uprising, which then rapidly burnt itself out. And yet this uprising represented more than what Otto Bauer so brilliantly analyzed in terms of economics and politics: its form and dynamics indicate something far beyond this.

Immediately following the tumult, the police noted certain peculiar occurrences that they could not comprehend and that thus confirmed their view of the riot as an act of senseless vandalism, the destruction of "completely innocent buildings." The storage boxes of a kiosk were dismantled, thrown onto the street, and broken open, and the postcards inside were torn up and scattered on the street. On Kaiserstraße and Lerchenfelderstraße stationery shops were attacked, their window panes smashed, and "various paper goods"—books and school supplies—torn from the shelves and left damaged or destroyed on the street.[47] When a police booth at a streetcar stop in Panikengasse was attacked and demolished, the demonstrators had already ripped down the metal timetable stand and broken up the entire installation; the destroyed telegraph was thrown onto the street like a trophy.[48] What according to the *Neue Freie Presse* were "almost grotesque mob demonstrations" directed against no fewer than ten schools in Ottakring indicates dimensions of the conflict that evidently went beyond the material character of more typical demonstrations and represented acts of particular social and cultural significance with specific symbolic content.

Obviously more than just the political economy of suburban poverty—food shortages and wretched living conditions—was expressed in these riots, and more than just a struggle for territorial control. What the police and the press diagnosed as their "grotesque" character indicates rather a cultural formation of difference, insubordination, and revolt, which eludes explanation in terms of political and economic conditions. The question must therefore be raised as to how such a cultural formation arises, what it brings to expression, what traditions it draws on, and how it both enters the discourse of power and at the same time remains removed from it.

The first question to present itself is that of the formation and differentiation of an urban modernity, for which the periphery of the city is in many respects an object of appropriation. This appropriation can be interpreted as an attempt to integrate, use, and exploit economically a particular territory with particular social configurations. The rationalization of this procedure—the exploitation of suburban "human capital" for surplus value—can only be achieved by a subtle and ever threatened balance between discipline and communication. The appropriation process develops in a field of power and conflict, of subjugation and revolt, and can signify a clash between different codes and symbolic systems.

Since the disciplinary power of modernization is not exercised exclusively or even fundamentally by the military and police apparatus, what takes place in this field of contention is a conflict between different attributions of meaning and significance. In the context of experienced urban life, the difference between town and suburb, between center and periphery, presents itself not only as economic and political, but also in symbolic and cultural terms as a struggle over the investment of the urban body with meanings and values. This process can be understood as an interplay of latent and manifest elements, of inertia and movement, of ostensible peace interrupted by sudden, apparently unmediated eruptions of violence. In this process, the center deploys the power of writing, in which the rationality and objectivity of modernity become an instrument of hegemony, against the traditional, oral culture of the suburb. The suburb's resistance is not simply confined to the territory of the street, that is, its own specific domain, but rather seeks to rupture the power and violence of modernity by attacking its public manifestations.

Articulated in this, in however vague, grotesque, obscure, or ambivalent a fashion, is an attack on the symbolic order of modernity. The destruction of writings and their apparatus seems to reveal not only a pleasure in destroying things in general, but rather a profound resentment toward the new social power that attends the inscription of the suburb. This inscription is not simply expressed in a superficial texture, in the form of advertisements and business signs, traffic signals, writings on buildings, and the distribution of various kinds of printed matter. It is rather a profound process of both the reification and abstraction of subjective and objective living conditions. It involves the newly emerging fields of social and health statistics, housing and work regulations, official certificates and documentation, police and military ordinances, health and death records, and the applied social sciences of criminal anthropology and criminology, which together seek to contain the existence of the suburban population scientifically while at the same time disciplining it.

In the course of urban modernization, the suburbs were re-formed and overlaid in writing. This process took the form not only of systematized regulation in work and education, or of advertisements for products of mass consumption that were becoming available; rather, the "suburb" in its totality was depicted as a world outside of bourgeois rationality and urban order. The precondition for this was the wide application of forms of knowledge derived from social statistics, medicine, epidemiology, evolutionary biology, and law enforcement, which first made modernity historically possible, bringing the social transformations of the nineteenth century into the iron structure of reason. These fields of knowledge produced an instrumental narrative designed to create the conditions for the "colonization" of the suburbs and their comprehensive ordering, when necessary deploying police and military means.

Writing and science thus became significant emblems of modernity, whose force the suburban population sought to escape through material and symbolic acts of destruction. The ostensible irrationality of their anger, the anarchy of their violence, expressed a logic that was foreign and incomprehensible to the ruling order. For the rebels, however, this violence most definitely had its own rationality, serving as both an outlet for aggression and a moment of liberation and freedom.

The question then arises as to how the symbolic force of modernity depicts, defines, and establishes the suburb as a territory and manifestation of the "other." Further, there is the question as to whether the suburb is simply the passive object of manipulation and transformation, or whether it does not also obstinately develop its own physiognomy and dynamic, thus undermining the ruling order and changing it. Can city and suburb, center and periphery, be understood only in terms of a linear polarity, or do not both need to be analyzed as elements of one and the same process of transformation? Are they not both historical formations and territories, intertwined and continually redefined by way of reciprocal perceptions, attributions, and investments of meaning? How is the city formed as an ensemble of different cultural processes, and how is the "suburb" established in this process as simultaneously a configuration of segregation and integration, of difference and identity? Do not questions of power and impotence, of self-determination and external determination ultimately present themselves in a radically different light from the standpoint of the periphery? And what are the lived experiences, the strategies of survival, and the challenges presented by change that endow suburban life with meaning?

If segregation and integration, cultural difference and identity, power and impotence all represent essential constitutive elements of the "suburb," the first question to tackle is that of its social manifestations. Where did the suburban population come from, what was their social composition, and what created their concrete living conditions? What did the topography and constructed form of the suburb look like? How did its social organization and everyday life function? To sum up, the question is one of a phenomenology of the suburban.

CHAPTER 3

ORAL COUNTRYSIDE, WRITTEN CITY

In the process of industrialization the suburb acquires a specific, dual character. It becomes a transitional space, the successive integration of the countryside into urban structures, a gray zone of diffuse passage from agrarian to urban culture, the negation of the countryside in the structure of the city. It is the simultaneous coexistence and interpenetration of industrial complexes and housing tenements, fields and construction sites, factory buildings and open land. The suburb, however, also denotes specific mentalities determined by an environment that indicates cultural transformation as well as rapid industrial development: rural and agrarian worlds and consciousnesses linked up with rapid processes of urbanization that reflect the transitional character of the suburb in general.[49]

While revolution in the city brought political freedom to the village, it also had the effect of subjugating the countryside to the new hegemony of industrial society. On March 13, 1848, Vienna revolted; by the third week of August there were armed confrontations between burghers and the urban proletariat. At this time of the greatest social ferment in the capital, the parliament passed the law abolishing serfdom. The revolt of the capital's proletariat thus paved the way for freedom for the peasants; counterrevolution and neoabsolutism could only liquidate the urban revolution by guaranteeing its achievements to the peasants. Through the abolition of hereditary subjugation, the peasants became citizens of the state and the free proprietors of their land. Forty years after the revolution, the last vestiges of serfdom were finally set aside, even as room was made for the reinforcement of new forms of dependence.

But, while the counterrevolutionary regime began, with massive administrative effort, to regulate strictly for the first time relations between state power and the village, and a considerable part of the old communal land was transferred into individual private ownership, certain forms of communal property, such as those of peasant communities, of neighborhoods, or of other collectives, continued to exist alongside. This created fundamental problems for the rural administration. The question of the usufruct and possession of the former agricultural communities remained largely unclarified at the turn of the century and, especially in the villages of southern and southwestern Bohemia, became the cause and object of profound social struggles. The reason lay in the conflict between the established peasants, who had formerly had a share in the communally owned land, and the members of the new political bodies seeking to restructure village communities, which since the liberal constitution of 1867 had traditionally been organized hierarchically, into egalitarian municipal structures.

Following the revolution, post-feudal forms of property came into being that were modified in the ensuing decades by far-reaching capitalist development. Liberalism brought the free disposition of peasant land, turning the individual holding into a commodity and leading to a dramatic increase in the price of land. An ever growing number of peasant households thus became dependent on mortgage borrowing. The economic depression that began with the Vienna stock market crash of 1873, and that was worsened by a series of bad harvests in 1872–76 and the increasing pressure on prices from cheap overseas grain, brought symptoms of agricultural crisis in all the Austrian crown lands, Bohemia in particular, which after 1879 led to the prolonged economic downturn of the 1880's and 1890's. If peasants had taken on heavy mortgages during the years of favorable economic conditions and organized their operations accordingly, their interest burdens now stood in an ever worsening relationship to profits, which were squeezed by supply crises, price pressures, and lower harvest yields. As Peter Heumos has shown in the case of Bohemia and Moravia, profits in some places were often so low that production costs for the next year could only be met by a further increase in mortgage borrowing.[50] The mobility of land introduced by liberal economics and its consequential increased division; the impoverishment of broad masses of the peasantry; the fragmentation of holdings and the small peasant economy to which this led; the social differentiation among the peasantry; the fall in prices of agricultural products, over-indebtedness, and the actual exhaustion of credit provision—all these proved to be key determining factors of a comprehensive crisis that was to destabilize the entire agricultural sphere for decades to come.

Combined as this was with the marked population growth that had begun in the 1860's, the result was a steadily rising flow of emigration, which reached a peak at the turn of the century and which above all affected the bottom strata of the peasantry and in some areas amounted to a veritable depopulation. The revolution of 1848 had made both people and landed property more mobile and led to a kind of agricultural *Gründerzeit,* which bore the seeds of later crises. This brief agricultural upswing, together with the new civil rights embedded in the liberal constitution, led to a demographic dynamic that coincided with the need for increased human capital arising from the proliferation of urban and industrial concentration. When the acute agricultural crisis developed in the early 1870's, the flow of migration, mediated and supported by new means of transportation and communication such as the telegraph, private postal service, and railroads, became a flood.

The escalation of the agricultural crisis further sharpened the dependence of agriculture on urban capital, thus bringing about a transition from self-contained domestic economy and self-sufficiency to market production and increasing dependence on the market. It is estimated for the 1850's that about one-third of Bohemian agricultural production was destined for the market, but by the beginning of the twentieth century the proportion had increased to two-thirds.[51] The steady long-term fall in prices for wheat, rye, and sugar beet affected the predominantly grain-producing regions in a drastic and dramatic fashion.

Karl Renner, who had grown up on the border between the German- and Czech-speaking lands and who was later to become Austria's chancellor and president, reflects upon this profound transformation by describing the destabilization and gradual destruction of the rural, agrarian realm as an interaction of agricultural crisis and large families, of usury and the "penetration of capital into the village." The increasing social differentiation of the village, the "proletarianization of a large section of its inhabitants," led to the reinforcement of social and cultural stratification to a degree previously unknown. The "relation between the peasant and his helpers" came to be completely "stripped of personal friendship and frequently acquired a quite hostile form." The old "honorary distinction of rank" was replaced by "the antagonism of two classes"[52] and the formerly "peaceful and friendly coexistence" was transformed into "an unpleasant and hateful antagonism."[53] If in the middle of the century the key criteria in the choice of marriage partners had been "ability and especially industriousness," and children had been seen "not as heirs but as labor power," the few wealthier farmers now resisted fiercely any "connection with poorer or even second-rank families," leading to "lifelong and bitter enmity between the households affected."[54]

This rupture in the reproduction of peasant cultures, with the powerful and complementary processes of market orientation and market dependency, of industrialization and capitalization, and of the expansion and intensification of communications, revolutionized the division of labor in the peasant household and subjected the entire rural and agricultural sphere to a profound sociocultural transformation. The village proletariat, village poverty, and the rural "surplus population" became the main reservoir for a colossal flow of migration within the Habsburg territories, which supplied the monarchy's few industrialized enclaves, above all its rapidly expanding and booming capital, Vienna. In sum, the modern city dominated, restructured, formed, and re-formed the countryside according to its own logic and needs, and the countryside thus transformed and given its new functional designation fed masses of cheap labor power into the city.

Migrants from various ethnic groups and cultures arrived from all the different crown lands of the monarchy. The overwhelming majority, however, hailed either from the scarcely industrialized regions of southern Bohemia and southern Moravia, in other words the immediate agricultural hinterland of the imperial capital, or from zones where, as a result of the agricultural crisis, farming could only be continued as a sideline.[55] They represented, in Otto Bauer's words, both the highest type of agricultural domestic migration and the lowest type of industrial capitalist migration.[56] They arrived as unskilled or semiskilled labor power for industry, commerce, and domestic service, and they adapted themselves to the functional differentiation of particular districts of the city, settling in the industrial workers' suburbs and thereby strengthening and reinforcing a segregation of social space that had already begun in the *Gründerzeit*.[57] This pattern, however, requires qualification with respect to female migration. Lacking any professional skills, women migrants in the big city could scarcely find any work except in private households, and to a small degree in jobs akin to housework outside the home. By 1890 Vienna had more than 86,000 female domestic servants, and in 1910 just over 99,000, composing 34 percent and 27 percent respectively of all female employment.[58]

In principle this migration meant urbanization and proletarianization and a challenge to traditional forms of work, housing, food, and clothing. But the migrants also brought with them into the urban context their time-honored rural and agrarian forms of life and thought, which were then adapted, modified, and transformed.[59] Czech immigration to Vienna had had a long tradition, and, especially as these migrants were almost all Catholic, it had been marked by a steady ethnic and cultural assimilation, a surprisingly rapid adaptation to the urban environment, which was noted even then by contemporary observers. Not until around 1900, with the arrival of large numbers of skilled industrial workers with a strong national identity and specific cultural interests, did a Czech community with its own associations, newspapers, and bookstores begin to develop. The social and cultural consolidation of the Czech minority acquired a political dimension; the struggle to establish public schools, for example, could involve Czechs from all social strata. In the same way, the nationalist separatism that had originally been confined to the small towns of Bohemia and Moravia assumed a new importance by around 1910 among the industrial working class of the imperial capital (all the more so as in Vienna there was not a single major industrial plant that was not completely mixed in ethnic terms), threatening to disrupt the internal organization of the Social Democratic Workers' Party, which was forced to implement new organizational reforms in the direction of strict centralization.[60] At the same time, however, the actual electoral behavior of a large part of the Czech migration indicated a rapidly completed process of assimilation. When the nationalist and separatist Czech Social Democrats in Vienna formed a coalition with the bourgeois Czech parties for the municipal elections of 1912, the list received only 13,000 votes, against 118,000 for the German Social Democrats. The overwhelming majority of Viennese Czechs cast their vote for the German Social Democrats and thus did not orient themselves politically along ethnic lines.

Throughout the second half of the nineteenth century, the flow of migration was dominated by individuals from the lower strata in agriculture and other trades. The agricultural crisis and its attendant process of social differentiation fragmented a rural culture that had previously been relatively homogeneous, disintegrating and destroying it at the mechanized pace of the new age. What was decisive now was the impact of an increasingly organized urban and industrial market, which forcibly stamped its partially "blind effects" (new structures of need and demand, falling prices, etc.) on an essentially subordinate and only partially still domestic and agricultural economic order. Yet the agrarian and rural sphere was marked by certain continuities, above all a conception of space and time that was quite different from the urban one, expressing a finite, locally bound, and circular annual rhythm of seedtime and harvest as opposed to the infinite and linear time flow of industrial production.[61]

The typical form of communal existence of the rural peasantry, the village, is the embodiment and epitome of direct connection and face-to-face contact. Individuals are identifiable and closely linked to one another within the community by a dense network of hierarchies and authoritatively fixed dependencies. Close communication and social contact is correlated with a high degree of normative cultural, religious, and political control and with specific village forms of social sanctions. The structure of the community is visible and transparent, induces "espionage," and rests on the "transparency of even the innermost space."[62]

The rural is, of course, neither static nor timeless. But economies and communities that are essentially closed, in which life and work and cultural expression are all located in one place, doubtless favor the tenacious persistence of traditional and pre-modern models and norms. Rural and agrarian life thus contains a representation of space, a "spatial grid," that presupposes a certain orientation, an ability to name and understand places that is dependent on and

5. A "village in the city." The Brunnenmarkt street market in
    Neulerchenfeld. Source: Historisches Museum der Stadt Wien.

determined by this integration in closed, cyclical, and organic communities. Simple rhythms and cycles become components of a larger, holistic mode of thought that embraces the entire lifespan and all its events from birth to death as well as the succession of generations.[63] To ensure social and cultural integration and give meaning to the cosmic cycles are the task of religion and the various confessions, which assume the function of institutions of socialization while at the same time being instances of social discipline.

The peasant culture with its closed life cycles and isolated social spaces encountered in the city a highly complex and contradictory context, which replaced cultural identity with the experience of difference and fragmentation, thus making the system of social relations visible and decodable. The tokens of urbanization are concentration, collection, accumulation, and compaction.[64] The city is a conglomeration of objects; it intensifies the complexity of social life and stages human social ties as an alienating experience.[65] It is not only a spatial and social form of modern life, it is above

6. The inscribed city. Corner of Lerchenfeldergürtel and Lerchenfelderstraße. Source: Historisches Museum der Stadt Wien.

all the bearer of a specific and decisive modern consciousness. The spatial and cultural change from country to town is momentous, and always signifies a rupture in an individual's biography. The seemingly unlimited urban growth, the increasing complexity and division of labor, the fundamentally changed relations between and within social classes, and the reduction to objective labor power—changes such as these render obsolete the almost Ptolemaic idea of an ordered cosmos in a closed community and replace it with the urban experience of a "Copernican shift," that is, a fundamental experience of subjective irrelevance in the crowd, rush, and roaring noise, the bewildering confusion and painful contingency of this new and complex social order. The coexistence of the systematic and the arbitrary, the visible and the invisible— this is the true significance of the modern city as a dominant form of life.

Ferdinand Hanusch, who arrived in Vienna in the mid-1880s as an indigent migrant and who subsequently became Minister of Social Affairs in the First Republic, described the dramatic experience of this Copernican shift as "the great sea of buildings from which the noise of the city dully resounded, filling someone who grew up in the country with terror and dismay." The masses of people that seemed to stream past one another arbitrarily, sometimes colliding, the apparent absence of contact and connection—the consequences of the new mobility were at once stimulating and threatening and coalesced into a profound experience of anonymity, loss, and isolation:

> I had become an ant like all the others in this great anthill ... The giant buildings, the great displays, the many people who hurried past without bothering about me, the scurrying cabs and the omnibuses stumbling against the sidewalks, the horse-drawn streetcars with their bells and cursing drivers—all this produced a tremendous noise, which the city-dweller was undoubtedly used to, but which had such an oppressive effect on someone arriving in a big city for the first time that he lost every ounce of courage, for it seemed to him quite impossible that he could ever find his way in this hustle and bustle ... Like so many others, to come to Vienna and seek my fortune had been my dream since childhood. Now I was in Vienna, in this city of millions, and found myself alone and forsaken as I had never been before.[66]

The rhetorical gesture of a repressive uniformity is not enough to explain difference, complexity, foreignness, and conflict as constitutive aspects of urban experience. What is involved here is rather a contradiction, a paradox: namely, the simultaneous coexistence of difference, arbitrariness, and order, of visible facts and objects with the invisible form of the city. The city's "form" consists in the first place of structures that are not immediately accessible to sensory perception: property relations, housing regulations, obligations, rents, taxes, etc. It is thus not simply a material formation, it is equally a construction of learned modes of perception, both conscious and unconscious.[67] It is not a given fact, but rather product and process simultaneously, the expression of a stubborn entanglement of the symbolic and material spheres. It is thus also a field of political discourses of identity and of potentially politicizing experiences of cultural difference.

The integration of immigrants into urban and metropolitan structures, the adaptation of their agrarian cultures of origin to an urban social context, the modifications of their ways of life necessary for survival in that context thus take place in a complex and contradictory interaction of adaptation, assimilation, and conflicting values. The immigrants brought their (unwritten) history with them, their "village in the mind," while they also had to learn new forms of social organization and understand new guiding ideas that were derived from the dictates of industrial discipline and rigorous schedules. The big city, "by the complexity and confusion of its external phenomena, accustomed them to continual abstractions, to indifference toward what was nearby and close connection to what was far removed."[68] The "village in the mind" created their world in the suburb, which was essentially an oral one. The social boundary between city center and suburb is thus not simply definable in spatial terms. While the center exerts power by written authority, the expressions of the suburb persist in their obstinacy and ostensible lack of history as dissonant voices in the public sphere. The culture of oral exchange and narrative transmission is a social disadvantage and obstacle as much as it is the local preservation of an orally articulated mode of life that creates its own identity in dialect, popular song, and street slang, in wit, mockery, and dirty joke. It is a form of life that defends itself against the encroachments of the center despite its inability to escape these:

> On Saturdays after we got paid, we would go to an inn for supper. Either to one nearby, where we could run a tab during the week, or to one further out, where things were cheaper and the portions bigger ... We stayed there after eating. Music played and popular singers sang joyful Viennese songs full of gentle everyday humor ... At moments like these the music and song melted the souls of all the guests, and we felt content and carefree. The Czechs were most affected by the songs and jokes of the singers ... I was very surprised that a large part of the boisterous, applauding guests, often the majority, was Czech, only a small percentage of whom spoke German to any significant degree. I found it quite astounding that these Czechs, journeymen and masters and their wives, were not offended or annoyed, but that they applauded and laughed at the jokes as if they were no longer Czechs, no longer had anything in common with those stupid rustics, and by their applause showed their complete assimilation as genuine Viennese.[69]

Foreignness in the city and speechlessness in public reinforce a sense of being alien and excluded. The fragmentation of life and work, its tracelessness, hampers individual integration and collective orientation, leading the immigrants to fall back on their rural traditions, to seek contact with others from their homeland, and to observe holidays and festivals along traditional village lines.[70] It is in this connection that Karl Renner writes of the "village in the city":

> They all still betrayed the village in their behavior, and yet they had all acquired a certain big-city polish. I had come to Vienna to get to know the capital, and here I discovered a segment of its population who in a certain sense represented a transition from country to town, and I asked myself how large, if one took the entire immigration from all the regions of the Empire ... this "village in the city" might be.[71]

In his description of a "five-kreuzer dance" in the Vienna Prater, that place of cheap entertainment so beloved by the lower classes, the Viennese writer and essayist Felix Salten comes to very similar conclusions. It was the "simple and humble folk" from every province of the Empire who found comfort here, the village and small-town youth who had moved to the big city and were working, serving, starving, and struggling. For Salten the big city was a Moloch, a difficult borderland, the no man's land for "an entire generation who are not at home in the enormous city, who are lost and lonely in the confusion of this roaring life." They are strangers in this "gigantic city, whose workhouses swallow them up, and which strips them of their nature and crushes and consumes them."[72] In the dark and smoky taverns of the Prater they found "a piece of home ... They turn with stiff backs and short shirts, which Upkra has painted so wonderfully. Now we're in Bohemia, in the sunny hill country of Moravia and the luxuriant plains of the Hanna."[73] The countryside becomes a metaphor for a particular form of being: active, physical, repetitive, unaware, and linked inseparably with the processes of nature:

But these young girls from the common folk, whose cheeks are still fresh and glowing from the fresh air of the fields of their homeland, whose arms are still sunburnt from working outside, these young girls with the firm gaits and the supple forms of their fresh and healthy bodies, with their gentle, curious eyes that seem intoxicated by dreams of love—they have the innocence of nature. Their dancing has a proud devotion about it. They dance the way they work: evenly, persistently, inexhaustibly.[74]

The idealized rural naturalness and (still) unbroken bodily vitality is contrasted with the wasteland of ugliness and emptiness embodied in the industrial urban system: artisans and workers whose "nature was stripped by the dull confines of their workplaces, by alcohol, and by the loathsomeness of the big city"; women who after just a few years in Vienna "had already lost all of their blossom ... who were already hopelessly devastated in their bearing, and whose earlier openhearted instincts were already tinged by burdens and lies"; and finally those countless beings who were "downtrodden, trampled, destroyed in the city," who vanish without trace, and whom no one knew.[75]

Felix Salten was one of the very few representatives of the cultural elite of fin de siècle Vienna who ever took immigrants and the "other" Vienna of the suburbs as a subject. Of course, his perception of the "other" Vienna was confined to its public presence in places of popular entertainment like the Prater. What interested him was the distance of popular culture from the prestigous culture of the bourgeoisie, the deep-rooted insubordination of suburban life, and the continuation or metamorphosis of countercultures. He was fascinated by its immediate presence, sensuality, and bawdiness, which contrasted with the fleetingness, contingency, and tracelessness of its social existence. Yet even Salten's gaze is directed exclusively at the performance and exoticism of suburban culture, while its forms of life and conditions of reproduction remain oddly vague or completely obscured. Evidently aesthetics, social perception, and the dominant cultural discourse coalesced into a collective tradition in which the suburbs were anathema, and the topography of Vienna was divided into visible and invisible zones.

CHAPTER 4

PROJECTION AND GRIDS

As Carl E. Schorske writes in the Ringstraße chapter of his book on Viennese modernism,[76] "a Baroque planner would have sought to join the suburbs to the city in such a way as to create a vast vista oriented toward the central, monumental features," in other words, to provide the suburbs with the precondition for the visual and political perception of the center as center. Instead of this, however, the Ringstraße was not built centrifugally out to the suburbs, but rather formed a figure contained in itself, and one that simultaneously defined a separation of society: the ruling classes, the nobility, and the upper middle class in the city center with its old palaces and modern refuges of bourgeois life, and, separated from this, the inner suburbs with the petit bourgeoisie and civil servants, and the outer suburbs with the industrial proletariat and lower classes.

The socially segregating architecture of the "Ringstraße period" is part of a double convolution in the urban terrain. This convolution is at the same time a spatial and territorial expression of power and dependence and an expression of sociocultural marginalization and economic integration. First of all, a "hard" signature is inscribed in the suburbs that creates facts and structures, a signature of factories, of the industrialization of everyday life, of rampant urban expansion, of tenement construction, and of transportation and communication arteries. This signature becomes a source both of political movements (the Social Democratic workers' movement) and of an immeasurable everyday misery. On the other hand, the suburb becomes a field of projection of domination, in which the interests of economic subjugation mingle with ideas of an "other out there" to form a distorted image of modernity. The Biedermeier suburb was real in its cultural value, that is, in its embodiment of an idyll. The modern suburb is real as a place of economic interests, but unreal as a field of cultural perception. Its actual form of appearance vanishes beneath a layer of indifference, ignorance, suppression, and effacement. One could say aphoristically that the real Biedermeier suburb was replaced by an unreal suburb of modernity constructed as a space of imagined threats. The self-reflective presentation of the splendor of the Ringstraße with its consequent confirmation of a bourgeois and aristocratic ruling elite identity corresponds to the complementary idea of an "other Vienna," a "dark continent" packed with imponderables and uncertainties, which needs to be domesticated and civilized by the center. The first thing to ascertain, therefore, is what concrete developments and transformations in the urban economy and in urban planning and topography led to this shift in perspective.

Between 1860 and 1890 Vienna underwent a decisive transformation in building and space. The advancing division of labor and differentiation of space was expressed, "on account of the pressure of ground rents, in an increasing homogenization of city districts and the spatial segregation of income and population groups."[77] In the wake of the 1848 revolution, new housing for the middle class increasingly arose in those old commercial quarters situated within the customs "Line," replacing the feudal recreational landscape. At the same time an early industrial underclass of day laborers and casual workers gathered at the periphery of these districts in slum-like reception quarters. Every evening the police dispatched thousands of homeless across the Line into "open country."[78] A population increase of around 40 percent between 1830 and 1850 was coupled with an increase of only about 10 percent in housing. By the second half of the 1850s, these conditions were no longer sustainable. The homeless began to camp out in public squares and were lodged by the police in stables and municipal jails.[79] The social situation of the capital was marked by wretched and scarce housing; "in its horrors and hopelessness it bore comparison with the Paris Cité or London's East End."[80]

That Vienna had at its center a huge tract of open land available for modern development was, ironically, a consequence of the city's historical backwardness.[81] The massive fortifications and the glacis surrounding the center were left in place even after they had lost their military function, when other European capitals had long since abandoned such strongholds. The revolution of 1848 gave new political and strategic significance to the open space of the glacis, not against a potential foreign aggressor, but rather a potentially revolutionary population. The military's main argument against civilian development of the glacis was the persistence of a revolutionary threat and the consequent need to secure the Imperial Palace against possible attack by the suburban proletariat. The dynamic of economic and social exigencies, however, made arguments along such lines increasingly untenable. In the arrangement of the Ringstraße, accordingly, military considerations were combined with the need of a bourgeoisie aspiring toward political power for an imposing, monumental boulevard. What had previously been a ring of military separation now became one of social division.[82]

A process was thereby initiated that was designed to create and stabilize a model of spatial division, reinforcing a social differentiation of the urban terrain in the form of a concentric narrative of domination. The two eastern suburbs that had grown up at the city limits, as well as the relatively remote

7. The city as projection. Favoriten district around 1900. Source: Historisches Museum der Stadt Wien.

fifth district (which included Favoriten until it was separated off in 1874) and the outer districts, experienced a further social downgrading as a result of the immigration of lower classes. The southern and western suburbs, which had grown up on the terrain of clerical and secular landowners, accommodated on account of their proximity to the center the middle-class population that was driven out of the inner city; following a thorough redevelopment these suburbs were converted into housing quarters for the middle class and civil servants. This led to a further expulsion of the lower-class population into the outer districts, as was paradigmatically demonstrated by the example of the working-class and artisan suburb of Alt-Lerchenfeld.

In this way, a solid barrier was placed between the luxury housing of the city center and the potentially dangerous working-class districts. The complex differentiation between center, inner suburbs, and outer suburbs corresponded to a hierarchical arrangement of the social space that was more evident and well-defined than in either London or Paris. By the turn of the century, a solid ring of densely constructed working-class suburbs had been drawn around the districts within the Gürtel and the city center. Only the thirteenth, eighteenth and nineteenth districts with their villa estates were designed for the upper- and upper-middle classes.[83] To the west, Währingerstraße formed the central connecting axis between the inner city and the districts of Währing and Döbling. As a whole, however, upper-class concentration in the outer districts was comparatively slight, a fact that was chiefly a function of the lack of adequate mass transport. Only in Hietzing, where the Radial railroad, which opened in 1900, established a quick and direct connection to the center, did any quantitatively significant concentration of the upper-middle class develop.

The fundamental shift in the distribution of population in social space took place between 1870 and 1890, a phase of increasing concentration of capital, and was reinforced and stabilized in the years that followed. A large part of the lower-class population who had been expelled from the old commercial suburbs now settled immediately adjacent to these, beyond the Line or Gürtel, not the least reason for this being that the western suburbs on both sides of Mariahilferstraße continued to form, as they always had, the center of the most labor-intensive branch of Viennese industry, the garment trade.[84] Given the lack of an adequate transport system, work places had to be within a manageable distance from the workers' homes. The disproportionate growth and massive concentration in building and population in districts such as Neulerchenfeld (where in the mid-1880s more than twice the population lived jammed together in only two-thirds of a square kilometer than there was in the square kilometer of the inner city)[85] can thus be quite plausibly explained. In eight suburbs directly bordering the Line, nearly two-thirds of the workers resident there worked outside their own district. A "memorandum on the suburbs" assumed that these masses of workers "sought their living in the city center but their housing in the suburbs on account of low rents and food costs."[86] And, in a social report from 1901, Max Winter saw already at six in the morning "the human ants emerge from their buildings and move to work in dense swarms." Life in the suburbs got under way earlier than in the city center:

Across the Schmelz, to and fro, through Lerchenfelderstraße, Thaliastraße, and Koppstraße, through Grundsteingasse and Burggasse, the main movements went toward the Neubau factory quarter, while across the Gürtel to the railroad stations and Gumpendorf swarmed the men and women who had to provide for their families, and domestic servants and adolescent youths, who also had to bring with them what they needed for the day ahead. The streets teemed with young and old, men and women, happy and sad, bent-over and able-bodied—the early risers at their leisure, reading newspapers, smoking and chatting, the late-comers rushing in haste [...].[87]

The new industrial districts of the south and northeast, on the other hand, generally followed a more "incremental" pattern of growth. Here, following the requirements of their location, dynamically expanding industries in major new sectors had sprung up on the edges of districts already built-up, thus creating the basis for the development of further workers' housing quarters in close proximity to the work place. The high rents and the frequent moves that were a result of this, together with the lack of cheap mass transport, were the factors making for this particular adaptation. Only in rare cases was it possible even for highly skilled workers to choose to live at any great distance from their work place or in quarters of the city that met their (relatively) higher everyday needs.[88]

In the wake of the new upswing in industrialization in the mid-1880s, a process of growth and concentration came about that was organized as a kind of archipelago, projecting the suburbs into the agricultural surroundings like a chessboard divided into lots. Large open spaces in the outer districts were built up with housing tenements in a bleak rectangular grid. The second Vienna building ordinance of September 23, 1859, which required for the first time that streets should be planned in as straight a fashion as possible, established the precondition for the rigid adherence to geometric principles that expressed the generally recognized planning concepts of the *Gründerzeit*; this later led to harsh criticism by Camillo Sitte of the "factory-like rectilinearity" of the developed space.[89] Even in cases where construction plans were drawn up by Ringstraße architects—Förster for Brigittenau, and Siccardsburg and Van der Null for Favoriten—the grid pattern was maintained, and in the best of cases expanded by the element of a stellar intersection after the Paris model.[90]

From the end of the 1870's, rail connection to the Westbahnhof was an increasing factor in determining location. Fünfhaus, Rustenfeld, and Breitensee attracted the large-scale land development work of construction companies. Their speculative projects were focused principally in Neu-Fünfhaus, the checkerboard strips outside the Line between the Westbahn and the Schmelz cemetery.[91] Already in the early 1870s, Neulerchenfeld had purchased the northern side of the Schmelz, which the army did not require and which had been allocated for construction, from the municipalities of Fünfhaus, Rudolfsheim, and Breitensee—still an undeveloped area at the time separated from the built-up area of these communities by the broad barrier of the military zone. Construction on the northern flank of the Schmelz was

among the most substantial in quantitative terms in the whole history of
Vienna; it followed a strict principle of grid development, with perfectly
straight thoroughfares. The reckless straightening of Bachstraße followed that
of Thaliastraße, providing the preconditions for a grid development of the
entire zone between the Gürtel and Possingergasse all the way to
Gablenzgasse.[92] The drawing-board town "on the American model" that
arose here brought to a conclusion the development of the area between the
Westbahn and Thaliastraße "in a completely uniform checkerboard system."[93]
The new urban patterns that emerged on the periphery and in the outlying
districts simply repeated, block for block, the same formation. These urban
quarters had no centers or focal points, simply sections, fragments, and
remnants. And yet, ironically, this "no-man's-land of social life" (Lewis
Mumford), this "repository of the metropolis"—a site of settlement of heavy
industry as well as of a mass concentration of working people—sustained the
image of a uniform city by the way the façades of the tenement blocks
frequently imitated the prevailing neo-Baroque architecture of the
Ringstraße.

   The suburbs thus followed a double, if interrupted, development in their
architectural and spatial formation. On the one hand, the territories newly
opened up to the south and east of the city represented the direct
materialization of capital in space, while at the same time seeking to establish
through architecture and transport both a symbolic and a real connection with
the center. In the outlying districts that developed from pre-industrial suburbs,
on the other hand, capital made use of tradition, and instrumental rationality
made use of history, to project a homogeneous urban entity. In the course of
the industrialization process, therefore, structural differentiations that had
already existed historically acquired increased emphasis. Ottakring, Hernals,
Penzing, Rudolfsheim, and Meidling, for example, had all developed from pre-
industrial settlements with small-scale trading centers, vineyards, and
agricultural holdings into industrial sites and proletarian districts. In Ottakring
a factory district had developed around the brewery by the mid-nineteenth
century, and by the mid-1880s the dynamic surge of industrialization swept
away the last remains of medieval viticulture and allowed a *Gründerzeit* grid
city to develop. The villages of Braunhirschen, Rustendorf, and Reindorf
(combined in 1863 into the expanded municipality of Rudolfsheim), together
with Sechshaus and Fünfhaus, which for a long period had a rather petit-
bourgeois structure, had by the 1830's grown into a continuous built-up
zone, which according to contemporary reports represented the "authentic
Vienna factory district" and which had come to resemble more a "major
town" than anything like the original villages. The textile industry of the pre-
1848 era was dominant here, while the Oesterlein rifle factory was already
gigantic by contemporary standards. As the process of industrialization and
concentration steadily continued (in Fünfhaus, for example, population
growth between 1830 and 1851 was no less than 400 percent), it was chiefly
Rustendorf and Braunhirschen, and Fünfhaus to a lesser extent, that were still
able to serve their traditional function as centers of recreation and refuge for
the Viennese population up through the last third of the century, as evidenced

by a whole series of large restaurants and entertainment facilities (Schwender's Colosseum, the Brauhaus, Pokorny's Sommerarena, the Zobeläum, the Victoria Hall, the Elisabeth Hall, the Stefanie Hall, etc.). Similarly to Rudolfsheim, Meidling had also become an important industrial center before 1848, while its agricultural structure and even the function it had acquired as a resort by virtue of its proximity to Schönbrunn fell into decline. With the loss of importance of the textile industry and its removal to other areas, Meidling became a site for metalworking and machine construction during the *Gründerzeit*, while Gaudenzdorf and Untermeidling had by 1890 become densely built-up quarters of factories and workers' housing, with their recreational function being taken over by the adjacent Hetzendorf, which had not yet been affected by industrial development.

With the exception of Hernals, Meidling combined like no other suburb a modern, industrial, and urban dynamic with the persistence of pre-modern, village, and rural idyllic structures: the synchronous coexistence and overlapping of different phases and stages of urban development (in 1890, 60 percent of the total land area was still made up of fields, meadows, and pasture). The art historian Hans Tietze declared that "these places were organic forms of life that were suddenly radically recast," a conglomerate of "city and village growth": "on the one hand the dismal blocks of speculative housing for the masses, extensive districts where the unrestrained greed for profit had completely throttled the elementary need for housing; on the other hand vestiges of village life still managing to put up successful resistance."[94] This juxtaposition of unearthly, drawing-board architecture and survivals of pre-modern peasant modes corresponded to the social division of the district. A good half of the population were workers in industry and commerce living

8. Industrial modernity on the periphery. The Simmering gasometer.
    Source: Historisches Museum der Stadt Wien.

in Meidling's central quarter in the notorious "Halbritter buildings" (a traditional Viennese tenement structure in the form of a double line of blocks), in the already built-up sections of the no less notorious Fuchsenfeld, in the newly erected proletarian quarter near the Philadelphia bridge, in the two-story and single-story houses of Gaudenzdorf and Altmannsdorf, and in the multistory tenements of Neumargarethen. On the other hand there were shopkeepers and business people, civil servants and teachers, office workers and railroad and streetcar employees, as well as a surprisingly high proportion of freelance professionals for an outlying district:

> The city did indeed press outward in every direction and seek to expand, but here and there all across Meidling we encounter the old village with its traditional features and only slowly, very slowly, is the city doing away with these considerable residues.
>
> In Meidling everything is juxtaposed: the old village and the modern city; industry and agriculture; the old proletarian suburb with stables for ox-carts and courtyards for cabs and drays right in the middle, as well as the dark and noxious workshops of the "little man" ... and alongside this, new quarters with towering tenements where the highest rents are charged for light and air. The patrician houses of Old Meidling have their idyllic courtyards blooming with flowers, and country houses stand right up against the arteries of urban traffic as well as in the secluded quiet corners around the Fasangarten and in Hetzendorf with its old-Viennese summer freshness. Everywhere there are expanses scantily covered with grass but also scattered with the dirt and refuse of the transformation process, which can be all too palpably observed in these places. This is typical of what remains of the notorious Fuchsenfeld, which is still bordered by Gaudenzdorf, Untermeidling, and the newest district Neumargarethen: goats and geese graze on it, hordes of children play in the dirt of these fields, a woman scavenger searches through the rubble.[95]

It was these profound changes in the pattern of urban growth to which the building ordinance of 1892 reacted, establishing the western city borders as a residential district with a limit of four stories on new buildings, and the south and northeast of the city as industrial zones, thus enacting into law a process that had long since been under way in actual fact. Indeed, the ordinance represented no more than an "adaptation to a fait accompli."[96] Expansive industrialization required space, extension, boundlessness: conditions that were satisfied, for example, in Simmering, Brigittenau, and the district of Floridsdorf, which was annexed to Vienna in 1904.

Simmering, a kind of traditional urban "depository," assumed a pioneer position as a center of heavy industry (a number of machine-building firms settled especially in the area bordered by the Arsenal and the Ostbahn and Aspangbahn railroads), while at the same time being the industrial district of Vienna that longest maintained its rural, largely horticultural, character. It was a terrain not coded by history, which allowed an unimpeded projection of the logic of capital and which did not even require symbolic integration into the city as a whole. There was no resistance to the transformation of open country, and it was precisely in this way that the territory received its multiple economic and

9. The city electricity plant at Simmering. Source: Historisches Museum der Stadt Wien.

administrative coding. It was at one and the same time industrial production site and social dumping ground. Dominant features here were the "giant, dirty gray mass" of the hospital for infectious diseases, the centralized cattle market and slaughterhouse at St. Marx, the municipal gasworks (established in 1899) with its imposing industrial skyline of gasometers, the electricity works (established 1902), and not least the central cemetery, which was laid out in 1873–74 on land acquired from the Kaiser-Ebersdorf municipality: "The land stretching out here is either the earth of the cemetery or desolate scrub. There is no joy here. Far around the cemetery everything pleasant and comfortable has been torn up or exterminated, and the misty gray landscape is punctuated only by factory chimneys and spectral monuments to the dead."[97]

In this peripheral district the city seeps away and the countryside increasingly dominates, with its farmhouses and peasant markets, and amid them the omnipresent scenery of the cemetery. Thus, alongside the rapidly rising industrial complexes of the *Gründerzeit*, the fallow land of a gigantic wasteland also typifies the district: the bare, gray Simmering "heath" dotted only on its edges with a few cottages and smallholdings, which served as a military training ground as well as a working-class recreation area—an "unenclosed wasteland," a "fallow land of poverty," an "area of untilled misery":

A few starving goats vainly graze on the crippled blades of grass trampled down by drilling recruits ... Gray, misty, unending. In winter snowdrifts bank up high, scarcely cleared for a narrow footpath, while in the summer months it becomes a campground of the poor: scrofulous children with limbs already crippled in the cradle and with no other toy but a scrap of dirty paper; ailing and careworn mothers old before their time; retired workers smoking their pipes; gaunt figures from *The Weavers*, who look as if they had just escaped from the grave to walk around on the heath.[98]

Like Simmering, Brigittenau—separated off from Leopoldstadt and made into a district of its own in 1900—was also considered a territory designated for industrialization and urbanization. In 1864 the quarter around Brigittaplatz was developed along plans drawn up by the Ringstraße architects Förster and Siccardsburg,. Practically unsettled, the area became a prized object of speculation, with regulation of the Danube and the construction of the Nordbahn and Nordwestbahn railroads as well as the Danube canal bridge at Alsergrund offering the decisive impulse for manufacturing. A second wave of building during the later part of the *Gründerzeit* brought with it the establishment of large factories (in 1913, three out of seventeen large factories in Vienna, with a total of 5,600 employees, were located in Brigittenau). The electrical works of Siemens-Schuckert alone, which lay on the boundary between Brigittenau and Leopoldstadt, accounted for a quarter of Vienna's large-scale industry in terms of workers and machinery. Housing grids arose in the immediate vicinity of the production sites, making maximum use of the partitioning of the land, and the district, referred to colloquially as "Affentürkei" (Turkey for Apes) and "Glasscherbeninsel" (Broken Glass Island), acquired the mark of an industrial site and workers' quarters precisely where its original landscape on the flood plain had kept it free the longest from urbanization,[99] and where the Viennese had held popular feudal spectacles and festivals since the early modern period.

The old settlement of Floridsdorf on the north bank of the Danube was already described in the 1880s as one of the "most impressive industrial sites of the Empire." By the turn of the century Floridsdorf had developed into the unchallenged leader of heavy industry in the Habsburg metropolis. A diverse industrial zone emerged here, with companies such as Siemens & Halske, Clayton-Shuttleworth (later Hofherr-Schrantz), and Fiat building new factories and storage facilities for their extensive large-scale production. Chemical plants, textile mills, and foodstuff factories, and, towering above all else, the locomotive factory and two railroad works gave the district its particular character and appearance. The area experienced an "almost American" growth, in the course of which the population rose by close to 50 percent in the first decade of the new century alone. By 1910 there were already over 100 manufacturing companies here, of which six employed more than 1,000 workers—a concentration not even closely rivaled by any other district of Vienna.[100]

The industrial sites in these outer-lying districts were soon joined by gigantic workers' housing quarters, the result being social segregation and functional separation, amounting to a radical change in the city's social space. But, if in Brigittenau, for example, a marked partition of the district remained as a result of the railroad route, dividing a closed-off residential zone around Wallensteinplatz from a less developed area bordering on the Danube, where grid housing, gardens, meadows, small factories, and storage yards lay in no recognizable pattern, Favoriten, on the other hand, displayed a more modern organization of its social space, both radical and comprehensive, systematic and complete. It was established in 1874 from the increasingly proletarianized parts of the third, fourth and fifth districts. Through the operation of land prices, an "economy based on division of labor" had led "under profit pressures" to "a functional specialization of the urban space" as well as a "marked social segregation of the population."[101] The steady expansion of development took place according to a strict pattern in which housing and industrial plots were intermingled. On the edge of the Wienerberg and Laaerberg hills there thus grew up what was for Viennese standards a uniquely homogeneous and dynamically expanding quarter. Medium-sized plants in metalworking and machine-building in particular were built here, as well as the innovative and capital-intensive electrical industry, without breaking the prescribed block-grid system.

A direct product of industry, this district, "which mushroomed in open country in the wake of the railroad construction,"[102] was a perfect example of the grid construction of the *Gründerzeit.* Projected onto space, designed with circles and lines following the premises of strict rationality, it was largely built on open land as a new and planned out urban agglomeration:

Favoriten is a town unto itself. Someone took a sheet of drawing paper, ruler and pencil, and drew horizontal and vertical lines. He started from Favorita, now known as Theresianum, colonized with his pencil the bare country road that ran toward Himberg, tore down the poplars on the right and left side, filled in the ditches, and made buildings, factories, and tenement blocks arise on their banks. The blocks were hatched in red on the plan but were sober grayish-brown buildings in reality. Toward Laxenburg as well, and along the line of the railroad, streets arose, converging like rays on a focus at the Favoriten viaduct of the Südbahn. There was a small building at this focus, the Steudel inn, and settlements also at the ends of the roads ... But what lies in between is the sober reality of the factory quarter. In bleakest uniformity the buildings, always gray or brown, always gloomy, combine into streets, lengthwise and crosswise, stretching from Simmering to Enzersdorf, with a few squares here and there, which are just as soulless as the buildings and alleys. No monuments decorate them, no ornamental fountain gladdens the eye; even the sole public buildings, the schools, are gloomy like everything else. The raw brick of a factory with its ridiculously even line of windows—four stories one above the other—is the only variation in the picture. Everything covered with smoke and dust, everywhere the roar of industry. Nowhere is there light or a place to relax. Everything bleak, everything gloomy, all gray on gray—*that is Favoriten.*[103]

The grid construction of the *Gründerzeit* provided the optimal valorization of land for private building contractors on a large construction zone: "This planning criterion was so strong and compelling that it even ignored those disadvantages in terms of street alignment and housing construction that arose from disregard for the topographical peculiarities of the landscape."[104] With no consideration for any kind of historical circumstance, landscape condition, or social requirement, the grid built up abstract units with the exclusive purpose of profit on the capital invested. The only differences to be found were between corner and central blocks, in the size of plots (standardized as far as possible), and in their specific position in relation to the urban agglomeration. Charged with the social control of linear form, the grid defined both alignment and geometric perspective. It was an endless geometry of equal blocks, an expanding chessboard with no edge or center.[105] It was determined by the dictates of logic, of reason; it was the effect projected onto space of "a creative act that occurred elsewhere, in the Mind, or the Intellect'.[106] Above all, however, the grid was determined by speculation: "[M]ore city came into being when speculators felt the urge to speculate."[107]

New legal regulations defining and securing private property independently from state and nobility opened the door wide to speculation and accelerated the process of a comprehensive social and cultural transformation. The grid construction, standard repertoire of *Gründerzeit* town planning, was the classic element of the privatized city, following the logic of private development of urban land. It embodied an increasing standardization of urban life. And standardization always means abstraction. The model for the private builder was whatever could be generalized as the lowest common denominator, i.e. as marketable demand.[108]

The combination of speculative building and immigration concentrated the suburbs into zones that were extremely narrow both socially and in terms of building space (housing construction from 1856 to 1917 amounted to 460,000 units). During the nineteenth century the population of the Vienna conurbation increased sevenfold, quadrupling between 1830 and 1900 and doubling in the last three decades of the century.[109] A high point at just over 2 million was reached in 1910, while at the turn of the century the annual increase was around 34,000 people, with immigrants making up just over 65 percent of this.[110]

The fundamental pattern was that of a zonal, peripheral growth. The suburban communities, which were increasingly integrated into the urban sphere of influence, grew at a higher than average rate. Growth in the suburbs could be put down to two factors, especially as an increasingly sharp decline in the birth rate had already set in by the turn of the century: on the one hand, immigration, which assumed entirely new dimensions after the abolition of serfdom and which was concentrated overwhelmingly in the suburbs; and on the other hand, the spatial displacement of the lower classes into peripheral districts outside of the Line or Gürtel in the wake of the Ringstraße construction and the concomitant radical transformation of the old commercial suburbs into living quarters for civil servants and the middle class. Favoriten thus became "a virtual refuge for numerous families who had no other resources but their children, could not manage to exist in other parts of the city given the significantly higher rents and provision costs, and were pressed into the low-rent tenth district."[111]

By 1880 the commercial and industrial classes in the suburbs made up more than 80 percent of the population, and in some areas over 90 percent— as in Sechshaus, Favoriten, Rudolfsheim, Neulerchenfeld, Untermeidling, and Gaudenzdorf (where a peak of 94 percent was reached).[112] In 1890, when Neulerchenfeld and Ottakring were combined into the sixteenth district, over 76,000 of the 107,000 inhabitants, i.e. 70 percent, worked directly in industry and trade, a percentage surpassed only by Rudolfsheim.[113]

Population growth in the suburbs and outer districts constantly outstripped new construction. Most reserves of land within the Line, however, were already built up in the 1880s, with the last adjustments being undertaken in the wake of the construction of the Gürtel avenues and the Stadtbahn railroad. The newly constructed areas, together with the concentration of those already built-up, led to an extreme exploitation of available land; at first there was no restriction at all on intensity, though in 1883 the building regulations were revised to set an 85 percent limit on any plot.

Housing conditions for the population in the outer districts were marked by extreme overbuilding, a massive burden on incomes as a result of high rents, and the permanent threat of eviction.[114] A vast number of contemporary studies by social reformers and social scientists describe life in the tenement blocks as a thoroughly claustrophobic experience.[115] The modern tenement was a transit camp that effaced all traces of the life of its inhabitants, "blocking the traditions and germs of empathy and cooperation just as it did the development of any right to freedom and the realization of desires for happiness."[116] Up until World War One, 85 percent of housing units in the outer districts were the smallest possible size (consisting of one room, or two including a kitchen). Four-fifths of the population here lived in this "poorest housing category." Even for the most wretched accommodation in cellars, outbuildings, and attics, rents were demanded that were higher per square meter than those for apartments on the Ringstraße.[117] The exorbitant level of rents led to overcrowding, subletting, and bed-letting, and by 1900 only 4 percent of the inhabitants of Ottakring had a room of their own.[118] Eugen Philippovich, in an investigation of housing conditions in the outer districts from 1894, established that, in the overwhelming majority of cases, standards of space were below those for army barracks. This was confirmed by an inquiry conducted by the newspaper *Das Abend* shortly before the outbreak of war, which showed that sixty-eight apartments in Brigittenau and Leopoldstadt had a total of 404 inhabitants, in 94 percent of cases falling below even the minimal standard of living space per head for prisons and soldiers.[119]

CHAPTER 5

A PANORAMA OF MISERY

While the misery of life in the Vienna suburbs is extensively documented and analyzed in a wide spread of journalistic articles and writings by social reformers, it finds virtually no mention or consideration in the Viennese "high" literature of the time—in striking contrast to the situation in other European metropolises. In Arthur Schnitzler's 1925 *Traumnovelle*, the protagonist Fridolin makes a secret nighttime excursion to a house in Gallitzinberg where masked characters from noble and upper-class circles meet for an erotic rendezvous. His journey by coach leads from Alserstraße through an unknown territory of dark side streets to reach a two-story villa in elegant minimalist Empire style with green Venetian blinds. "They drove along Alser Strasse, then passed under a railroad viaduct and continued on toward the suburbs through dim, deserted side streets."[120]

This sentence, a mere aside in the course of the story and its construction, betrays in the context of Schnitzler's overall work and for the image of Vienna in literary modernism a particular, class-patterned model of the city. Vienna is perceived as a "centrifugal" city read and textualized from the center outward to the periphery, an urban area socially segmented concentrically from the first district out to the inner and peripheral suburbs. Each district has its specific housing clientele, who according to their social position are placed higher or lower on the scale of values. The inner city is allocated to the higher nobility and the nouveaux riches, with the lower nobility having the district of Wieden, the merchants, petits bourgeois and middle-rank civil servants the fifth to eighth districts, and doctors and university teachers those portions of the ninth district adjacent to the Ringstraße. This view of the urban landscape is reproduced by Hilde Spiel[121] in her autobiographically inspired essay on turn-of-the-century Vienna, as well as by Stefan Zweig in his memoirs:

> Within, however, one felt that the city had grown like a tree that adds ring upon ring, and instead of the old fortification walls the Ringstrasse encircled the treasured core with its splendid houses. Within, the old palaces of the court and the

nobility spoke history in stone. Here Beethoven had played at the Lichnovskys', at the Esterhazys' Haydn had been a guest; there in the old University Haydn's *Creation* had resounded for the first time, the Hofburg had seen generations of emperors, and Schönbrunn had seen Napoleon. In the Stefansdóm the united lords of Christianity had knelt in prayers of thanksgiving for the salvation of Europe from the Turks; countless great lights of science had been within the walls of the University. In the midst of all this, the new architecture reared itself proudly and grandly with glittering avenues and sparkling shops. But the old quarreled as little with the new as the chiseled stone with untouched nature. It was wonderful to live here, in this city which hospitably took up everything foreign and gave itself so gladly; and in its light air, as in Paris, it was a simple matter to enjoy life.[122]

The gloomy, smoky Vienna of poverty and dirt, peopled with immigrants, proletarians, hawkers, servant girls, unemployed, criminals, and so-called good-for-nothings, was not a subject for Zweig, though it far overshadowed the center in terms of area. Zweig's subject is rather an imagined, historicized, and naturalistically ordered Vienna, in which all the strands of European culture have intersected, and whose multi-ethnicity proves to be not a source of political and cultural conflict, but rather the almost alchemistic precondition for a special genius loci, which in Zweig's vision somehow manages to dissolve all tensions into harmony and thus create a special Viennese flair. The texture of the city and the topos of its streets and quarters are interpreted as an organically grown totality, whose spiritual center of gravity is formed by the inner core.

To the bourgeois gaze, as expressed in the literature of bourgeois memory and perception, the suburb remains curiously invisible and blanked out. If it appears at all, this "world out there" does so in connection with imaginings of the female. Schnitzler recalls in his memoirs his walks through the inner suburbs of Neubau and Josefstadt. The outer belt of proletarian suburbs remained a refuge of obscurity and strangeness; if he ever found his way there, it was still an empty and undescribed zone for him, where one might encounter things repulsive, disquieting, and frightful. In the "intermediate zone" of the inner suburbs with their bourgeois imprint, opening up toward the periphery at their outer limits and being characterized by social intermingling and cultural heterogeneity, Schnitzler found inspiration for certain female characters in his literary works. The "sweet girl" appears here alongside the "doubtful-looking women" on their "pitiful attempt to bag their game."[123] Schnitzler could thus write in his autobiography, *My Youth in Vienna*:

> On a November evening in the year 1881, on one of our walks through the suburban streets of the Neubau and Josefstadt districts, it so happened that we joined forces, after a few pleasantly received introductory flourishes, with two young girls. The designation *"süsses Mädel"* didn't exist in those days, but at least one of them could justifiably have claimed to be not only a sweet girl, but although hundreds of thousands might have preceded her, the *first* sweet girl.[124]

What does emerge about urban conditions in Arthur Schnitzler's fiction—and this applies not only to his own work, but to the overwhelming majority of writers in turn-of-the-century Vienna—is a division of the city into accessible and inaccessible territories. The mental cartography that underlies these fictions seems to have formed an *imaginaire* of the urban that was obligatory not just for the world of the writer, but for the perceived cosmos of the bourgeois classes in general.

The "other Vienna" of the poor, the declassed, the proletarians, the casual laborers, and outsiders remained something removed from bourgeois perception, indeed outside the world they had created. A perspective oriented toward the norms of court and bourgeois culture largely excluded the suburb from the context of urban life—except as a place of crime and disorder, infamy and unpredictability, a place to be avoided at all costs. It was left to the new brand of metropolitan reporters and journalists, like Emil Kläger[125] and Max Winter, and to police officials and police doctors to document this other Vienna and bring it into the perspective of public perception:

> Look at these people wracked by hunger, crippled by disease, sleeping in dirt. Men and women in torn rags, hunted out of our shining streets whose wealth they might besmirch, pressed back into the sewers and pursued even there by the wrath of our order. Their love is bread, their ambition a place for the night, their hatred the bloated society.[126]

In the course of his reports on the city and its miseries, Max Winter made extensive trips through the proletarian suburbs (Favoriten, Floridsdorf, Simmering, Ottakring, Brigittenau, etc.), describing the prevailing conditions of work, housing, and life in great detail. His picture of Vienna has little in common with the luminous and exhilarating memoirs of Stefan Zweig, or with Schnitzler's *La Ronde*. When Winter strolled through the proletarian quarter, he wrote of "old buildings" characterized by "humble, sooty passages, windowpanes often blind with age, courtyards filled with junk no longer needed in the workshops, a complete lack of gardens, occasional stables, and in newer buildings ... door after door of tiny dwellings, the prisons of children."[127] Winter's texts frequently associate workers' housing with lockups and prisons: all private life is played out in narrow, dark, and gloomy "dungeons," the life of adults marked by overwork, too little free time, and sexuality displayed before the eyes of bedfellows and children, children who for their fun are confined to playing in passages and stairways and those pitiful courtyards of the mass housing quarters that land speculation has spared:

> Halbritter buildings, then Muhr buildings. A whole book could be written on these double blocks, a stimulating book that would tell the tremendous suffering of the working people, their joyless youth, their early wilting under hard labor, their sad demise. "$75\frac{1}{2}$" reads the last door on this old-Vienna tenement, whose only place of recreation is the narrow courtyard running along the rear side of the back block. This is where all the activity takes place, where all day long a great horde of children play, fleeing the tiny apartment cells; this is where the old people sun themselves on flimsy open corridors. Everyone is familiar with the history and fate of the others, knows and shares their worries ... basically the same sad stories, the same remorseless fate, the same pressing cares. Here is the domestic worker who has to have her crippled husband with her in her little room, there the widow

WORKING
conditions *(handwritten)*

who has outlived everyone, even her children, serving the young proletarian woman in the dungeon next door as a vision of her own future: a tiny room for a monthly rent of just over eight kronen. An incubator for every kind of disease, this whole great building with its hundreds of people … Everything personal seems to be obliterated. But in the rear lies the bedstead, with straw sacks and covers put out to air, air being indeed the rarest thing in these dwellings.[128]

Child labor was common, often hard, and practically unpaid. Work in the flower, knitwear, and tailoring trades was not confined just to female workers; to gain a minimal wage, children had to help as well. Men worked in the factories, such as the large plants established in Floridsdorf along the Nordbahn and Staatsbahn railroad lines. Life in the suburbs started at an early hour.

At four in the morning the endless train of cabs were already stumbling on their way, as well as the two-wheeled carts that carried soil through the streets; the bread wagons drove by too, often in a burning hurry, piled high with loaves from several bakeries and vanishing in all directions in the dark of the night so as to arrive on time with bread for the awakening population.[129]

Those who had work—whether in transport, in factories, or in homework, as servants, casual laborers, apprentices, journeymen, or whatever—Max Winter counted as the fortunate ones, who had not yet been driven to the margins of existence by the city and its new economy. The unemployed and those seeking work had to be on their feet even earlier. They formed a standing line of misery, a reserve army of labor who were available for casual work and could be mobilized at any time:

In the early morning darkness they hurry into the city, to Schulerstraße where newspaper advertisements are displayed, then to the cooperative employment agencies and the city employment office, running their feet sore in the competition for bread, only to return home to their hungry children and careworn wife all the more discouraged … Others creep into the emergency shelters for the homeless, or out to the Wienerberg or Laaerberg where on cold December nights they might find a warm place in the brick kilns.[130]

Yet those able to find shelter in the brick kilns were better off than the hundreds of homeless who had nowhere to sleep but in "underground Vienna," the ramified system of drains and canals built along the river. Emil Kläger described his excursion through this "accommodation" as follows:

← potential source *(handwritten)*

The final hide-out for the homeless in the Vienna drains we found was outside the dome at the Stadtpark. We had to climb up a shaft rigid with dirt, behind which the so-called "Schmittn" was to be found, a small room with a tiled vault where a forge was installed while the drains were being built. Here a couple of young lads were sleeping on an upturned wheelbarrow, their faces showing the expression of a powerful desire for rest. Their bodies literally wrestled for a bit of room. A step further on I stepped into a space scarcely a meter wide under the iron spiral stairway leading up to the Karlsturm tower. Here three men were lying on the ground, covered in filthy rags. It was a picture the imagination of an artist driven by social outrage might have created.[131]

It was not just in the drains that the city's homeless and poor spent their
nights, but also beneath bridges and viaducts, in parks and meadows, and in
the Vienna Prater. Under the Franzens Bridge, the Ferdinand Bridge, and the
Stephanie Bridge (the last of these now the Schweden or Salztor Bridge)
camped legions of homeless and vagrants; the drains converging on the
bridges, with their side chambers and niches, also provided desirable
accommodation on cold, raw, wet, snowy nights. These tunnels were used
not only for sleep; people also cooked there, cleaned themselves, or just sat
around. The drains and their access tunnels were favored not just because
they offered a certain protection from the police, but because the moist warm
smell of the effluent raised the temperature on these ice-cold nights and made
the stay there somewhat more bearable. On nights such as these, people
sought close and direct physical contact, as this shared bodily warmth could
provide additional insulation, however meager:

> The next shelter we found above the Ferdinand Bridge, with once more the same
> outward appearance. The tunnel was somewhat wider than most, but the floor was
> thick with dirt and the air full of repulsive odors. On the left side some poor devil
> was asleep on a board, covered completely in rags. Close to his head were the so-
> called "cooking stones." On the passage to the right, however, lay some twenty
> people, their tangled limbs serving each other as bolsters. They had literally buried
> themselves together so as to share the warmth emanating from their bodies.[132]

In summer, the homeless used the city's green spaces, especially the Prater
meadows, spending the night behind bushes, shrubs, and undergrowth, a kind
of accommodation and night shelter that in popular parlance was known as the
"green bedfellow." Entrances to the brush and undergrowth were disguised
and made inaccessible by cunning barriers, so as to escape attention in the event
of police raids. Disused cranes on the Danube and barns were also used as
shelters.

Anyone who had a bit of money could find an overnight stay in men's homes
such as the one on Meldemannstraße,[133] where, besides food, washing gear and
a bed for the night, even a small library with newspapers and other reading
matter was provided. Another form of cheap accommodation was to be found
in dormitories scattered across the suburbs, such as those Emil Kläger described
on the Kleine Schiffgasse, Haidgasse, and Hofendergasse in Leopoldstadt.
Many of these facilities were illegal and enabled the owners to make a good
business out of the poverty of their customers. These were crammed together
in the smallest possible space and the most unhygienic conditions:

> There are dwellings in old, semi-decrepit buildings, generally consisting of three to
> four rooms, in which eight or more people of both sexes spend the night. They are
> partly accommodated in beds, but most of them lie on upturned boxes or planks
> on the floor, even on window shutters. The cost averages between 20 and 30
> kreuzer per night ... On entry we breathed a thick and heavy air. The smell of old
> eating utensils, the dry waft of moldy towels, an awful smoke burdening the air, the
> frightful human stench—all combine into an ensemble that does violence to the
> lungs.[134]

In these texts of social reportage, as in the work of those writers who textualized the city from its periphery following their own experience of immigration and social marginalization, Vienna appears as a divided urban space, internally cleft and broken. The Slovenian author Ivan Cankar arrived in Vienna as a twenty-year-old student and enrolled at the College of Technology, though he did not complete his studies, returning to Slovenia after a few terms. In 1898 on his second stay in Vienna, he began his career as a writer, finding quarters sublet by from a seamstress in Ottakring. In his writings Cankar sketches time and again an almost stereotypical image of the figure of the proletarian seamstress, most impressively in the short story "Die Näherin":

> She was a remarkable woman. She sewed from five in the morning to eleven at night, to midnight, or even the whole night through without lying down to rest. On days like that she was almost ugly—red-rimmed eyes, raw lips, a fallen face … Ever since our liaison she worked a great deal; and if I would wake up in the night at one o'clock I would still hear her outside, hear how her needle pierced the hard material, and especially when it struck against the thimble … No, she did not complain, at least I never heard her do so. And it would not have suited her—she was brought up as a workhorse to keep silent and work and finally lie still when she'd done enough.[135]

In the eleven years of his second stay in Vienna, Cankar wrote a wealth of literary sketches based on his experiences in the city, taking the "other Vienna" as his subject, the shabby, wretched Vienna of the suburbs and industrial districts. His story "Before the Goal," written in 1901, is a precise example, dealing with what he saw as an unbridgeable social gulf between center and periphery. If contacts and encounters did take place between these two worlds, they did so under the sign of shame and a sense of humiliation and exclusion, of degradation, devaluation, and marginalization by members of the bourgeois world.

The story's protagonist, Jereb, is a fictional figure in whom elements of the author's own experience are depicted. Alhough he has been to college, he lives in poor conditions in the outer suburbs, light-years away from the splendor of the Ringstraße, on the fourth story of a newly erected tenement. He sublets from a factory worker with a wife and three children. To get to his room he has to make his way through the hallway and kitchen in which the family sleep, as quietly and unobtrusively as possible. His everyday life is sad enough—he works as a bookkeeper in an office, which seems to him an end to all his dreams. His social and material situation strikes him as an unchanging "awful procession."[136]

Jereb's life runs its course in the divide between an unbearable existence in the suburbs and his inappropriate and utopian projections. He dreams of being rich and having power over others, imagines himself in a tall mansion on a tree-lined avenue, as the greatest adulterer in his milieu, having beautiful, cool, and proud women of bourgeois origin easily at his disposal, and seducing them all in succession.

Yet Jereb's actual world is far removed from that of his dreams. No seductive women modeled after Klimt's paintings are within his reach: he is alone. His connection to the world of the bourgeoisie is ephemeral, generated entirely by his imagination. Jereb feels inferior and socially excluded. He is embarrassed by his outward appearance, by the shape of his forehead, the curve of his lips, his chin, and his narrow neck. He perceives himself as a flabby and grotesque figure, formless, bony, and repulsive. The world of desirable women lies infinitely far beyond his grasp and only reflects to him his basic clumsiness and lack of talent in relations with the opposite sex. Jereb perceives his social origins as rotten, a hereditary burden he cannot slough off. The memory of his youth—which cannot be long ago, since he is depicted as a man who still feels young although he is not being given a definite age—seems like a walk through a graveyard. Everyone he knew, let alone loved, is already dead, destroyed in those suburban alleys that form the inescapable boundaries of his world. He recognizes how the gutter has become his fate, the insoluble riddle of a world that has condemned him and his kind to misery:

> Everyone he had loved in his early youth had died one by one in the gutter, damaged and dirtied. With shameful and repulsive work he had prolonged his own life, driven by that harmful and bestial drive: the fear of death. Jereb could never understand how it was that so many unhappy and despised people lived in the world, why they tormented themselves with work they hated, since it brought them no benefit and scarcely even a crust of bread, and was dishonorable and hateful into the bargain. They sweated and slaved away simply to keep their blood circulating in its turgid course, demeaning and dirtying themselves even for this end.[137]

The only thing that brightens Jereb's disconsolate existence is an occasional visit to the theater, which provides a certain connection, however fragmented, with the city center. But this only brings painfully home to him time and again how inaccessible the world of the rich and beautiful will always remain, and how an impenetrable network of glances, gestures, evaluations, and devaluations excludes him from the desired bourgeois existence. His path from the periphery to the center, from personal and social misery to the shining world of the theater, leads him through the bright and splendid streets where the bourgeois live and work. He experiences a tormenting sense of alienation, as he only feels protected in the society of outsiders and losers that has become his home. On the other hand, the sporadic short moments of confrontation with the shining world of bourgeois culture reinforce his sense of inferiority and uncertainty, leading him to the conclusion that he is regarded exclusively with contempt and repugnance, as a mere disturbance, as a displaced intruder:

> Jereb avoided the wide streets with their dense crowds of people. The alleys through which he passed were already deep in shadow; lampposts were few and far between. He met workers returning from the factories, seamstresses, servant girls, drinkers, and casual strollers. This was the society in which he felt at home, where he walked free, was natural and let his thoughts wander without fear or shame. It was a different matter, though, if he accidentally found himself in a main street with tall, splendid

buildings and an elegant public. He immediately crawled into his shell, bent his head, and no longer knew what to do with his hands and feet. He was ashamed, he felt small, unkempt, and ridiculous, as if his appearance, his threadbare suit, his frightening suburban image, and his awkward gestures were a scandal to the elegant face of the metropolis.[138]

The suburb for Cankar stands in sharp contrast to the center with its shining brilliance. It has no elegant boulevard inviting one to go for a walk, no flâneurs like those who happily lost themselves in the bustle of metropolitan Vienna, no intellectual coffeehouse culture to stimulate poetry and literature, no private contentment to support a contemplative distance from external conditions. The urban periphery in Cankar's novella is a world of darkness and dirt, a world without sunshine. It is a dungeon of dilapidated streets and buildings; the air is unhealthy, full of noise and dirt. There is no escape from this world—it is a prison, even if it has not been officially declared one. In his story "Mimi" Cankar writes:

> The heavenly sun did not shine in this district. Over the roofs wafts smoke from the factories, and when you walk along the street, soot blows in your face. The buildings are tall and boring. The people you come across here are poorly dressed, their faces hollow, their look unhappy. This barren suburb stretches far around; whether you go east or west, it still doesn't come to an end. I knew a man who already had a gray beard and a crooked back and had never in his life traveled to the end of that unconscionably long street leading to a brighter world. This suburb is a gigantic prison, without a single free person. I sometimes wonder what crime these prisoners have committed. One morning I crossed the street and looked at them coming toward me in long lines, with tired and heavy steps and sleepy eyes; it seemed as if I heard the iron fetters clanking beneath their clothes. They disappeared into great gray buildings without windows, and the doors shut tight behind them.[139]

This "marginalized Vienna" that Cankar depicted, the wide, dark, and sunless belt that surrounds the central districts, is a zone of social implosion. The concentration of local fixation, existential inescapability, and lack of mobility is coupled with escapes into an imaginary world and inappropriate utopias. This belt of hopelessness and social misery is an intermediate zone of the urban, a negation of society and a materialization of inhumanity. The "internal colonialism" of society expressed in this de-civilizing process leads to disease, infirmity, and alcoholism. Ivan Cankar's perspective, marked by empathy and personal engagement, runs in a certain sense parallel to the social text that the medical, coldly distanced, and objectivizing view of the city administration inscribed on suburban conditions. The instrumentality of modernism that finds expression here protocols a "total archaeology" of desolate living and working conditions, social deviance, and pathology:

> The need for stimulation or, as it is euphemistically called, "strengthening," to eventually reach a state of numbness, is all too frequently apparent in connection with the many worries and miseries of poverty experienced by this population. Their wretched condition permits them only in the rarest of cases to satisfy this need by consumption of beer or wine, so that they are forced to take refuge in

spirits. The alcohol counters that are so numerous in all the streets, side streets, and alleys show the extent to which this is demanded and drunk. In point of fact, it is consumed partly in the form of schnapps of various kinds, partly in the form of tea (!) and punch (!), to such an extent that not only is its effect manifest in the form of hilarious intoxication, but, what is much sadder, its deleterious operation marks the entire conduct of life—in the domestic sphere, in terms of health, and, most troubling of all, even in an unknowable way on future generations.[140]

The excessive alcohol consumption of the suburban population of Vienna, so frequently an object of complaint by doctors, bourgeois social reformers, and Social Democratic theorists alike, served as a drug of social escape, designed to compensate for a completely inadequate nutrition. Flight into the delirium of a cheap and readily available mass narcotic is explained by the exhausting and confined conditions of industrial work as well as the wretched state of suburban housing:

Housing conditions of the poor are generally quite unsatisfactory; they often have only a single room at their disposal, in which adults live with several children, where cooking and washing also have to be done, and which in winter, so as to spare fuel, is ventilated as little as possible, if at all. Better-off workers generally have a separate kitchen, but in this case the living room often also serves as the workshop of a tailor, shoemaker, weaver, etc., which means that the air is permanently impure. In the case of those trades that generate a considerable amount of dust, such as locksmiths, the respiratory organs of children of tender age are permanently irritated ... The high level of rents, partly a function of the housing tax that is much higher in Vienna than in other big cities, oppresses the poor in a frightful manner and prevents them from taking sufficient care for their food and clothing.[141]

Around the turn of the century, therefore, the urban panorama of misery had become apparent to journalists writing on social conditions, as well as to social reformers and the new social sciences. Yet critics of the time already noted a contradictory phenomenon that strikingly differentiated modern Vienna from other European metropolises: suburban misery here had a façade and an architectural context that concealed it and hedged it in. The Viennese tenement, at least in its outward appearance, did not follow a purely functional factory aesthetic, as was the rule in Manchester, Liverpool, and other dynamically expanding industrial centers of Western Europe, but rather a contradictory and ironic one. On the street side, splendidly decorated *Gründerzeit* façades contrasted with the confined, overpopulated, and inadequately equipped dwellings within, creating a contradictory "grammar" of the suburb. As early as 1860, thus long before the real expansion of the working-class districts of Vienna, the two Ringstraße architects Rudolf Eitelberger and Heinrich Ferstel already wrote how speculative landlords would dress up the outside of their buildings as splendidly as possible to seduce prospective tenants and charge a higher rent. "A colossal building like this then looks like a regular palace from the outside; it has all the outward appearance of this."[142] Shortly before the incorporation of Lerchenfeld, Hernals, and Ottakring into the municipality, the Viennese diarist F. von Radler wrote:

The culture of the second half of our century, which impoverishes everything, has even created a number of palatial apartment blocks in these districts around Vienna that seem to bear the mark of complacent comfort and even ostentatious luxury. In the streets of Hernals, far from the precincts of the Residenz, stand a large number of gigantic four- and five-story tenements with imposing façades, which building companies hungry for speculation erected in the era of so-called economic upswing. There is a complete contrast here between the shabby interior of the needy inhabitants and the exterior of their dwellings. The stranger who finds his way here is surprised by how, on a short tram ride to Dornbach, for example, individuals and groups looking like a Hogarth caricature peer from the windows, and that surprise grows to astonishment when he observes how balconies supported by artfully executed caryatids are adorned with shabby laundry put out to dry.[143]

10. A poor quarter on the Lerchenfelder Gürtel. Source: Historisches Museum der Stadt Wien.

Two decades later, after the full capitalization and privatization of the suburban terrain, the ninth international housing congress held in Vienna also noted "the peculiar mixture of the outwardly palatial and the internally indigent that gives the suburbs the stamp of disconsolate barrenness and the most striking shabbiness."[144]

This contradiction between appearance and reality, aesthetics and misery, can be read as a social text that indicates a characteristic interaction of the hard and soft signatures of the city. The grammar of the city creates "facts" by social projections of terrain, space, and territories, thus producing its internal dialectic as an interaction of surface and depth. The deep grammar here is simply the "hard signature" of the city, by which we mean the structured ensemble of socially generated spaces and segregations that directly appear as fixed features of the urban geography and topography. It is the apparently ahistorical arrangement of the city, which at first sight seems always to have been the way it is. It derives the character of its hardness from its power of definition over transportation, communications, and the hierarchized displacement of social actors and subcenters of production and distribution. By the "soft signature" of the city we understand the ensemble of its aesthetic formative components—silhouette and perspective, ornament and context, the establishment of public and private space, as well as the fixing of differences as ontologized categories of the beautiful and the ugly, the high and the low. While the hard signature lays down a seemingly unchangeable order of center and periphery, of space and social status, by declaring the suburb as the chaotic counterpart of the urban order, the soft signature seems to create a homogeneous urban entity integrated by an aesthetic of continuity.

11. Suburban poverty in Neulerchenfeld. Grundsteingasse. Source: Historisches Museum der Stadt Wien.

Max Winter also thematized the topic of fastidious shabbiness in his reports on the poverty and social conditions of "darkest Vienna": the giant modern tenements had French doors, brass fittings, framed mirrors, cast-iron railings on the staircases, and colored tiles in the passageways, "all pretty, all new, so who would think you need only enter the first dwelling to encounter the direst social and moral squalor?"[145]

Many tenements in the Viennese suburbs were in fact marked by a characteristic double function: their façades imitated the aesthetic display of the Ringstraße architecture, and yet inside they lacked any luxury or spaciousness of the kind that was so characteristic of the bourgeois buildings of the *Gründerzeit*. Their internal arrangements were patterned according to a pure rent-extracting functionality, giving a minimum of space for a maximum outlay. Adequate sanitary facilities were absent, as was any functionally "useless" space that could be used for leisure, relaxation, and the more complex aspects of social reproduction.

The mass housing construction in the suburbs followed chronologically on the building of the Ringstraße from 1857 onwards—that spatial and architectural documentation and conservation of a high bourgeois aestheticism in contrast to its feudal and aristocratic counterpart, which shows on all sides "the pathos of a *Gründerzeit* in thrall to capital," for which "no form was too empty, and no business purpose too mean, to justify self-presentation."[146] Given the monopoly position of the landowners and building contractors in the housing market, the high building standard developed for the Ringstraße and the technical and aesthetic norms it adhered to were equally articulated in the construction of mass housing. The insistence of a housing authority independent of economic pressures on "respectable" façades is evidently connected with basically pre-modern representation interests of the capitalist contractors that harked back to feudal models. In the context of this aristocratic and high bourgeois building tradition, there arose in the outlying districts the typical multistory tenements with fashioned façades and decorative ornaments, generous doorways, and spacious stairwells with appropriate paving:[147]

> Cheap striving for effect, academic clichés, and ersatz materials are the dark side of this style, with dire results especially in domestic architecture. Even in the suburban districts that have replaced the rural buildings of yesterday, this beggarly swaggering prevails, falsifying and distorting the genuine material and noble forms of mansion construction. The shabby elegance of tenements and business blocks and the low proportion of villas—giving the whole street its characteristic image in the new and renovated quarters—forms the other side of the greed that symbolizes the enhanced self-satisfaction of the new Vienna in the triumphal way of the Ringstraße.[148]

As Peter Haiko and Hannes Stekl[149] have suggested, however, the detail of the façades on the suburban tenements cannot be explained simply in terms of the representation requirements of the building contractors, especially since to an increasing degree these no longer inhabited the objects of their speculation. This apparent contradiction, i.e. to inscribe on the shabby world of the suburb almost the same surface aesthetic as on the display architecture of the Ringstraße and the central districts within the Gürtel inhabited by the bourgeoisie and civil servants, does, however, make complete sense in terms of the technology of domination. Our contention is that the façades must be decoded also in relation to their "policing function," for a similar outward appearance of façades in center and periphery, inner city and suburb, generates elements of urban continuity, a homogeneous urban body, without abolishing the social distance between the two. At first glance, no great differences are noticeable. Architecture thus celebrates an identity inscribed on the façades, whereas functionality cements difference. The lower social strata are given the impression that there is not an absolute and deliberate distinction between them and the bourgeoisie, but simply a gradual one, which can be bridged at least in imagination. The city is produced in the imaginary as a homogeneous body, but its aesthetic is formulated as a bracketing ornament of social difference and political domination. Its outward effect, the seeming continuity of the urban space, corresponds to a political and social internal effect that can be described as pacification and social narcosis. The uniformity of the façades is supposed to lead the declassed to behave quietly and passively in housing conditions that in an objective sense are wretched and impoverishing.

The appearance of the suburban façades is thus not just a lie; it cheats their inhabitants of the political awareness that the social differences of capitalism penetrate from the street into the very interior of the buildings. The domination of the public sphere is duplicated and has its complement in the domination of the private sphere, where it is deeply inscribed; or, to put it another way, the aesthetic becomes coauthor of the private. This aesthetic, which decrees the private as the refuge of misfortune behind impressive façades, is designed to prevent social and spatial marginalization from becoming public, and thus the object of cultural articulation and political consciousness, by creating an appearance of urban continuity and homogeneity.

Although the mass poverty hidden behind the illusion of the façades sought an outlet time and again in spontaneous, short-lived, and ineffective riots and was only finally articulated as a political factor in the wake of the great "popular movement" of the suffrage campaign of 1905–7, it was ever present in municipal politics as a significant hygienic, medical, and epidemiological problem. For the quite desolate state of health of the suburban population caused by wretched housing conditions, alcoholism, malnutrition, and inadequate clothing threatened to make them unsuitable for both work and military service. It was not so much humanitarian considerations, but rather demographic, industrial, and instrumental ones that led the state administration to describe, measure, and medicalize this misery, and make it the object of a socio-technically motivated discourse of planning.[150]

This process can be understood by analogy to processes of colonization, as Michel de Certeau has demonstrated with the example of colonial ethnography.[151] He perceives the textualization of the "uncivilized" as a hegemonic discourse, by which oral cultures are removed from the domain of rationality and transformed into a strange and "exotic" object. The textualization of the "world out there" (i.e. of the suburban life-world of the illiterate underclass) foreign to and incompatible with the project of modernization, dissolves this life-world and "translates" it into mere signs, numbers, and facts, which can be (scientifically and politically) manipulated independent of particular time and space. Only by this process of signification is the "other" of bourgeois civilization generated as such and brought into position for rational encounters and domination, whereas the untranslatable residue becomes an object of demonization, obsession, eroticization, and desire.

CHAPTER 6

THE SUBURB AS THE "OTHER"
OF CIVILIZATION

In contemporary reports, the suburb appears as the disorder inherent to and concealed within the urban order, a cosmos of social and cultural marginality and a byword for urban alienation. The suburbs are "dark landscapes along the railroad," characterized by "heavy breath," "gloomy, stupefied joylessness," and the concentration of the "joyless, sterile, and gruesome."[152] They are quarters of "naked, crude, razor-sharp force" that are marked by the "sign of coarseness" and that give way to "dirty, loamy country roads stretching far into the distance," "unchanging in their empty monotony, boringly uniform, dead straight, and endless."[153] Schermann, a columnist for the *Arbeiter-Zeitung*, saw, "in the most lamentable of all Vienna's suburbs," the grid quarter of Obere Donaustadt that sprang up along the Engerthstraße in the late 1880s, nothing but a conglomeration of "smoking chimneys, untidy shops, spirit counters, stench and dirt, slovenly women, neglected children, prostitutes."[154]

Modernization and industrialization had stripped the lower classes of their traditional social character and their largely homogeneous folkloric appearance, both of which had defined them in clear subordination to the feudal hierarchy and given them an appearance more animal than human in the perception of the elites. They were now dissolved into a heterogeneous mass of outsiders to bourgeois society and perceived as threatening—needed for their functionality as human capital while being feared for their deviance (criminality, prostitution).

The distinction between suburb and center was not defined simply in terms of space or historical time, or by any specific ensemble of architecture, technology, and infrastructure, but above all by the projection of difference and the establishment of social and cultural distance. Social distance was variously produced according to the epoch and the form of rule. When Donald Olsen[155] speaks of the social distance between the Vienna suburbs and the center being greater between 1750 and 1850 than it was subsequently, he is at the same time right and wrong. For the symbolic difference between the nobility and the feudal lower classes was of course an absolute one, seemingly irremovable because anchored in a religiously determined system of precisely differentiated social hierarchies.

This distance did not decrease with the development of capitalism and industry, but it was certainly redefined, as liberalism challenged the previous formation and supplied a new coding. The social distance from the lower classes is no longer defined in terms of a God-given order, but by the new rationality of money—the ceaseless stream of production brings dominator and dominated abstractly onto one level, that of valorization by capital. The conceivable utopia of the abolition of class distinctions, against which no theological barrier any longer stands, must be countered by a police and military system. The new social distance between bourgeois and workers is determined by the dialectic of economic integration and social exclusion with its spatial segregation. In this way, however, the suburbs become territories that are strictly separated off socially and culturally, in other words "dark landscapes." They are projection surfaces for the threats that seem to challenge the triumphal procession of modernism and bourgeois utopianism in the wake of enlightenment, liberalism, and economic and technological progress. In place of the reality of the suburb, with its factory workers, artisans, shop girls, and home workers, arise stereotypes of prototypical agitators, potential revolutionaries, vagabonds, criminals, and an ambivalently charged cosmos of female sexuality in the form of obliging and amoral girls and professional prostitutes. As the Vienna police doctor Josef Schrank wrote in 1886:

> The proletarian does not strive to approach the rest of society, or higher society as one might put it, and the criminal avoids the other popular classes not, as the proletarian does, to be of use to refined society but rather to lie in wait to ambush it; the prostitute for her part, who is outwardly equipped with the comfort that is required for movement in higher circles, presses into fine society, robs honor, destroys marital happiness, and infects rich and poor, high and low with the same dreadful poison of syphilis.[156]

It is the polymorphous terrors and anxieties of this "imagined suburb" that separate it more sharply from the center than does the segregating architecture of the Ringstraße. The interplay of bourgeois monumental architecture and the political imagination of the threatening terrain of a "shapeless other" generates a boundary that in Georg Simmel's words is established not in space but in society: "It is not pieces of land, not city and rural districts, that border one another, but rather the proprietors and inhabitants who exert a reciprocal effect ... The border is not a spatial fact with sociological effects, but rather a sociological fact that takes spatial form."[157]

The sociocultural transformation of the suburbs, however, happens in a manner that is anything but linear and mechanical. Rather the process is ambivalent and interrupted, both centripetal and centrifugal—particular segments of the lower classes become part of industrial modernity and its rhythms of time and work, while others are stigmatized sociopolitically and by the police as they either cannot or will not submit to the new discipline of labor. They resist incorporation into the industrially organized and disciplined masses. The suburbs thus become sites of difference and of social and political disturbance in the eyes of the center.

The fears of the ruling classes are no longer directed at the "other" in its form as "dehumanized rabble" and "mob" crying for more bread or demanding the overthrow of nobles and priests. These old fears dating from the pre-modern order of domination are replaced by new ones, deriving not least from the rise of the industrial proletariat. The male bourgeois gaze is no longer sure of its social and political control over the suburb and begins to develop a systematic suspicion and disdain. Symptomatic of this is a further observation by Josef Schrank:

> In order to get even an approximately faithful picture of the present moral state of Vienna, it is necessary to bear in mind the three enemies of civilization: crime, the proletariat, and prostitution. In the big cities we find all three of these represented in a threatening superfluity. It is from the proletariat that criminals and prostitutes are recruited. Almost all criminals fall into the proletariat after serving their punishment. Prostitutes, with few exceptions, either stem from the hungry proletariat or eventually become proletarians, whether as criminals or beggars.[158]

The episteme of bourgeois suspicion differentiates the following categories: the suburb as site of potential rebellion and revolt; the suburb as site of sickness, infirmity, and prostitution; the suburb as site of criminality and vagabondage; the suburb as site of ethnic-cultural disorder and miscegenation (and thus also as a projection surface for anti-Semitic resentment); and finally the suburb as social-pathological wound, which seems to threaten the ostensibly healthy urban body.

The pathologizing of the suburb, however, is only the surface of a discursive process that is much more profound and that depicts the urban periphery as a territory of the seamy and repulsive, of scum and the lack of culture, and thus as the "other" of bourgeois society. This biological and cultural positing of difference relates to specific features in the construction of bourgeois male subjectivity in the nineteenth century. The social exclusion and marginalization of the "other" played a functional role for the constitution of the bourgeois as universal subject of enlightenment and progress. As Peter Stallybrass and Allon White have shown,[159] the anti-hierarchical theme in bourgeois discourse is not only a rejection of the feudal culture of the nobility, but at the same time a devaluation of popular culture, which is denounced as "low," "vulgar," and "impure."[160] The bourgeois "purifies" himself in this explanatory model, unaware, as it were, of the historical contingency of his origin, of the socially polymorphous, of the sensual, erotic components of popular culture. The "underside" of society is discursively extra-territorialized, just as (bourgeois male) sexuality and instinctuality are internalized as a component of the political unconscious.[161]

The popular is both kept at bay and desired. The culture of the suburban lower classes, which is socially rejected and marginalized, thus generates a constitutive dependence of bourgeois identity on the "other" by making the social periphery into the symbolically central.[162]

Fear of the unruly political formation of the "suburb" thus not only was the result of an inner dialectic of bourgeois subjectivity, but had real causes in a changed political function of the European city in the course of the nineteenth century. Cities were no longer just one center among others in a territory of domination, forming part of a far-reaching polymorphous feudal system of domination in which non-urban centers such as monasteries and feudal estates also possessed political power. Rather, with industrialization and the formation of nation-states, cities become the sole centers of political and economic power.[163] Whereas in the pre-modern context the lower classes could be segregated with little problem (even in the urban context), and their role in the production process, however important, was not seen as culturally and politically essential for the economic order, industrialism now brought both male and female workers closer to the center of power. It was not just that the position of the working class in the production process grew more important, but that through the workers' movement a form of political self-organization developed that had no equivalent in the political prehistory of mercantile production.

In this way the lower classes became both more dangerous to those in power, more significant, and also less calculable and less predictable. In their very diversity, which in many respects eluded traditional social categorizations, they became the "amorphous other," that is, a sociocultural discursive construction in which the traditional marginalization of the lower classes mingled with new forms of social exclusion. These derived on the one hand from the form of industrial production (factory discipline and wage labor), and on the other from the psychic and cultural identity requirements of the new bourgeoisie. In this way, the excluding gaze of the male and female bourgeois was equipped with an additional, phobic dimension. The social "others" in their imagined rootlessness were turned into urban nomads and vagabonding specters, who at any time could challenge the center of power, erect barricades, set up workers' militias, and deliberately prepare the overthrow of governments. This is made clear in a celebrated quotation from the *Neue Freie Presse* of 1890: "The soldiers are ready, doors are shut; households stockpile provisions as if for a siege, businesses are closed, and every countenance bears the mark of deep anxiety. This is the physiognomy of our city on the workers' holiday."[164]

In the suburb as projection surface of bourgeois fears, however, it is not just political revolts that threaten, but disorder in general, in the form of the "industrial reserve army," the sum of all those unwilling to work, the loafers and hoodlums:

> A hundred thousand arms capable of work are available, complaints of a lack of labor power are constant, and the most honest efforts of our best employers are thwarted. A hundred thousand sinewy hands stick in the empty trouser pockets of

the flâneurs on the remaining Prater meadows, the "Schanze," the Liniengräben, and similar rendezvous of our patented vagrants, but despite a temporary shortage of schnapps, these gentlemen refuse the most lucrative enticements that echo from every work place with a constant "No dice!" Thousands upon thousands of foreign workers are imported at heavy cost and much local complaint, while thousands upon thousands of our own domestic rogues lie idling in their refuges as splendid examples of the classic *dolce far niente* and laugh over the laments of trade. A legion of veritable athletes, regular full-blooded Hercules, huddle dead drunk all day in the fake-spirit counters, or while away the "eternal long time" until the next opportunity for trouble with new kinds of cardsharping and other forms of practical cossackry, and they would be most upset if any kind of industrial champion sought to purchase and obtain their cooperation even for the slightest honorable tinkering. For "What we don't like and what ain't no fun/For that kind of work we ain't got time."[165]

Yet the pathology of the suburb was not defined simply by the specter of rebellion and upheaval, but also by xenophobic, anti-Slavic, and anti-Semitic fears, and above all sexual fears. This connection becomes evident, for example, in a report by the Catholic priest and subsequent Reichsrat deputy Father Eichhorn on Floridsdorf and its surroundings:

> If you stroll through these broad but dirty streets you meet modernized Jews with cunning eyes, and Slovaks in their traditional dress bearing heavy bundles with all their possessions, often even including their children. At certain hours the streets and pavements are swarming with gaunt figures; many men's faces are stamped with sullenness and even discontent; many women's faces show stupidity. These unhappy people are the workers.[166]

The sharing and exchange of women, Eichhorn continues, are not uncommon phenomena in the workers' districts; free love and common-law marriage are "the nurseries of a large part of the coming generation." Among the "grisly things" of suburban life is the widespread child labor, and, whenever the authorities are forced to intervene, it can be established that the majority of young girls who are still of compulsory school age have already lost their virginity. The general view has thus formed that "Floridsdorf and surroundings are nothing but a breeding ground for vice, infected both physically and morally."[167]

Fear of the "other" in its many guises thus also had a sexual and erotic component. In this way the identity of the ruling bourgeois male could be maintained, though these components had to be bracketed out of consciousness and repressed into the unconscious. The bourgeois ego and its morality corset, in which a dynamic of sexual anxiety and defense combined with attraction and desire, thus constructed the suburb not only as a threat to the sphere of politics and the public, but also as an undetermined and yet dangerous territory of sexuality, a secretly attractive and seductive terrain of lust. The cultures of the lower social classes and the prostitution that was connected with these were recast by a phantasmagoria of the sexual.[168] The sexuality of female members of the lower classes, and of female workers in particular, was fantasized as unruly, "free," libidinous, and available to bourgeois male desire, in contrast to the sexuality of bourgeois wives, who were subject to strict, "Victorian" moral rules. Felix Salten could thus write in his description of the Wurstelprater:

> Here, as in no other place, the basic human drives are simply revealed. The desire of woman for man, the desire of man for woman. The atmosphere in this hall is completely filled with this direct force ... There is no innocence here, at least not literally, no notion of social morality ... Their embrace is both expectation and prediction. And many of them already have in their expression a shimmer of gentle acquiescence, that silent surrender that leads women too often to pay for the brief pleasure of their spring days with long travail.[169]

Yet the suburb was not only configured as a place of almost ethnographic reconnaissance, or as the description of a "freer" sexuality: it was also feared as a place of commercial vice, of moral decay and infection. In *The World of Yesterday* Stefan Zweig describes prostitution as a major evil of his romantically tinged bygone world of turn-of-the-century Vienna, employing a military metaphor to express the forceful sense of threat: "The gigantic army of prostitution, like the real army, was made up of various branches, cavalry, artillery, infantry, and siege artillery."[170] In this sexual topography of the city Zweig locates the "siege artillery" unambiguously in the suburb, though he does not name this as such, speaking only—since this zone clearly lay beyond his conscious perception—of "the places where in the Middle Ages the gallows had stood, or a leper hospital, or a cemetery had been, or where the 'freemen' and other social outcasts had found shelter. In other words, vicinities which the citizens had preferred to avoid as residential quarters."[171]

Zweig compared prostitution with a dark cellar, an underground Vienna, over which the immaculate façade of bourgeois society was erected. The chapter on sexuality in this memoir of his youth contextualizes the city unambiguously within a sexualized cosmos. The Vienna of his youth seemed "Victorian" to him, morally two-faced and threatened by an infectious sexuality (syphilis being both a real and an imagined danger). The cities of his maturity, on the other hand, struck him as "progressive," sunny and healthy, characterized by youth and free from the evils of sexual guilt and prostitution by the healing effects of women's emancipation and Freudian psychoanalysis, and by the athletic cult of the body and the liberation of young people.

This dramatically enhanced fear of "vice," which is expressed in a large number of texts and debates of the time,[172] cannot be attributed simply to the increased number of prostitutes in the wake of rapid population growth, or an improved medical diagnosis of sexually transmitted diseases while the prospects of cure still remained poor. It is also connected with the way that the "hetaerae" did not stick to the spaces and quarters that were officially designated for them, the suburbs, but were also present in the inner city.

Reading the memoirs of the Ottakring whore Josefine Mutzenbacher[173] not simply as the literary fiction of their presumptive author Felix Salten but, in the context of contemporary sources that construct the city as social text, there appear behind the male fantasies, projections, and poetic fiction also patterns and sketches of an everyday sexuality at the turn of the century. Undoubtedly the suburb had little in common here with the commandments of bourgeois morality. The sexuality of the lower classes was not marked by complex courtship rituals, romantic codes of love, and property-oriented forms of marriage and expectations of inheritance, but rather by coarseness, haste, the immediate satisfaction of drives, a prevailing "immorality" and material poverty. Comparatively low hygienic standards, heavy physical labor, omnipresent infection and illness, and a short life expectation left little room for erotic refinement. This becomes clear in an episode from Mutzenbacher's life when, at the age of thirteen, after the death of her mother and her seduction by a Catholic school assistant, she fell into an incestuous relationship with her father:

> My father had formed the habit, after the first stormy period was over, of regularly screwing me early Sunday mornings, before I got up. I now realize that this is the custom of all workers, who are tired and have to get up early during the week and so generally mount their women on Sunday, when they have had a good rest. This became our custom as well, and during the week I got my desired treat only now and then in the night, and even then only when I took the initiative myself.[174]

Salten's "Mutzenbacher" lays over the suburb a dense film of omnipresent sexuality, in which "male fantasies" of bursting sensuality, phallic pleasure, and refined eroticism are materialized in and represented by the protagonist. If these fantasies are removed, the text can be read as a depiction, in the form of social reportage, of social desperation, the fleeting satisfaction of drives, and existential hopelessness. And in this respect the text is comparable with many scientific treatises of criminal anthropology and criminology from the turn of the century. Max Pollak, for example, court and judicial advocate in Vienna, reported on a "monster trial" of some young people from Ottakring and Hernals from the year 1907.[175] This involved the misdeeds of the so-called "Scherzer Platte," a loosely organized gang of male and female youths aged between eleven and sixteen who had specialized in theft and prostitution. Accused along with them were two procuresses who had led their underage daughters and other girls into "commercial vice," as well as a large number of male clients who were accused of sexual abuse of children and included a number of waiters, a baker, a delicatessen supplier, an academic painter, and a doctor.

Pollak, who had full access to the files as defense counsel for the accused youths, spoke of the "sore wounds in the social and moral conditions of the capital." The girls, who were all under fourteen and had grown up fatherless, pursued their prostitution in a semi-commercial way and had already come into conflict with the law for vagabondage, theft, begging, and hawking. They were already "masters," said Pollak, of "deliberately combining theft and vice."[176] Their clients, according to their own testimonies, had first noticed them owing to their "defective looks" and "impertinent expression." They wandered "barefoot and neglected" on the lookout for customers in the

Lerchenfeldstraße and Thaliastraße area, took them to two "regular child brothels" run by the accused procuresses in Ottakring, and there earned a "pittance" of a few coins. A key role in the girls' testimonies was played by a so-called "child-breaker" not identified by the police, who was described as a man "with a gray-streaked beard, obviously belonging to the educated classes," and who had introduced a large number of them to the procuresses.[177]

The trial ended with prison sentences of six months to a year for the procuresses, and penalties ranging from a few weeks to a few months for the young gang members. The accused men were acquitted, "given the minimal credibility of the witnesses."

Pollak's account provides a kind of scientifically "objectivized" parallel text to Salten's literary fiction. He cites in detail the testimony of the painter Rudolph Klingsbor, who encountered some of the girls on Lerchenfelderstraße and took them to his apartment for nude studies, where he frequently became intimate with them:

> A few weeks later his apartment bell rang one evening, and he also heard kicking at the door. Klingsbor, who happened to be having a visit at that time from an actor L., opened up, and in came the two girls again. Klingsbor did not want to let them in, but they pressed inside, and, when they saw the smooth-shaved actor, Klingsbor told them he was a priest, thinking that would make them want to leave. But the two girls declared that was all the better, that priests were the "real thing," and that maybe this one was a "catch." They leapt about the room and started discussing the most vulgar things, deliberately to arouse the supposed priest, who remained perfectly still. In the meantime Klingsbor's roommate, the painter Mahr, came home. The girls grew still more wild and impertinent; asked to leave the apartment, they lay down on the ground, lifted their skirts up, spread their legs apart, and demanded with vulgar expressions that they should be sexually used, and so on. Only when they were given some money did they leave. They repeatedly came back again, were given no more money, and therefore made a noise in the building or stood on the street outside and shouted offensive expressions at the windows.[178]

But this sexuality situated dramatically outside the bourgeois system of values did not just remain confined to the twilight zones of the "siege artillery." In the male bourgeois gaze, its crude and brutal factuality was transformed into a field of desire, an object of divided and repressed wishes. It thus also became something transgressive, serving the bourgeois male youth as a sexual initiation and training ground before and outside of marriage. A Viennese scholarly magazine from 1912 conducted an inquiry among young doctors, who were asked about their first sexual partners: only 4 percent mentioned a girl who might be a potential wife, against 17 percent a servant or waitress and 75 percent a prostitute.[179]

It can be readily assumed that these percentages were not specific to young doctors, but were representative of whole generations of adolescent sons of the bourgeoisie. In their sexuality, the "suburb" was present both in fact and symbolically: in fact as an experience of initiation and refuge, symbolically as the dangerous terrain of both attraction and repression, of seductive pleasure and the omnipresent pathological danger of venereal disease, of desire and the defense against it. The suburb thus embodied the "other" of bourgeois male sexual morality in the figure of the prostitute. Desired as a "grotesque" object of pleasure, she symbolized the sexual identity of the man that he rationally had to reject. As the obscure object of desire, she reminded the bourgeois male of his own "baser" dimension, his animality, and thus of the discrepancy between sensuality and instrumental reason. The suburb with its feminine coding was therefore rationally marginalized, though it remained effective and consequential in the collective unconscious as a culturally significant element of bourgeois male experience.

Prostitutes thus combined much of what the center feared most about the suburb: vagrancy, rootlessness, ambivalent female sexuality, and the threatening loss of spatial and social distance between inner and outer city. The attitude of the bourgeois male toward the hetaera, desiring-rejecting and at the same time dividing off, ultimately corresponds to what Georg Simmel established as the attitude of the bourgeoisie toward vagabonds: they "did not pursue vagabonds simply out of hatred, they hated them also because they had to pursue them in order to maintain themselves."[180]

This brings us to the question of the mechanisms of this social division of the city and the psychodynamic that lay behind it. It is clearly not sufficient to grasp the polymorphous "other" simply as projection or as a process of sexually motivated demarcation. The plethora of anxiety- and aggression-ridden moments that the "other" of the suburb is invested with indicates a more complicated process.

In his analysis of the aftermath of the Ottakring hunger riots of September 1911, the Social Democratic leader Karl Renner, for example, discusses the pharisaical morality of the upstanding bourgeoisie as the necessary antipode to the "vice" and "depravity" of the suburban dispossessed. But capital as the decisive vector in the division of the city escapes the immediate perception of both the bourgeoisie and the proletarians. It is "generally fluid, and all that is visible are the places where it is managed and handled, the banks and stock exchange." Capital is "everywhere and nowhere, wandering through town and country and is immediately rendered invisible as soon as it is confronted with resistance."[181] It is this "wandering" of capital that rearranges not just the material form of the city but also the imagination of it as conveyed through desires and projections. The transformation that the capitalist economy performs on pre-modern societies and their urban forms can be viewed, after Gilles Deleuze and Félix Guattari,[182] as a modified production of desires, which reconfigures a social field, in this case a city. Capitalism here does not simply mean a change in the economic relations between people, but also a restructuring of the desires, fantasies, and imaginations a society bears within it. Put another way, every form of society is characterized by a specific ensemble of manifest and latent, unconscious desires and drives. The economy and the sphere of drives thus interpenetrate and create a "production process" in which neither sphere is the root cause of the other, but rather both are produced reciprocally and modeled into an urban entity. This process is not dialectical, but takes place in interrupted fragments.

"Production" thus always also means its opposite, namely, social control or anti-production, which brakes and breaks capital's tendency toward endless accumulation.

This continuing spiral of production and anti-production, delimitation and relimitation, is only possible, however, at the price of ever new divisions at ever new levels. It is precisely at this point that we find the process-like entanglement of center and periphery, inner and outer city. As capital incorporates the rural suburb, that is, dissolves and restructures the old social relations and roles, producing the lower classes as male and female workers, so it also creates its opposite: a multifarious and unchanneled mass of potential agitators, vagrants, idlers, and prostitutes. The political and cultural economy of the bourgeoisie thus corresponds to the anti-product of the sexualized and vagrant figure of the suburb. Its "other" is the field of unruly desires that escapes the machine of bourgeois desire and society, representing at the same time both a potential rebel zone and a colonial territory.

CHAPTER 7

COMPRESSION AND DECOMPRESSION

Modernity, which divides the city and creates the "other" of civilization, is strikingly transformed in the world of the suburb, now principally defined by the axis of time. The acceleration of everyday life, the constriction of disposable time by a sixty- to seventy-hour work week, and the concentration of reproduction, recreation, and leisure on Saturday evening and Sunday all combine to generate new biographical models marked by an alternation of movement and rest, pressing work and fleeting pleasure, compression and decompression. Desire and enjoyment are increasingly focused on short, intensive, fragmented forms of satisfaction, some of which are invested with violence. Ivan Cankar described this as follows:

> I entered a lowly, smoky, and dirty inn that was full of guests shouting loudly and singing. The women sang and shouted too; they were dressed in colorful rags; their faces were ruddy and wet with sweat, their cheeks bloated, their eyes dull. Another room a few steps higher was decorated with paper flowers; thick dust floated around; there was a low stage and people were dancing. Everyone was thoroughly aroused, rushing about loudly—as though a slave driver with his whip were standing behind them. This is how feverishly one would live were one summoned from the grave to live just one more night ...
>
> There was a young worker. He, too, was excited and restless, and was drinking a lot. "Quick, Tini!" He took her by the arm and they hastened into the swirling dust. Music struck up, noisy and crude like the music at a fun fair ... When they returned, they were both strangely aroused; they breathed heavily and rapidly, and their eyes glowed as though through a red mist.[183]

The wretched social conditions that modernity brought with it created zones of concentration and deconcentration in the suburbs. While housing and family life were confined to the most limited space in tiny overcrowded apartments, social relations spread out onto streets and public squares and into specific zones of amusement. The rise of the first mass popular culture of modernism seems closely bound up with this "social-physical" interaction, for, where housing and family life lead to forced proximity, aggression, and hopelessness, the compulsion arises to escape this misery and transform it on the street, or outside the home, into a lighter, more fluid, and positive experience of relaxation and distraction. The suburbs with their show booths and music halls, their bars and spirit shops, their inn gardens and dance halls served as colorful counter-worlds of forgetting and social aphasia.

For an outside observer at the end of the century it must have been a picturesque and bizarre, even grotesque, procession that advanced each Sunday to the newly constructed amusement quarter of the Bohemian Prater at Laaerberg at the extreme periphery of the tenth district. They came from the depths of Favoriten (especially from the so-called Kreta, where Czech immigrants were concentrated around Quellenstraße), from Simmering and Erlaa and the brick works settlements close by, in short, from "a generally unknown part of the Imperial city, which comprises a quite foreign world, enclosed in itself."[184] Thousands upon thousands found their way here to spend their scant free time boisterously dancing and flirting and consuming copious amounts of alcohol at inns and recreational establishments with names like Bartonicek, Bezdek, Brozek, Budar, Dworacek, Klimes, Pokorny, Sklenarik, Swoboda, Wanya, etc. The loamy narrow footpaths leading up to Laaerwald between Drascheschlössel and the Simmering line of the Staatsbahn railroad overflowed with what the *Constitutionelle Vorstadt-Zeitung* described in 1884 as a "population of a quite distinctive breed." "Hideous women selling schnapps, hawking their wares in the Czech idiom" marked the path of this "remarkable colony," as did "old women caked with dirt asking for alms, cripples showing their deformities, and out-of-tune hurdy-gurdies making a deafening noise."[185] From everywhere, though, came dance music from the inn courtyards, to the sounds of which swayed young couples and lovers who had found each other for the day and a brief night, or possibly for longer:

> It is here where many ties of love were joined; an admirer needed only to pay for the delight of the carrousel and take the adventurous ride with the girl of his choice, and she was his. The screams of girls and the roaring of young men alongside the jarring and always out-of-tune barrel organ formed the encouraging accompaniment to this piece of earthly bliss ... and the couples wended their way home in intimate embrace through the idyllic paths of the Laaerwald.[186]

The proletarian pleasure zone of the Bohemian Prater was constructed in the early 1880s in Laaerwald on the grounds of the Wienerberg brick works and building company.[187] Starting with two inns run by the proprietor of the brick works canteen and a Vienna Prater entrepreneur, others followed in rapid succession, generally built without regulation and only licensed afterwards. Around the central inn, called the Pokorny Castle, which did indeed give the impression of a "regular medieval castle," there arose an amusement park along the lines of a traditional annual fair, whose operators were established showman families in Vienna and who for the most part were subtenants of the Laaerberg innkeepers. As early as 1884, the *Illustrierte Extrablatt* reported on a "richly decorated resort with restaurants, roundabouts, swings, test-your-strength machines, and panoramas of all kinds. It goes without saying that the characteristic Prater clown is here too."[188] Alongside the numerous bowling alleys, shooting booths, and carrousels, swings were an enormously popular attraction in the Bohemian Prater, including the evocatively named "catapult swing" and the so-called "Hutschenschleuderer," to which Franz Molnar paid literary tribute in his play *Liliom*.

Toward the end of the century, modern amusement technology increasingly made its mark. There were for instance the "steam man" exhibited at Pokorny's (a human figure mechanically driven by a steam motor); the "electric writing machine" presented by Josef Hossinger; the "electrizing machine" in the inn garden of Adolf Kliemesch (a kind of electric massage apparatus that generated frictional energy on the basis of electrostatic charge); a mechanical shooting booth at the Mrquan inn (where the target figures were constantly changed in both their horizontal and vertical positions); the so-called "trolley carrousel" of Mathias Kloff, which ran on circular rails around an "airship" (its four-wheeled cars were moved by hand); and the "velocipede carrousel" of Franz Schiller (bicycles at the ends of centrally fixed spokes). The many panoramas exhibited in tents or wooden booths, presenting pictures and views of the animal and plant worlds as well as various landscapes, can be seen as direct forerunners of cinematography.[189]

Undoubtedly, however, the most popular amusement for a working population that had only recently been subjected to the dictate of industrial time organization and discipline was the "five-kreuzer dance," which in the Bohemian Prater was a feature of virtually every establishment. This type of dance corresponded particularly well to the value orientations and expectations of a suburban population whose life was structured by the rhythm of machines and the weekly rhythm from each payday to the next, while their available free time was restricted to Saturday evening and Sunday. Alfons Petzold described in "Raw Life" what he saw as the prototypical escape from everyday life:

> The air in the inn was a mixture of smoke, dust, and sweat, where intoxication, sexual excitement, and pugnacity festered. Some soldiers started laying into some noisy, babbling foreigners; some ladies were sick and had to be taken out by their friends. The dancing grew wilder and wilder. The women flaunted their inflamed sexuality through the hall, and the men danced lustfully around them. One rapid polka followed another; other dances were not fast enough for their raging desire. From time to time the harsh music was drowned out by the mad cries of the dancers, who incited each other on with their shouts. But there was also noise from the tables, bawdy female laughter and the babbling song of drunken men— new melodies and old, the tear-drenched verses of a Vienna "hit," and the songs of whores and prisons rose through the night.[190]

Like Petzold, Felix Salten also saw the five-kreuzer dance as an alternation of compression and decompression, a refuge from a bleak existence. For him even the cheap, fleeting, and escapist mass amusements were an expression of immediacy and authenticity; they seemed to open to the detached metropolitan flâneur a perspective of escape from and a projection screen for the ambiguous feelings of his own social relations:

> A country song struck up, a modest little tune, which turned contentedly around on itself and then paused again before cheerfully continuing. And now the children of the city and the newcomers from the country could clearly be distinguished. For the former, this was just another waltz, while the latter began rocking in little steps as if at a church ceremony, in that serious calm with which peasants treat the dance as ceremonial work, and the peasant costume seemed to be visible under many a uniform. Jubilant shouts arose here and there out of the memory of the far-off village; dancers clapped their hands and wove through each other laboriously. In the midst of the stamping, cheering, laughing, and loving youth arose the desire not to have to stand here aloof like a stranger, not to watch the participants like strange animals enjoying themselves in primordial and unbroken pleasure, not to pass these happy hours brooding and hesitating, but rather to take part, without afterthought or reservation. We can imagine a young man who, with all his mental finesse, knowledge, and culture, still has sufficient strength to escape this subtleness from time to time, to free himself from restraint, and immerse himself in this steaming tumult of simple basic drives, then to return newly bathed to the others, who know only melancholy and ambiguous sentimentality.[191]

Salten's perspective on the five-kreuzer dance is that of the flâneur, whose description of the city projects a breach in his own subjectivity. Where Salten sees the power of youth and erotic desire as a moment of authenticity and freedom, the gaze of the policeman Josef Schrank creates scenarios of prostitution and violence:

> In the suburbs of Vienna, more than in Vienna itself, there are dance halls where the sum of a few kreuzer is charged for each dance. These places are visited by the lowest classes of the population, and the females among them are none too strict in their morals, but give themselves over to prostitution at the slightest opportunity, even to street prostitution. In these bars, which are also much frequented by the garrison, bloody conflicts over girls often erupt between soldiers and civilians.[192]

These contrasting visions of the suburb are not inconsequential, but form genres and narratives of the modern city. They fuel both romantic and menacing images of the metropolis. They relate metropolitan life as novel, as reportage, later as film, and as notes in police files. In this way a contradictory imaginary of the city is constituted, which is itself reinscribed on the urban realm.

The multicultural mingling of metropolitan Vienna and the resulting processes of cultural fragmentation and alienation, of separation and ghettoizing, intensify social compression and decompression; they produce the need for demarcation, assimilation, and escape, radicalizing the problem of social and cultural identity for both groups and individuals. While ethnicity, nationality, and class membership have separating and excluding effects,

consumption, diversion, and relaxation work to homogenize, since in the act
of enjoyment they make the "problematic other" into an "anonymous equal"
with the same yearning for a lost home. In the collective experience of music
and dancing bodies, which relates to a lost past identity, difference and
reciprocal foreignness is momentarily suspended and replaced by a common
destiny:

> The orchestra struck up a czardas, and we were back in Hungary. Everyone was
> dancing and whirling around. It was lovely, and they all enjoyed five minutes of the
> magic of home. No one here begrudged the songs of the others, and without it
> having to be said, without it even occurring to their simple minds, they were all
> familiar with the homeless sense of loss, the yearning for home and roots; they
> recognized this in themselves and in others. And whether the music was a waltz, a
> folk song, a polka, or a czardas, everyone here had one thing in common: they
> were strangers in this gigantic city.[193]

The question could be raised at this point whether the capital city of a
multicultural empire was not the very place where differences between
cultures and ethnic groups might be concealed by way of popular
entertainment. The inclination toward appearance, aesthetic superficiality,
and everyday hedonism that is part of the Viennese stereotype could then be
seen in historical context, as is often the case in relation to the Biedermeier
period, not simply as the expression of a servile attitude toward authority. It
would be above all the manifestation of a politics of public space and public
presentation that did not simply have an interest in preserving feudal-
bourgeois domination, but that tolerated, if not promoted, specific forms of
popular amusement in traditionally designated places in order to provide a
safety vent for multicultural tensions that threatened the system.

In any case, the difference between inner city and suburbs is determined by
domination and certainly not articulated merely in forms of popular
amusement. It is expressed in the interior architecture as well as in the
convolution, i.e. territorial segregation, of public space, and not least in the
movements and perceptions of its inhabitants, i.e. in their imaginary
cartography. The "city" not only absorbs the surplus value of industrial
production and financial speculation, it facilitates in this way the rise of
socially differentiated and graduated cultures of perception and mobility. It
creates on the one hand the culture-consuming bourgeoisie, who enjoy an
increasing amount of free time outside of work, and the idlers such as voyeurs
and flâneurs, who can live unemployed but in luxury from the yield of capital
and property. On the other hand it creates a mass of harassed people who
inhabit the suburbs in wretched conditions and whose labor provides them
only with the bare necessities for survival.

In his autobiography Alfons Petzold described his life as an apprentice and
unskilled worker in Ottakring as a nightmarish, fevered march through a
suburban limbo, an inescapable cycle of malnutrition, physical deformation,
overwork, illness, and both mental and physical breakdown. "Suburb" was
synonymous for him with those places "where neglect is no longer a bodily
sin, because poverty can no longer protect the body."[194] Laid low by his

incurable tuberculosis, he passed the time of his forced unemployment strolling through the streets and squares of Ottakring:

> In all these buildings, from the cellar to the roof, lived my people, the damned of the earth. Torment pressed here against thin and damp walls, impotent rage trembled at me from the passageways and floors, dog-like humiliation gaped at me from the windows ... How wretched were the youths playing there before my eyes. All these children with potato bellies, ape-like limbs, watery brains, scrofulous wounds, and the poison of their caste in their bodies.[195]

In striking contrast to the harassed crowds of the suburbs was the flâneur, as Walter Benjamin theorized him in his study of Paris under the Second Empire,[196] and whom Arthur Schnitzler presented on stage as a Viennese character. While a disinterested and almost zoological view of the city and its ways of life was permitted the flâneur, to the harassed it appeared as a threatening arena of social Darwinism. The flâneur can wander between home and café, street and theater, or park and restaurant without any concern for time. He can refine his subjectivity, cultivate his senses, and construct complicated codes of consumption, eroticism, and relaxation, whereas the harassed remain impotently trapped in the cycle of simple reproduction. They find relaxation and diversion only on Sundays in the inns, amusement parks, and music halls, or at the circus and panopticon.

The movement and spatial mobility of the harassed always remain under the dictate of time, i.e. of the undeferrable resumption of work in factory and shop. For the flâneur, time is not a scarce resource, but an opulent surplus and a rich reservoir of his social and cultural existence. For him, the amplitude and unlimited extent of space and time are guaranteed from the start, whereas the

12. The legendary suburban inn "Zur Blauen Flasche". Source: Historisches Museum der Stadt Wien.

harassed remain tied to their locality. While the "local" in the pre-modern town essentially corresponded to closed-off life-worlds[197] and isolated spaces of social experience, the modern city creates an illusion of continuity and spaciousness. Here the "local" is constituted not hermetically, but rather as the social construct of an economy that produces social limitation and cultural isolation via the nonavailability of free time and mobility.

The rise of the industrial classes produces its specific dialectical irony of mobility and settlement. The most mobile social strata (newcomers and migrant workers) become the most sedentary, as their position in the production process and their class situation rob them of any further mobility and confine them to their places of work and production, while the traditionally sedentary bourgeois, through the possession of (new) means of production and capital gains, can make use of all the opportunities offered by the new technical means of mobility (railroads, ships, automobiles, airplanes).

The opportunities that the various social actors have for perception and knowledge are differentiated accordingly. For the flâneur and the new bourgeoisie in general, the experience of the cultural difference, novelty, and complexity of modernity that arises from mobility and from artistic, technical, and scientific innovation is readily available. Whether he opts for conservative persistence and confinement in tradition or whether he surrenders to the ambiguities of "progress," which suppress classicism and historicism and open up a new field of expression, abstraction, and rational (re)construction, is ultimately a function of the options of "class perspective" and individual biography.

[handwritten margin note: Classes become further segregated]

13. Popular entertainment in the Vienna Prater. Source: Historisches Museum der Stadt Wien.

The harassed of the suburbs, on the other hand, have no choice in the matter. They have no options; they cannot accept or problematize the cultural ambivalences of modernity in their contradictory synchronicity in the way that lies open to the educated bourgeoisie, but are simply reduced to the brutal positivism of the here and now:

> It was 1885 and I had already spent two months out of work in Vienna; my money was used up and the ten kreuzer left in my pocket were my last chance of survival. I made the firm resolution to spend no more than two kreuzer a day. Out of this I still needed new shoe leather, but I calculated that I could manage for another five days and hope to find work in this time ... If a poor person suffers from hunger in a remote village, this is certainly unpleasant; but in the big city, where so much is offered to the eye and all wealth is placed on show in the street, where shop windows displaying objects that cost thousands are brightly illuminated, where sated people sit around in coffeehouses and restaurants, often not even tasting the daintiest dishes—to go hungry in a city like this is a hundred times worse and can reduce a man to a beast. He is forced to see how all these people who are more fortunate than he is pass by indifferent without even noticing him, or else they growl contemptuously if the hungry man staggers against their fur-trimmed coat.[198]

Social life in the suburb is constituted by a dialectic of fleeting, fearful, and aggressive glances and a counterpart of seemingly iron, unchangeable facts of an industrialism whose effect is loud, dangerous, dirty, fast, and threatening. Factory and shop are not just sites of production but constitutive elements of cultural practices, "world views" and worlds of experience. While the urban rootlessness and nomadic imagination of the flâneur conjures up the appearance of several possible worlds, for the suburban population there is only one world. The flâneur enjoys or else suffers from the availability of time to the point of insipidity and boredom; the harassed suburban population experience decompression as a painfully short stay in the world of nonwork. While the flâneur can cultivate and aestheticize the discovery of multiple inner worlds as an identity experience, the mass culture of distraction appears to the harassed as a place of relaxing and transgressive nonidentity. The need to get out is experienced less as "alienation" than as an interval won and a welcome interruption in the rigid life span and biography demanded by modernity. Self-realization for the harassed—spontaneous expression, freedom from work and discipline—can be decompressed in and through the arising mass culture. The social energy of the harassed that is not expended on labor and basic reproduction can be exiled, lost as though in a dream, in the "superficiality" of mass culture, its spectacularity and crowdedness, its unaccountable variety and exoticism denounced by elites. A contemporary observer, for example, wrote of the Bohemian Prater:

> On Sunday by midday the gay life has already begun. Swarms of girls, women, men, and boys wander over all the paths across the fields leading from Favoriten to Laaerberg ... The "ladies," who with few exceptions dispense completely with hats, walk singly or in pairs, their hair brushed tidily in modest Sunday style, while along the way stand "bons vivants" from the most distant parts as well as the

gilded youth from the tenth district and the swells of the Ringstraße, taking up their posts to select with sure gaze a "heartthrob" for the day or longer ... Music reaches us from a dance hall, by a band that claims the great Smetana as its countryman, though it has scant other connection with the musical world. *Mtata, mtata* forms the eternal theme of all its dances, to which the dancers rush in, and the intervals are devoted to flirting, which has very little in common with either the "ball conversations" of the gossip papers or the well-known primer of "good tone." The beer mug is passed around, and the motto "wine, women, and song" is varied here to "beer, Marianka, and brass band."[199]

While the flâneur can construct and confirm his individuality in a free choice of scene, place, and self-presentation, all that mass culture allows the harassed is the experience and confirmation of their existence through the enjoyment of its noncolonized parts. The "other" of mass culture that the elites despise and reject, its supposed lack of "taste," "depth," and "culture," thus becomes for the harassed an authentic social space and a site of positive difference and autonomous self-assertion of their own identity.[200]

In this social constellation it is no longer place but rather time that becomes the dominating principle of the urban order: "The technology of urban life is quite inconceivable without all activities and reciprocal actions being most precisely arranged in a fixed time plan that transcends any subjective determination."[201] The factor of time, its free availability or the subjection of the individual to the dictate of work schedules, is decisive for the imaginary cartography of a city, inasmuch as it is developed and laid down in the minds of its inhabitants. "Time" produces both the bourgeois flâneur and the proletarian harassed. For the harassed mass who populate the suburbs and whose labor provides them with only a bare subsistence, there remains only the iron edifice of simple reproduction in the interplay of a ten- to twelve-hour workday, the consumption of food, and the sleep of exhaustion.

CHAPTER 8

FROM POPULAR TO MODERN: MASS CULTURE AS DESIRE MACHINE

The transition from the rurally constituted pre-industrial to the modern industrial suburb thus went together with the rise of early prototypical forms of mass culture. Mass culture in a certain sense creates the industrial suburb as a cultural form of life, configuring it via an ensemble of cultural practices. It is, so to speak, its new face.

If pre-modern popular culture with its grotesque and carnivalesque forms of expression can be seen as the recreation of a population living under a regime of feudal ranks, the arising mass culture should be understood as the organized amusement of uprooted and displaced populations, who had to recompose their life in the impoverished urban environments, in conditions of harsh industrial and commercial work, wretched housing conditions, and poor nutrition. The early mass culture was the culture of those who possessed no symbolic capital in the bourgeois sense and had to create their own world, appropriating and arranging symbolic forms of praxis and conduct into an everyday life that would foster their identity. This was of course not an autochthonous, self-determined process, but a mixture of new supply and demand variables, a continuation as well as a reordering of inherited traditions, sexual roles, and survival strategies.

The rise of mass culture can thus be seen as a gigantic social testing ground of an aesthetic and hermeneutic of the mundane, where the attempt was made to establish a new rationality of life under conditions of exploitation through labor, exclusion from "high" culture, low life expectancy, and poor health. It was a rationality that allowed labor power to be sustained, a minimum of fulfillment to be achieved, and, despite the lack of resources and self-determination, a semblance of possible happiness to be appropriated, a moment of beauty, and a glimpse of the utopia of a different, better life. The creation of personal and collective identity in precarious external conditions oscillated between two poles: on the one hand the work-place-centered forms of struggle of the politically organized workers (for the most part skilled), who could derive from the nonmechanized and nonrationalized remainder of their labor power a political and cultural capital that they brought into the organizations of the workers' movement; and on the other the leisure time cultural praxis of unskilled workers, who sought escape from the annihilation of work or unemployment by their often excessive participation in the world of amusement. In the venues of popular entertainment, different forms of cultural practices intersected and crossed. The tavern was a place for political activity as well as for play, recreation, and the consumption of alcohol; Vienna's most famous recreation ground, the Prater, was used on May 1., for the self-assertion of the organized workers just as it was on other days for simple reproduction, sexual encounter, and spectacle.

Mass culture can accordingly be conceived as the lived reaction of ordinary people to the "work shock" of modernity.[202] It arises with the forcible transformation of the lower classes by the world of industrial capital, and accompanies it as a compensatory refuge of the promise of happiness and identity. On the one hand it creates new if limited opportunities for consumption, on the other it is the material expression of a cultural praxis designed to give the bare world of everyday life a meaning, an aesthetic, and a biographical perspective. By cultural praxis here we mean those attributions of significance that make less into more, lower into higher, banal into purposive, and mundane into valuable, thus giving bleak life a meaningful shape. Cultural praxis translates the conditions of life into a context of meaning and significance, thus establishing a life-world whose function is to guarantee the order and continuity, the identity and routinizability of the connections of life. Life-worlds reduce social complexity and are designed to guarantee the "usability" of the environment even in conditions of poverty, difference, and contingency.

The pre-industrial age had popular media of communication such as printed sheets with easily understandable illustrated proverbs, short texts with religious, moralizing, macabre, and apocalyptic contents. But especially typical of the age was oral communication for the illiterate majority through tales, practical jokes, song, and performance. All this was linked into a rhythm of everyday life in which work was not categorically divided from nonwork, but one flowed into the other, and which simultaneously linked material production into a more general ritual of symbolically conducted existence. "Work" was part of a more comprehensive cycle of elementary events, combining baptism, childhood, adulthood, marriage, and death into a theologically systematized form of life.[203] The popular appeared here as a horizontal bond that ran from production through to (mainly religious) holidays. The entertainment available to the mass of people took the form of fun fairs, church fetes, troupes of actors, itinerant storytellers, animal trainers, presenters of monstrosities, miracle healers, peddlers, folk singers, conjurors, and comedians. The aim was fun, fright, and sensation, tension and nervous excitement, and above all boundless and uninhibited jollity. Festivals often continued for several days and were sanctioned by both church and nobility.

Although this popular culture was associated above all with the religious calendar, its function and social character were shown nowhere more clearly than at the hunt and at popular fetes, which might even involve public executions. The liberal essayist Friedrich Schlögel gives an example of this in his description of the last public execution in Vienna on May 30, 1868. By one o'clock in the morning large numbers of expectant spectators had already gathered at the "Spinnerin am Kreuz" to take possession of the enormous area "laughing and shrieking and howling and joking":

> These were the habitués of the gallows, of both sexes—pinched faces, regular customers of the noisiest bars, inmates of the dirtiest cellars of poverty and squalor, a composite mixture of the many-headed company of knaves ... All who had not been detained in prisons, asylums, and other Imperial establishments for improvement had come out for crude pleasure. Right through until dawn, the mob made the most appalling nuisance; then when day eventually broke and the food sellers came around hawking their "criminal sausages," "poor sinner pretzels," "gallows sandwiches," etc., all hell broke loose and thousands upon thousands became as frenzied as was the fashion at the Brigittenauer Kirtag in days long past.[204]

At dawn the so-called better society also arrived, driving up in their carriages, the elegant ladies equipped with opera glasses and ushered to the best places by a special entrepreneur.

> Then the "poor sinner" arrived [the 23-year-old robber and murderer Georg Ratkay] and the official procedure took its undisturbed course. Was the crowd enraged? Was it shocked by the frightful sin? A jubilant cheer echoed through the air when, at the moment the executioner adjusted the candidate's head, a pole broke and hundreds of curious spectators pressed forward. The joyous cries of at least a thousand throats went on to reward the clever trick of a man who knocked a coachman's hat off because he "thoughtlessly" kept it on when the priest began his prayer.

There were more of the same merry pranks. As you can see, a "respectful majority" can richly amuse themselves beneath the gallows.[205]

If the public executions that continued into the *Gründerzeit* are interpreted as prototypical articulations of a still feudally marked popular culture, contemporary descriptions that connect the spectacle of executions with publicly experienced sexuality are instructive, showing the close connection between death and eros, the public world and the "dangerous" classes. These classes are visible and present en masse, they flaunt themselves in the spectacle and find expression here precisely by manifesting themselves as an organic collective that has its own language and rules. This of course involves forms of sexual and erotic expression that necessarily appear foreign and threatening to the bourgeois observer. Thus the spectacle forces him to express in his own way the foreign and the sexual, which he fantasizes as a wild collective orgy. In an almost Canettian sense, the mass builds up its excitement toward a sexual climax, finding release and self-abandon in the very act of execution:

Until the early 1860s, i.e. when executions still took place in Vienna at the
"Spinnerin am Kreuz" outside the customs barrier toward Matzleinsdorf, long
flocks of dissolute women and their pimps would arrive toward nightfall of the
previous evening at the execution ground, where the wildest orgies were celebrated
right through the night until dawn. Amid the playing of guitars and harmonicas,
cries of "Buy these piping-hot sausages!" and the sale of spirits, the most bold and
shameless vice was practiced, for which the surrounding fields and bushes provided
a most suitable setting.[206]

In spectacles such as these that express a pre-modern popular culture still in
transition toward modernity—forms that we define here as feudal-popular—
desire circulates within itself. In its inner life the feudal-popular has a moment
of autonomous enjoyment. While its symbolic forms of expression, its
customs and practices, were certainly subject to the hierarchy of God and the
nobility, in terms of domination they were essentially structured only by a
public and formal apparatus. The sphere of reproduction still allowed a largely
free circulation of desires and drives. Because the labor process still took place
within feudally structured forms of life and was not governed by an industrial
discipline imposed from outside, the sphere of everyday culture was
determined by domination only to a lesser degree. The spaces of public life
left to the lower classes thus remained porous and were pervaded with niches
that were free from domination. Domination stepped in only when this
microcosmic public sphere passed over into the more general public sphere
controlled by nobility and church. The feudal-popular is therefore self-
reproducing, and determines continuity and change largely on its own basis.
The ordering power of the dominant is certainly present, but in no way does
it cover the entire surface as a policing authority. The pre-modern difference
between "below" and "above" is expressed in the forms of life of the lower
classes through the tight restriction of social mobility and the identity of
place and significance. The sphere of culture and desire can thus be left
potentially to range and circulate freely.

The feudal-popular does not display any overflowing symbolic content
subversively directed against the prevailing order, such as could grow out of
the trauma of a disturbed circulation of desire. Hence neither does it know
any "mass politics" that could conceive of a unity of desire in the form of a
liberated future society. The "Wurschtl" clown—hero and symbolic figure of
the ordinary people in pre-modern Vienna—lives and survives from day to
day. He respects no "lordship" but knows how to camouflage this; he is
bawdy and sensuously, even sexually, desiring, but he cannot be caught and
tied down.

Contemporary descriptions of Vienna popular festivals and
entertainments[207] in the first half of the nineteenth century give a good
depiction of this free circulation of desire in a feudal-popular culture. One
especially popular event was the Brigitta-Kirtag, which was held outside the
city gates and which attracted up to 40,000 visitors each year. There was
"food"—the roast chicken that the Viennese were so fond of—and "drink"—
beer and wine from giant barrels—as well as music, dancing to barrel organs,
performances by local and military bands, circus shows, wrestling, stages with

actors, "dwarfs," performing apes and dogs, and of course the mocking appearances of the clown. In 1834 a great establishment was erected, the so-called Colosseum, a kind of general amusement park, in which all possible forms of entertainment were combined: swings and Russian slings, roundabouts, English carrousels, skittle alleys, clay-pigeon shooting, wrestling, William Tell-style shooting with crossbows, fortunetellers, boating on a pond, trick riders, and puppet theater. Favorite attractions included a giant elephant made of cardboard and linen, as well as an enormous barrel containing an elegantly furnished dance hall, not to mention the so-called Brigittenau railroad, drawn by horses and linking the Augartenstraße with the amusement ground. The Brigitta-Kirtag was celebrated for decades as a popular festival of gaiety and enjoyment until the authorities decided in the revolutionary year of 1848 that "with regard to the exceptional situation"[208] this popular pleasure had to come to an end.

The feudal-popular involved large gatherings of people, celebrations, amusements, turmoil, and madness, but its inner moment of freedom, the circulation of desire, gave the spectacle a form that despite its intensity was politically inconsequential. It reveals a circular choreography—it begins, it swells up, it discharges and disappears as if nothing had happened. This rhythm is given paradigmatic expression in Franz Grillparzer's description of the Brigitta-Kirtag in his story "The Poor Fiddler," published in 1848:

> All pain was forgotten. Those who had arrived by carriage stepped out and mingled with the pedestrians, the sounds of distant dance music echoed, answered by the shouts of the new arrivals. And so on and on, until finally the wide doors of pleasure opened, and forest and meadow, music and dance, eating and drinking, shadow plays and tightrope walkers, illuminations and fireworks, all combined into an Eldorado, a pays de cocagne, which sadly—or perhaps fortunately—lasted for just one day before vanishing the day after like a summer night's dream, leaving behind only a memory, and perhaps a hope.[209]

Contrary to modern society

The feudal-popular knows neither the separation of performers and spectators, nor that of stage and audience. It is not something you look at from outside, but rather something you join in with. It is self-descriptive, and in its festive rituals it points to something beyond the existing order. In the here and now it contains the myth of eternal recurrence and the sacredness of the undivided universal-human beyond rank and hierarchy. It is as it were the self-assertion of creation. In intoxication, enjoyment, and sensuality, in the temporary suspension of social inequality and division, "the people" seek themselves as the "*pagan-divine.*" This turns the ruling hierarchies of court and city, of nobles, priests, and people, upside down, without, however, changing the political body of society. By putting the lowest on top for a brief while, suspending the symbolic order so that "the real hierophants of this dedication are the children of servitude and labor,"[210] everything is changed only to remain the same. These are, in a word, saturnalian festivals, and just as in the Roman Saturnalia, which celebrated the (temporally limited) return of the golden age, these church and popular festivals also involved the renewal of the world. Transgression and reversal of hierarchy were the means of staging this, and the "people" created themselves on the border of art and life, grotesque event and historical time. Foolery, farce, and laughter are the media of transformation and transgression. The goal is the creation of an intermediate time and world of universality, of freedom and surplus—in a word, the pagan-divine:

> [A]s a lover of humanity I say that especially when people forget their individual aims for a while, they feel themselves part of the whole, which is ultimately where the divine resides, yes, God—I thus see every popular festival as a genuine celebration of souls, a pilgrimage, a prayer ... An invisible yet unbroken thread leads from the drunken exchanges of transport workers to the strife of the sons of gods, and the young girl who, half against her will, follows her pressing lover into the whirl of the dancers contains in embryo all the Julias, Didos, and Medeas.[211]

As Mikhail Bakhtin[212] has shown, the pre-modern popular festivals also contrast with the official holidays of the nobility and the church, which directly reproduce the hierarchy of society and place status before being and seriousness before laughter. The carnivalesque articulates the feudal-popular as counter-world to the formalism of baroque social etiquette. The geometry of courtly forms of behavior is counterposed by a "grotesque" and unbounded space that seeks temporary release from the dominant discourse and the existing social order and allows communication free from station, social status, wealth, and property.[213]

After Joseph II opened the former Imperial hunting ground in the Prater meadows to the common people in 1776, this became a central place for popular amusements. Contemporary reports from the first half of the nineteenth century depict a colorful, multifarious popular culture of entertainment, partly anchored in the traditions of the Middle Ages and the early modern era: grocers, bread and sausage sellers, beer and wine counters, roundabouts, skittles, mechanical models, waxworks, panoramas, camera obscura, and stages for comedies formed a varied infrastructure for the recreation and relaxation of ordinary people. In 1846 there were no fewer than "four coffeehouses, seventeen billiard saloons, nine roundabouts, fifteen skittle alleys, three swings, nine art exhibits, three Punch-and-Judy shows, one swing, and ten gardens, as well as fifty-four taverns selling wine and beer."[214] The Prater was a divided world—the central avenue was where the aristocracy and nouveaux riches paraded in splendid carriages and in the latest fashions, displaying their wealth and social rank before thousands of eager onlookers, while the Wurstelprater proper was where the ordinary people gathered: "Only a few of the dazzling crowd, or the crowd attracted to the dazzle, strayed into the neighboring Wurstelprater; indeed many hundreds of fine people, who with religious conscientiousness would not neglect any parade, had no more knowledge of the poetic Wurstelprater than we do of inland Madagascar."[215]

The Wurstelprater was not only a place of penny theaters, carrousels, skittle alleys, ape shows, magicians, players, menageries, and waxworks, it was also a place for the "carnivalesque" and grotesque, for clowning and the ironic transformation of reality. As Alland makes clear in the text just cited, the police censorship of the pre-1848 era reduced the Prater clowns to silence and pantomime. Despite this, their appearance evidently made a great impression and a colorful sight, which relate to the organic embedment of the Prater clown and his performance in the world of the lower social strata:

> The show had scarcely come to an end when a frightful trumpet blast in another corner of this permanent fun fair gave the signal for the beginning of the next performance. A large part of the spectators immediately ran in and watched the whole show from beginning to end once again. It goes without saying that any criticism is quite excluded; yet there are among the habitués of the clown theater some smart lads of a decidedly critical bent, who have studied the character nuances of each of the clowns and distinguish between one clown and another with the same keenness as our shrewdest critics distinguish between prima donnas.[216]

The performance described by Alland, however, is also instructive because it shows how the clown cannot be understood as just a social-romantic figure of popular subversion and rebellion. As the epitome of the specifically Viennese variant of the feudal-popular, he always articulated fear of the foreigner and the "other," xenophobic resentment of all kinds, including an often militant anti-Semitism. This latent xenophobia, however, remained hidden in the everyday existence of the celebration as identity reinforcement of the "people," forming a contingent though not causal formation.

How beloved the Prater was in the years before 1848 is shown by another contemporary depiction:

> But just cast your eyes over this motley thronging mass of pedestrians! Is it thousands or millions strolling around, chatting, sitting, drinking coffee, smoking, laughing, and flirting? Is there anyone left in Vienna today, you wonder, or is the whole population here in the Prater? Rather than just many, or even very many, it is a sea of people, a surging, showering sea! Oh little drop! Look over at the Wurstelprater, hear its joyous cries, its crazy tears, its cheers and shouts, its drums and trumpets. And now think that today thousands of happy Viennese are walking in the hills, thousands sitting in coffee houses and bars, thousands promenading on the Bastei and the Glacis, thousands smoking pipes and chatting in the pleasure gardens of the suburbs, and many thousands celebrating in the Lerchenfeld.[217]

The "New Lerchenfeld" was second only to the Prater as a center of popular culture in the years before 1848. It had been laid out in the early eighteenth century on the open space belonging to the Klosterneuburg monastic foundation. Right from the start, the (feudal) lower classes gathered here in unusual strength. The greater part of these were workers from the western suburbs of Vienna, especially the clothiers of the Neubau and Schottenfeld "Seiden- und Brillantengrund," drawn by the lower cost of housing and the better price of foodstuffs outside the customs barrier; then there were beggars, pantomime actors, bagpipers and other musicians, conjurors, wandering servants, messengers and waiters, rubbish collectors, clothes menders and cobblers, apprentices, embroiderers, and not least the celebrated

Engelmacherinnen, or back-alley abortionists.[218] The Danish poet Adolph Wilhelm Schack von Staffeldt wrote about his stay in Vienna in 1796 that poverty was a familiar sight here: "In the Lerchenfeld naked children tussle with dogs over bones, here beggars have their taverns and banquets, here they discard their wooden legs and bandages and ridicule their beneficiaries while enjoying meat and wine."[219] Here, after the fire in the Hetztheater, animal baiting was held at the inn Zum Weißen Schwan, and here, along with Lichtental and Erdberg the police doctor Josef Schrank located a key breeding ground of prostitution. The "ne plus ultra of all vulgarity"—kitchen porters, washerwomen, wool beaters, and factory girls—had already been "trained from childhood for this celebrated branch of industry."[220] Nor did Schrank forget to point out that it was precisely the Neulerchenfeld prostitutes of the pre-1848 era who were particularly popular with urban gallants. They took special care of their bodies, tolerated no competition from outsiders, and developed a comprehensive system of self-control, which substantially reduced the risk of infection from sexually transmitted disease. If one of them did fall ill, she was banned from further practicing her trade and financially supported as best they could by her colleagues.[221]

In 1804 this suburb, where, as a contemporary report noted, it was not rare during the summer months for twenty to thirty people to find shelter in a tiny attic, well over half of the 5,300 inhabitants were women, with over a third being "born elsewhere." A relatively young branch of business, which employed an increasing share of the population, was the selling of wine and beer. In the early nineteenth century, according to the land registry of the Klosterneuburg diocese, 103 of the 156 buildings had an alcohol concession, eighty-three of which made active use of this.[222] Franz de Paula Gaheis wrote of "the biggest inn in the Holy Roman Empire," where, particularly on weekends, "good-natured gaiety" turned into "a caricature of savage bacchanalia," dominated by "noise, shouting, and every kind of excess."[223] Almost all the inns had at least a certain expanse of garden, where popular singers, fiddlers, and comedians performed, and where on fine Sundays up to 16,000 people are said to have congregated.[224] Franz Gräffer saw in pre-1848 Neulerchenfeld "the veritable Tusculum of the lower classes of the Viennese population, who seem to celebrate an unending popular festival there in the summer,"[225] while Adolf Schmidl described the suburb in a guide to the districts around Vienna published in 1843 as a region where "the Vienna mob has its country *saison*," and "the realm where Bacchus and his whole retinue call the shots."[226] The democratic German journalist Adolf Glaßbrenner, a supporter of Young Germany and a masterly portrayer of daily life in Berlin, saw in Neulerchenfeld a cheap copy of the Wurstelprater:

> Merriment of the lowest classes of the people, but with no intermixing of respectability as in the Wurstelprater. Popular life as it is really lived, without refinement. Here harpists sing and shout, tell dirty jokes, and laugh at them themselves, there Punchinello is waggling. Peasants and their children, young lads with their girlfriends, slovenly whores, conjurors.[227]

The entertainment landscape in this era was diverse—an internal structuring and differentiation that in its essential features remained unchanged right through to the first decade of the twentieth century. Directly on the customs barrier, close to the Filiale home for war veterans, lay the so-called Little Prater: two circular buildings (where in the mid nineteenth century the celebrated daredevil horseman Gillet appeared), a waxworks display, shooting booths, roundabouts, refreshment tents, and stands offering almond cookies (so-called Mandoletti) and other delicacies. Then there were a great number of taverns and dives, meeting places for the suburban demimonde. This is where prostitution, both open and concealed, flourished, with countless incidents of stabbings and fights. They had names like Bahöll-Tinerl, Füchsl, Drei Säulen, Jägerhorn, Kleeblattl, Burgundisches Kreuz, and were the realm of roughs and pimps, of the underworld and suburban bons vivants: "Dissolute females sat around in colorful groups. Their favorite instrument was the zither, but you would rarely hear such a thing as a waltz. Almost invariably it was the so-called "Tanz," a brash, shrill, mad noise to which the lads whinnied and clapped. Nor could you escape among this class of people something that would be called yodeling."[228]

In the 1850's, to the fury of the police authorities, so called "naked balls" were held,[229] and later, after these were banned by the police, masked balls, whose focal point was women disguised as men:

> Masked balls were later held in the most obscure inns of Neulerchenfeld, and it was the mask of the hawker that best corresponded to the intentions of the demimonde, especially the low and bold. The young hookers generally started out with, "Give me money for an ice cream"; later this was upgraded in the low-class bars to a piece of cake or even a lucky sixpence.[30]

Finally there were the large well-established inns like the Rote Bretzen, Blaue Flasche, Weißer Schwan, Goldenes Fassl, Goldener Luchs, Goldener Strauß, Schwarzer Adler, etc., which were clustered around the amusement avenue of Gärtnergasse (later Grundsteingasse), Brunnengasse, and Neulerchenfelderstraße, and whose public was likewise recruited, though not exclusively, from members of the "lower classes"—skilled workers, small masters and their apprentices, shop assistants. In their spacious gardens and dance rooms, military bands played, Josef Lanner and Johann Strauss Sr. gave concerts, and the young revolutionary Johann Strauss Jr. performed his polka "Ligurian Sigh" at the Blaue Flasche, poking fun at the Redemptorist order for their support of absolutism. This is where great concerts of popular singers were given, the legendary "Wäschermädlbälle," and after the world exhibition year of 1873 the so-called "Lumpenbälle." This is where the poet of suburb and proletariat, Ferdinand Sauter, a well-known lush, could be found, as well as the young Friedrich Schlögl, who researched his early journalistic essays here. It is also where Johann Nepomuk Nestroy went to seek inspiration for the characters of his dramas and satires. The "Lerchenfelder" increasingly served as the quintessential and visible ideal type of the original Viennese male, as the satirist Märzrot depicted him around

mid-century in his *Wiener Daguerrotypen*: "A historical character whose fame
stretches far beyond the borders of Austria, with his breathtaking coarseness,
crude jokes, effusive pleasantries, and an instinctual tendency toward scraps
and kicking out … In sober condition, the Lerchenfeld man occupies himself
with idling and drinking."[231]

The acquisition by the Fünfhaus municipality in 1872 of a large site on the
northern side of the Schmelz, and the speculative construction there, which
was essentially completed by 1890, formed the precondition for a dynamic
urban development and intensive industrialization. In contrast to Favoriten or
Floridsdorf, however, it was only a very small number of large-scale modern
firms in leading sectors of industry that established themselves here, the
preponderance being locksmiths, plumbers, carpenters, engravers,
upholsterers, goldsmiths, and metalworkers, who set up their workshops in
rear courtyards or basements, working with one or two colleagues and
apprentices. The most common trade was that of craftsmen in mother-of-
pearl, whose high level of skill was as proverbial as their unspeakable social
wretchedness. It is more than a mere symbol that plots at the top end of
Gallitzinstraße, on the outer periphery of Ottakring, where an exclusive villa
quarter was to be built, were leveled with mother-of-pearl debris.

The Berlin writer Julius Rodenberg, visiting the Vienna world exhibition
of 1873, found "something between a manufacturing city and a village,"
with "a noisy population and much dust":

Every building was an inn or at least a tavern with its own singers,
musicians, and long, smoke-filled rooms full of carousers … Wine and song
at any rate, to say nothing of women. It is a good, pleasant land, this district
of the old "fields of Vienna" … There is singing and ringing all through the
night … There are concerts and music halls, it was where poor Madame
Mansfeld appeared, and now Amon and Seidel and the gorgeous Ulke sing
there.[232]

This repeatedly described conviviality, the so often-mentioned quest for
entertainment and almost maniacal zest for life of the Neulerchenfeld
population, stands in peculiar and seemingly brutal contrast to the social
development of this suburb, which in 1890 was combined with the Ottakring
municipality and annexed formally to the city with the second extension of
Vienna's boundaries in 1892. Its extraordinary urban dynamism with the
attendant wretched social conditions went together with a renaissance of the
traditional inns of the early nineteenth century but also produced large new
establishments. In the 1850's after the collapse of his renowned Zobeläum in
Fünfhaus, Franz Zobel took over the Goldener Strauß at the start of
Gaullachergasse, expanding it with a generous garden room and making it a
key venue for the city's most well-loved popular singers. Around the end of
the century, the inn was taken over by Georg Neufellner and, its name
changed to the Ottakring Orpheum, and finally, after substantial rebuilding,
it was transformed into the Weltspiegel cinema, the largest film theater in the
Viennese suburbs. The Rote Bretzen, Luchs, and Blaue Flasche were also
turned into cinemas soon after 1900; the large dance hall of the Bretzen with
its characteristic pillars was preserved in the Alt-Wien cinema.[233]

In 1860, the Neulerchenfeld citizen Johann Kunz acquired a building on the corner of Grundsteingasse and Brunnengasse and the land adjacent to it. Here he established a large, elegant ballroom, which he named the Apollo Room in reference to a celebrated earlier place of entertainment located at Schottenfeld. This gave out onto a splendid garden facility that stretched to Thaliastraße, ending at the very popular Seufzer-Allee, kept in decent semi-obscurity. The heyday of the Apollo Room did not last much more than a decade or so, as it was sold in 1875 and subsequently served as a so-called workers' hostel (shelter for the homeless) and later as a gendarmerie barracks, before finally falling victim to building speculation at the height of the *Gründerzeit*.

It was just around this time, on October 20, 1883, that the new Thalia Rooms were opened nearby in the Grundsteingasse, on the site of the former celebrated Grüner Baum. Besides the actual inn, there was also a concert hall (where the bands of the Hof- and Deutschmeister guards frequently played), the Amor Room (for dances and balls), and the Flora Room, where popular singers often performed.[234]

Neulerchenfeld was indeed an El Dorado for popular singers, who flourished above all in the last quarter of the nineteenth century.[235] They owed their enormous popularity to the fact that their songs, performed in the broadest Vienna dialect, masterfully mixed comment on contemporary events, humor and irony, subversion and ambiguity, with the crudest dirty jokes, lascivious miming, and matching gestures:[236] "Productions of this kind were therefore generally avoided by respectable young ladies. You found there a large number of milliners, flower girls, saleswomen, shop girls, etc., debauching with their lovers, whom they frequently changed and generally took from the ranks of shop assistants, commercial travelers, and the like."[237]

Edmund Guschelbauer, in the three decades of his professional career (1869–98), which he painstakingly documented,[238] appeared in some 550 Viennese inns, performing more than 300 times at the Grüner Baum and more than 150 times at the pinnacle for popular singers, the Rote Bretzen. The home ground of these suburban celebrities was the Café Seidl in Neulerchenfeldstraße, while from 1856 to 1910 the music exchange for both unemployed popular singers and the so-called "*Bratlgeiger*" (café violinists) was the Weißer Schwan. It was in Neulerchenfeld that Johann Fürst, the "lascivious faun and merciless jester, with his perfect contempt for good taste and manners,"[239] had his first success, as did the local legends Ignaz Nagel and Anton Amon, whose home ground was the Blaue Flasche. Until the early 1860s, women were excluded from the stage. Subsequently, however, the "divas of the Pawlatschen"—every one of whom took their lead from the uncontested queen of the Vienna demimonde of the time, Emilie Turecek-Pemer, known as Fiaker-Milli—had their regular triumphs in Lerchenfeld. These included the melancholic Antonie Mansfeld, who combined cancan with dirty jokes and ended in a mental hospital at the age of thirty-five; Fanny Hornischer, whose "Aufmischer" became hits, who was even freer in her words than Antonie Mansfeld, and who became the absolute master of "tootling" yodels, recalling Luise Montag (by birth Aloisia Pechaczek); and

14. Show booths in the Prater. Source: Historisches Museum der Stadt
    Wien.

finally Anna Ulke, who always appeared on stage in an elegant silk dress with
a train held by a liveried lackey, and whose performance was seen as the
absolute pinnacle of sauciness.[240]

The late blossoming of this popular genre, which was clearly out of sync
with the rapid urban development of the high *Gründerzeit*, relates to the
contradiction between urban Gestalt and collective consciousness. It
displayed that "village in the mind" that was no longer present as a signature
of the city. The music hall singers derived from the oral culture of the pre-
modern; they articulated the primary relationships of village life and in this
way set speech against text, mime and gesture against official euphemisms,
dirty jokes against high culture, and erotic talk against the double standards
of the bourgeois. By their use of resistance, subversion, and irony against the
rationality of modernity, they created a myth of community before this
dissolved in the anonymity of metropolitan life. They represent a culture of
transition.

With the advancing capitalization of the urban economy, these transitional
forms of an anarchic-organic popular culture come to an end. Naturally this
end is not abrupt, but the feudal configurations of the popular steadily fade
away, and particular moments find a new context as components of early
mass culture. The transformation of feudal-popular elements into the arising
mass culture runs against the social demarcation under capitalism that derives
from the mobility of labor power. Just as capitalism seeks to make use of mass
culture as a means of producing social homogeneity, so the articulations of
the "typically Viennese," the recourse to "*Gemütlichkeit*" and "lampoon,"
and the ironic distance toward those in power all represent an old potential of

difference and subversion. They can be interpreted as an attempt to gain an identity in a fragmented, internally ruptured world. The popular here loses its original and seemingly organic historical determination and is transformed into new and artificially produced structures, into something that may be called the "*popular-modern.*" Traditions were thus redefined, restructured, and adapted to new conditions of life. The yearning to "find oneself" was of course fulfilled only incompletely, and reduced to momentary experiences, petty entertainments, diversions, and everyday escapes.

Mass culture compensates for the shock of modernity by a wealth of material and technological devices, designed to facilitate these escapes from the misery of work and the time dictates of industrialization. The dream machines can assume varying guise, whether the "sensation technologies" of the Prater (carrousel, big dipper, ghost train, great wheel, etc.), the "imagination technologies" of cinema and football, or "narcotic technologies" such as alcohol and tobacco. Their essential function consists in providing moments of happiness, diversion, and relaxation, and in endowing life with a meaning and significance beyond the everyday, which is experienced as a dungeon.

The transition from feudal-popular to popular-modern, however, is not adequately characterized by the notion of transformation. This process is not a simple linear consequence of capital, technology, and urbanization, but reflects a complex and multiply coded alteration of cultural fields and context, of social hierarchies and relations of production. It involves the dissolution and reconstruction of social strata, and the redefinition of forms of cultural

15. Everyday escapes. The Präuschersche Museum in the Vienna Prater.
Source: Historisches Museum der Stadt Wien.

praxis in an urban context. In short, the social becomes economic, the cultural becomes political, and the political theology of the pre-modern is converted into the bourgeois Manichaeism of individuality and alterity.

With the dissolution of the feudal order, the autonomous, self-determining, and self-reproducing force of its popular aspect is lost, dissolving into a fragmented universe of projections and constructions. The popular-modern is thus created as a field of divisions, in a process of transgression.[241] To the lower classes, the discursive field that now surrounds and defines their culture is as little comprehensible as their own existence determined by it. This is accessible to them only as a fragment and becomes an existential and political question. The fragmentary is the form of existence of the popular under modernism, producing at the same time the yearning of the marginalized for wholeness and identity. The memory of the vanished pagan-divine of popular culture acts as a barb in the popular-modern, making this into an endlessly producing desire machine of the social imaginary—of dreams, everyday escapes, and fantasies.

In speaking of the beginnings of mass culture at the start of the twentieth century, we are accustomed to associating this with technically mediated devices of consumption such as cinema, phonograph, photography, and mechanically equipped amusement parks, as well as the sensational press and pulp fiction, cheap and standardized goods such as off-the-peg clothes, household goods, and kitsch. The preconditions for all these are mass production, infrastructures for distribution and consumption, and the provision of easily accessible consumption landscapes, and thus also mass communications, street advertising, and the charging of the banal with the aura of the special. Mass culture is the medium that makes more out of less and makes it possible, for a small outlay, to spend a short time in another world. Mass culture is also a bridge into the distance, insofar as, by way of the new visual power and the use of technically produced pictures and images, foreign worlds are transported into the here and now and previously unbridgeable distances into seeming proximity. Through mass culture, the "other" seems to be brought without hindrance to the self, and the object to arrive quickly at the subject—in short, through the new coding of fantasies, producers and consumers are brought together in a massive and rationally organized way. The accelerated circulation corresponds to the irredeemable aura of commodities; in other words, enjoyment is charged with fantasy, desire with consumption. Inasmuch as mass culture provides substitutes, it conditions a transgressive hunger for commodities, expanding to ever new terrains.[242]

The conjuncture of the sensational and gossip press, trashy novels, and cinema and hit songs that set in around 1900 addresses the gulf between dream and reality, mobilizing fantasy as everyday escape. In this sense, mass culture is permanent cinema, i.e. the projection of something different and better, of which only the reflection is accessible. The projection articulates and actualizes a difference of spectator and reflection, action and observation, being and appearance, wish and wish fulfillment. Insofar as desire is withdrawn from the world of lived experience and inscribed in the imaginary, with the real thus being consumed symbolically, reality is also coded with the grotesque.

A significant example of this for the development of mass culture in Vienna at the turn of the century was "Venice in Vienna," an amusement park established in 1895 on the site of the Wiener Prater.[243] In a form not previously known, traditional forms of popular spectacle were reinforced here with new technological and organizational infrastructures. Different forms of popular entertainment—musical performances, theater productions, music-hall shows, historical stagings and presentations—were mixed with "popular shows" (e.g. a "Somali village with genuine natives" and folkloric dance performances) and the latest entertainment technologies (giant slides, carrousels, giant wheel, cinema). Vienna's "Venice" was certainly not the first European theme park,[244] but it was the one most forcefully shaped according to the idea of a "total artwork." The Viennese Venice consisted of detailed and accurate replicas of Venetian buildings—palaces, canals, gateways, piazzas, bridges, houses, boulevards, and even a small convent. The total area was 50,000 m^2, of which 8,000 m^2 were waterways, canals, and a basin of almost 1,000 m^2. Buildings made up approximately 5,000 m^2. This Venice included shops, travel agents, restaurants, cafés, champagne pavilions, wine booths, beer gardens, halls for theater and musical performances, and even a post office. In peak periods a staff of over 2,000 was employed, serving more than 20,000 visitors per day. This was both a promenade for the bourgeoisie and a favorite destination for large families with modest incomes. It was a place where different social classes and cultures mingled—bourgeois and workers, soldiers and demimonde, elegant ladies and serving maids from the suburbs. The Viennese Venice was most popular in the summer, when the city's theaters and concert halls were closed. It had electric lighting, phonographs, and cinema as well as a great wheel modeled after London's Gigantic Wheel in Earls Court, opened in 1897. The wheel was a steel construction some sixty-four meters high, weighing about 500 tons and resting on eight pylons, which were each anchored in a great pyramidal concrete base. In the first year after its opening it carried 240,000 visitors to see the Prater and the city from a panoramic vantage point. Its so-called *wagons séparés* were taken at face value, so that many people believed they really were in a closed compartment and were arrested by the police for indecent behavior.[245]

In 1899, a further technical attraction was erected, in the form of a seventy-meter-long water chute. The degree to which these "entertainment technologies" delighted the Viennese can be seen from the memoirs of Gabor Steiner, proprietor of the Viennese Venice:

> In the place the Hochschaubahn now occupies, behind the great wheel, a splendid large lake was excavated and the "water chute" constructed. Already acclaimed in Paris, visitors similarly thronged to this Viennese version, and there were very engaging scenes when ladies fearfully refused to board the boat, cried and screamed when it got under way, and then calmly smiled again when it floated on at a leisurely pace. Reserve clothing was always provided for guests who fell in the water, but this was often insufficient. Of course it was always the fault of the

voyagers if they tumbled out. The public pressed around the lake and accompanied the ladies' cries for help with ironic shouts, there was a lot of laughter, and the proverbial Viennese sense of humor was much in evidence.[246]

The Viennese Venice offered a wealth of attractions. There were not only gondola rides with gondoliers imported from *la Serenissima*, but also the new artificial world of the phonograph and "living and singing photography," the highly popular tattoos of military bands, international specialty restaurants (Italian osterias and the celebrated Restaurant Français), an "automatic buffet," a sports palace with roller-skating, wrestling championships, and— clouded in scandal but much renowned—a Moulin Rouge with cancan and African dancers. Gabor Steiner writes that the Moulin Rouge had "tremendous success and no problems," and that the Viennese Venice had "a ground-breaking effect on all levels of entertainment."[247]

But the Viennese Venice could also be viewed in a more ambivalent light, as we can see in various references by Karl Kraus in *Die Fackel*, where he wrote that "it is impossible to visit the much-praised Viennese Venice in decent society, especially in the company of ladies; it is only a clique of shameless gutter journalists who praise it to the skies." It would give a foreign visitor an impression of Vienna "that he could get more cheaply and with less trouble— let's say, 'somewhere else.'"[248] The Vienna police chief at the time, Franz von Stejskal, viewed the "border district" of the Prater and the new amusement park more pragmatically, saying, "Finally we've got somewhere we can find all the crooks together."[249]

Although the original Venetian version of the amusement park was taken down in 1901, since after five years it had become too familiar and boring, the tag "Venice in Vienna" continued, becoming a synonym for popular mass entertainment in artificially adapted urban structures. Imitations of buildings from all over the world were constructed—Japanese, Egyptian, and Spanish streets. In 1902 this "international city" was transformed into a "city of flowers," with plants imported from Holland, and in 1905 the artificial "suburb" was illuminated by an electric sea of light, with 300 arc lamps, 60 floodlights, and over 10,000 light bulbs.

In 1912, after financial problems due to high borrowing costs, Gabor Steiner had to file for bankruptcy and "Venice in Vienna" was permanently closed. In the scarcely seventeen years of its existence, Steiner's artificial city had made a fundamental contribution to the formation of the mass culture of Viennese modernity. It was not only an opulent and playful testing ground for all kinds of contemporary theatrical and musical presentations for a wide popular audience (comedies, farces, reviews, ballet, variety, cabaret, wrestling, etc.), but also one of the most important venues for Viennese operetta.[250] Carl Michael Ziehrer, Leopold Krenn, Carl Lindau, and Josef Hellmesberger enjoyed great success there, as did singing stars much admired by the Viennese public such as Mizzi Zwerenz, Fritzi Massary, Carl Tuschl, Hansi Führer, and Ludwig Gottesleben. Songs such as "She's the Pride of New York" (transformed into "*Sie ist der Stolz von Hernals*") or "Oh You Girl of Mine!" became popular hits heard everywhere.[251]

But the Prater, which we initially identified as a traditional venue of popular amusement, not only provided an ideal site for the early theme park "Venice in Vienna"; it was also where the cinema was introduced to the Viennese public as a mass entertainment.[252] Its terrain favored the decoding and recoding of cultural praxis, since it had long been associated with popular entertainment in the collective memory, thus facilitating the introduction of new forms of popular culture and "cartographies of taste."[253] In the years between 1990 and 1914, six cinemas were opened in the Prater, with a total of some 1,500 seats. In the same era, both Ottakring and Neulerchenfeld became suburban cinema districts; thirteen cinemas opened there, with some 3,000 seats.[254] Though this initial expansion phase of the cinema was really nothing more than a primary "colonization" of the suburb—since in the inner city and the districts within the Gürtel more cinemas were built than outside this zone and the inclusion of the suburban periphery was only comprehensive after 1910—it is possible to say that the cinema was from its beginnings a site and an instrument of mass culture. Film theaters were built on main thoroughfares that were easily accessible, and located in those urban "landscapes of entertainment" that already looked back to a long tradition as popular amusement sites.[255] Many suburban inns and venues that were well-known and loved in the nineteenth century were turned into cinemas, such as the Blaue Flasche, the Ottakring Orpheum, the Rote Bretzen, and Zum Goldenen Luchsen. Cinema offered a favorable imaginary space for the recreational needs of the poorer social strata as these had developed in the wake of industrialization and changed social conditions. It was cheap and for a small outlay provided a great diversion from everyday cares. It was warm in the winter months and offered a refuge to women.[256] Cinema materialized the need for transgression and exoticism by the visual import of distant worlds and cultures, as was already suggested by the names of some theaters such as the "Weltbiograph." It provided children with a new escape for their free time and a place for adolescent subcultures. It symbolized progress, speed, and technology while also promising drama, emotion, diversion, and sensation. It refined the forms of presentation of the music hall, variety, and circus, and until the 1930s still kept its links with these, in that variety, interval shows, dance reviews, and performances by singers and artistes were still offered alongside the actual film. Sometimes the film actors even appeared in person in front of the screen, providing the juxtaposition of illusion and reality.[257] Cinema was an intermediate zone of new possibilities on the border between private and public. It offered space for the two sexes to come together, enabling pairs of lovers to escape the disturbance of parents and overcrowded apartments. It provided room to be alone as well as for company; you could be by yourself there without being lonely. It mixed people of different social classes and backgrounds together into a "mass" of cinema-goers.

The cinema is a symbolic universe. It creates parallel worlds and counter-worlds, it transmits intimations of something better, and it focuses fantasies and at the same time effects a lingering in the moment. As a dream and desire machine, cinema presents on the one hand a momentary happiness, and on the other the unchangeability of one's own existence, since its symbolic universe remains external and is not accessible in reality. By mobilizing dreams, it reinforces topographical and social destiny, and, by melting socially different agents into a seemingly homogeneous mass of consumers, it confirms the social segregation of the city at the same time as it refers to the ambivalent apparatus of modern mass culture as a whole. For, although mass culture "imprisons" the lower classes in the suburb, it still builds in a certain sense a bridge between these classes and the elites. A wide flow of symbols, commodities, and fantasies is at work in it. The dynamic of this flow produces both territorializations and transgressions. On the one hand mass culture suggests the illusion of a consumption that transcends barriers, the universal availability of goods and spaces, while on the other hand it continues to materialize barriers and displacements. It promises the whole but delivers only a fragment.

Mass culture should thus be seen as a multifunctional pattern, having to fulfill both psycho- and socio-dynamically a welter of often internally contradictory tasks of compensation, innovation, and standardization as well as integration and discipline. Not only is it a medium in which the "modern city" is inscribed, insofar as it secures the uniformity and standardization of the "human capital" required for industrial production, but it also makes possible the recognizability and routinizability of the proletarian-suburban way of life and thus lightens the everyday usability of the "city."

Mass culture "commodifies" the flow of goods in the form of cheap, industrially produced articles that are distributed to their customers via new systems of signs (advertising) and rationally organized outlets (department stores). This perfects a "political" manipulation of social distinctions. Mass culture writes not only a political text of difference, but also a cultural text of homogenization, in which ethnically and culturally different agents are made into an anonymous mass of apparent equals. It is the cultural medium of capital's articulation, but it is at the same time and consequently the opposite of this, i.e. a sphere of rebellion, resistance, and the search for happiness.

CHAPTER 9

A HERMENEUTICS OF THE MUNDANE

The suburb is at one and the same time a place of external marginalization, a place of internalized inferiority, and time and again also a place of revolt and a site of transgression. This is articulated symbolically in fantasies and imagined worlds of consumption (and in kitsch and appropriated petit-bourgeois elements) and practically in forms of resistance ranging from minor disturbances to revolts and uprisings. Both rebellion and social utopia are part of suburban reality, which cannot exist without this ferment. This is where the political mass organizations of the industrial working class emerge; from the workers' riots in Sechshaus of the late 1860's and early 1870's, and still more so from the 1880's onwards, there were ever new eruptions of spontaneous and violent disturbance—as when a state of emergency was proclaimed in Floridsdorf and Korneuburg following some astonishing anarchist attacks in Vienna.[258]

It was in no way merely the myths of progress of modern technology, science, and material production that offered, as a symbolic excess of the rational and feasible, the promise of evolution toward a new civilization. This symbolic excess included not only the new experience of wage labor, but also the overwhelming experience of a rapidly changing industrial environment in which reason, planning, and speed found direct powerful and local expression. This should be understood as the massive shock of expansion and innovation in direct everyday experience, which alongside the moment of violence displays a rationality capable of having a liberating effect. For, while the logic of industry enforces discipline and restriction, it is also the germ of a different, reverse rationality, which finds expression in the forms of struggle and organization of a growing workers' movement.

The urban aggregation, which seems to spread in all directions, naturally brings with it an omnipresent social atomization, but it also generates, as a response to overflow, chaos, and contingency, struggles, social self-assertion and for both individual and collective self-conception. These struggles are focused on the one hand on the improvement of working conditions, and on the other hand on participation in public and cultural life (universal male suffrage, municipal co-determination, access to general education and public establishments). They took place in the modern city, and from the early 1890s onward they were led and organized in an increasingly centralized fashion by a steadily growing democratic mass party that found its social basis overwhelmingly in the industrial working masses of the suburbs.[259]

This growing political self-organization of the work force, however, was created, accompanied, and supplemented by short-term, isolated, rapid, and unexpected revolts, and even successful instances of collective resistance and civil disobedience. The strikes, riots, and disturbances that were from now on an increasing factor in everyday suburban life expressed for brief moments the utopia of a different urban order based on mutuality and respect. The suburb then really did become, if only for a short while, that territory of unruliness, danger, and the unfathomable "other" that the fearful bourgeois gaze imagined.

From the chaos and misery of the metropolis, therefore, there grew—contradictorily, belatedly, and in quite violent struggle—the civilizing force of a social vision that took up the hopes and sufferings of the declassed and the urban pariahs, and that grew in this form into an emancipation-directed response to the "shock ensemble" of modernity that marked and shook up both city and country. This was at first nothing more than a possibility, an inkling. But, despite serious failures and disappointed hopes in particular concrete cases, the idea and possible perspective of a higher form of organization and cooperation not only found its original expression in spontaneous acts of resistance, but it also propagated itself in this way, gaining ground and coming to life precisely in those territories and zones where the deforming and transforming conditions of urban life were most stubbornly concentrated and visible.

The inhabitants of the suburbs, dislocated in the literal sense of the term, the unskilled economic migrants hailing chiefly from the ranks of poor peasants, together with the socially declassed lower strata who were driven out of the inner city, could latch on to a long tradition of social resistance. What they now had to learn, however, in the context of a radically changed experience of urbanization, were completely new forms of organization. This learning process should not be understood as a continuous linear advance; it was rather a procedure of steps forward and backward, a movement of trial and error, and a process in which spontaneity and violence could signal regression as well as progress. The creation of new forms of struggle and contention was fueled both by the traditional resistance of the popular and by the violent transcendence of this. Tradition and violence formed a common field of experiment in social action, the ultimate goal of which was the improvement of everyday life in the urban context. The two things ran in contrary directions, however, and resulted in a particular mixture of retardation and emancipation. This mixture was not an ideological narrative but the structural precondition for it. The symbolic surplus, i.e. the accumulated learning experiences of the struggle for new forms of organization, only grew into an ideology of the workers' movement in interaction with the narratives of progress invented by the Enlightenment. While violence as an act of transgression of boundaries imposed by tradition was certainly innovative in its way, it became dysfunctional in the sphere of ideological struggle with the state, a struggle that sought to deploy the newly acquired organizational forms of the workers' movement against the system of domination. Karl Renner could thus remark in his analysis of the inflation revolts of 1911 that the task of the organized workers' movement was principally that of "educating the proletariat for ever greater tasks in the future, and to look out for itself in the present." It was not just workingmen and women that the demonstrations had brought onto the street, but the people itself, "the people in the whole sorry extent of the term." Situations like this bore in them the "pains of a general confusion," they dissolved all fixed guidelines and delimitations in "nebulous exuberance," making everything possible, the impossible probable, and the determined and delimited infinite:

> The most crying accusation against the pitilessness of this social order crawled out of its quarters and joined the demonstration: those desperate ones for whom this bourgeois society provides no shelter, offering them no work place, and keeping no shop open for them; disinherited not only from property, but even from law, the lack of education and existence driving them to crime; desperate people whom the Christian press despises because this Christian society has deprived them of education by mother, teacher, and example, whom the state offers not establishments for improvement, but spirit counters and licensed pawnshops ... To redeem these people, and to kill the fateful monster of capitalism that permanently reproduces their ranks, is one of the holiest tasks of the proletariat. *It can march for them, but not with them.*[260]

Yet the difference between contingent social learning processes at the base and the progress narratives of the Social Democratic elites was a constitutive tension for the utopian dimension of the workers' movement. Despite the fact that violence was necessarily a taboo zone of public discourse, part of the innermost core of the state's symbolic order, its social energy remained a driving force of dreams for a new and better life. This particular tension between inconvertibility (violence being excluded from the public sphere) and conversion (making rebellion the object of political discourse) was ultimately what gave the early workers' movement its utopian drive. The accumulated learning experiences of the lower classes simultaneously cite and transgress tradition. A sense of respectability informed by their social and historical experience is mixed with a moral economics and a code of autonomy. Thus, in actions of social protest and resistance, pre-modern traditional elements, frequently drawn from the canon of rural and pre-industrial codes of behavior, mingle with "modern" models derived from the struggle against harsh industrial discipline. The old traditional individualistic male concept of honor is expressed together with a collective notion of organized and rationalized social protest. The coexistence of tradition-governed resistance and protest narratives, their simultaneous intermingling and incongruence—in short, the ever interrupted learning process of the social—gives voice to silent protest, articulates the ferment of the masses, and gives their "oral" forms of revolt a political demand. In and through these forms of protest, their protagonists find a voice; subjects speak whose stories and fates have never been written down. The traceless modernity acquires in this way a historical texture.

The learning process in the public space corresponds to a specific change-resistant tendency that persists in the private sphere. The symbolism of the private in many cases refers to something quite different from a narrative of progress. The private is dominated by an "economy of survival," which strives to ensure not just material subsistence but also a minimum of everyday poetry, an aesthetic of survival, and an intimate compensation for unbearable living conditions. Besides the attempt to secure food and clothing, this implies a cultural practice that can offer a certain meaning, over and above mere vegetation and the incessant compulsion to alienate one's labor power.

In December 1903 Max Winter visited an impoverished household in the "worst quarter" of Floridsdorf, known as Mühlschüttel.[261] In a decrepit hut in Scheffelgasse he found two adult women and three children living in a single room of scarcely 11 m² and with a ceiling height of 1.9 meters. At the time of Winter's visit, the father of the family was serving a sentence of several years' imprisonment in the Stein penitentiary, and his workshop adjacent to the family room was now used for storage. The family's nourishment consisted on weekdays of a loaf of bread, a liter of milk, ersatz coffee, and sugar. Only on Sundays did they also have soup, or pancakes made from potatoes that the mother and her grown-up daughter had gleaned during the week as scavengers on the garbage dump located on the land of the Klosterneuburg monastery (the refuse depot for the twelve Vienna districts between the flood barrier and the old course of the Danube at Floridsdorf).[262]

In the midst of this utter misery, Max Winter made a remarkable discovery:

> On the walls of the room, painted with a light blue distemper, there hung alongside a few holy pictures an almost colorless oil painting of the former Crown Princess Stefanie and an engraving in a small gold frame, with the double portrait of a princely couple of the Coburg dynasty. A certain Maria Immaculata and August were eternally depicted for patriots. Our further discussion hinged around these pictures.[263]

The Catholic cooperator and teacher of religion at the elementary school in Mühlschüttel, Rudolf Eichhorn, had recorded a similar observation nearly two decades previously:

> In this room inhabited by thirteen people (nine paces long, eight paces wide) there hung holy pictures and the portrait of one of our most serene princely couples. The lady of the house said to me about these pictures: "They're from a time when things were better here. I'd be quite all right here, if the Jew gave us as much as we've paid him."[264]

This indicates precisely a key aspect of the logic and reality of urban life with its contradictions and contingencies. It is impossible for people to find a home for themselves, somewhere that they can live, without having something beyond themselves: a connection with the possible or the imaginary, whether this is expressed in a noble and valuable form or in the ugliest of objects, in the most select taste or the vilest kitsch, what Lefebvre calls "derisive poetry"[265]—only such an objectified connection to the imaginary makes possible any kind of survival, even and especially for such urban pariahs vegetating in the worst conditions.

The reification of the imaginary in the construction of the private and of subjectivity is evidently fed by several sources. On the one hand it is a self-displacement in the public space as well as in the private, which is thereby given borders and contents, and on the other hand it is an alienated code of inwardness, oriented to esteemed figures in public life and from the religious and spiritual sphere. At the same time, however, it is a projection of the inside outward as the only possible poetry of the everyday: it is sentimentality and the attempt to create by way of kitsch a recognizable trace of something better amid the bad, appearing thus as a waiting room of utopia, as happiness amid misfortune, and as a home in a homeless world. The banal is made sacred, the valueless valuable, with kitsch as a surrogate for the possible, its traumatic empty place. As Lefebvre puts it, to discover living space and its meaning, concepts and categories are needed that refer to the "here and now of experience," to what is unknown and misunderstood in everyday existence. The relation of the inhabitants to nature, to being, and to their own essence, in other words, has its immediate place first of all in their living space—this is where it is realized and becomes readable.[266]

The Vienna tenements and the wretched quarters of the suburbs with their "tiny living rooms, high rents, frequent quarrels, and perennial dirt" were invariably described as sites of "economic and moral ruin,"[267] which must necessarily bring about the physical and mental crippling and the regression to savagery of their inhabitants, given their lack of quiet and air, their lack of stimulus, and their unhappiness.[268] On top of all this was the permanent fear of unemployment, hunger, and eviction: "In the multitude of suburban tenements the apartments, passages, and stairs were filled with this fear, which hung over the life of the workers like a constant dark cloud; it could drive them crazy, disturb the deepest sleep, make them shudder in broad daylight, and even spoil their hours of love."[269]

A decade after his research in Mühlschüttel, Max Winter published a social reportage on childhood poverty in Lichtental, in the ninth district of Vienna. Situated between Franz-Josef-Bahn and Nußdorferstraße, Lichtental was generally viewed as a run-down and dangerous slum quarter, "slums in the worst sense of the word, as unhealthy and uncultured as you could get." Since the end of the eighteenth century the formerly separate settlements here and the village of Lichtental on the Liechtenstein land had grown together into a suburban agglomeration, though great topographical variations in urban territory hindered private land speculation during the *Gründerzeit*. Lichtental thus presented itself in the early twentieth century as a conglomeration in dire need of cleaning up, composed of gloomy narrow side streets with low crouching suburban houses, overlooked here and there by three- or four-story tenements; inside the houses were "cramped and gloomy dungeons, which may well still be let out as apartments by the owners ... but which are in fact no more than sleeping quarters at best, flouting the most elementary rules of hygiene."[270] These "dungeons" were populated mostly by unskilled workers, drivers, and wood and stone cutters, who made their living loading barges on the nearby Danube canal. Then there were road sweepers, medical orderlies, workers on the streetcars and railroads, postal workers, as well as a minority of skilled and organized workers whose family incomes were insufficient to rent a tenement flat in one of the newer working-class districts, or who had simply remained in Lichtental as they were born and bred there. Winter wrote of the "multitude of urban slaves" who possessed nothing more than the symbolic capital of local identity, connection to the most confined "home," a vague pride to be Lichtentalers. And again here he was struck by the prominence of kitsch and the most valueless junk, most often encountered precisely in the poorest of dwellings: "The whole apartment is falling to pieces. The once bright blue walls have crumbled. Holy pictures on the walls. Everything gloomy and disconsolate."[271]

The reports of Winter and Eichhorn were in no way isolated cases. In December 1888 the doctor to the poor, psychiatrist, and Social Democratic party founder Victor Adler got into the works of the Wienerberg company with the help of a brick cutter and published sensational social reports on the living and working conditions there in *Gleichheit*, the paper he himself had founded.[272] The Wienerberg Brick Manufacture and Building Company possessed eighteen plants and a site of 900 hectares on the southern edge of Vienna. Eight thousand employees—the overwhelming majority of whom were Czech though Slovaks and Italians also made up a significant portion—produced some 200 million bricks each year, amounting to half the total manufactured in Austria; in the peak building season they could supply a million bricks per day. Production was highly labor-intensive; despite the investment in circular kilns and brick-cutting machinery that had been made in the *Gründerzeit* by Heinrich Drasche, who was both innovative and highly successful, the overall process was only only partly mechanized. As late as 1903, only 20 percent of the bricks were produced by machine, the rest still manually. This was family work: men, women, and children, joined by seasonally employed single men, made up small groups who worked on a piece basis for up to sixteen to eighteen hours a day, especially in the summer months. Most had a rest day in the middle of the week, but the Wienerberg company kept no record of working hours. It paid according to a bonus system: for every thousand bricks, the groups received ten kreuzer, but only if they had produced at least 80,000 bricks in the whole season. This enabled groups to earn from twenty to fifty gulden in late autumn, according to their productivity, but it was hard for them to survive through the winter when work was sharply limited. Payment in company tokens, the truck system, and similar methods reinforced the total dependence of these Viennese "brick slaves."[273]

After the retirement of Heinrich Drasche—who had succeeded the firm's "feudal" patriarch Alois Miesbach—and the transformation of Wienerberg into a joint-stock company, social achievements that had previously been exemplary were successively dismantled, and the wretched working and living conditions met ever more widespread criticism. When in April 1895 the 6,000 men, women, and children at all of the company's forty-one plants came out on strike, ever new revelations about conditions in the brick works grew into a public scandal.[274]

The *Neue Freie Presse* in an article of April 25, 1895, referred in particular to the inhuman conditions in the workers' living quarters. Four or five families—mostly Czechs who had arrived many years previously, with children already born in Vienna, "all speaking perfectly good German as well as their mother tongue"—were sometimes forced to share a single room. Each family's living space was drawn with chalk lines on the floor. On the upper story of a disused circular kiln lived twenty-six people, without any kind of sanitary facilities whatsoever. Water for cooking and washing was brought from ponds in the clay pits, and drinking water from the works canteen. Marital and family life seemed "completely abolished in these mass quarters."[275] Engelbert Pernerstorfer spoke in a parliamentary debate on the brick-workers' strike of "plague cellars of indecency" and "breeding grounds of all possible shamelessness," in which every event in life took place in public: "People slept in these rooms; they were born in the same room, they died in the same room; this was where they had sex, naturally in view of everyone else present."[276] The newspaper could scarcely conceal its amazement "that the children seem quite healthy, and some of the young girls even pretty." Most rooms had holy pictures on the walls, colored curtains at the windows, cupboards with glasses and dishes. It was "thanks to women's hands" that order and cleanliness could be maintained "in this tormented corner."[277]

The materialization of the imaginary in kitsch and junk is initially a defensive strategy, designed to make possible and bearable a life in such claustrophobic conditions tending to the dissolution of privacy and intimacy. From a life-worldly perspective, however, this implies an offensive move, especially insofar as it involves the production, continuity, and preservation of a private life amid the extreme conditions of incalculability, rapid change, material uncertainty, and social marginalization. What is articulated in kitsch is thus less a difference between "high" and "low" culture than a cultural strategy as part of an economy of survival. This strategy is necessary, but at the same time insufficient, needing as its complementary dimension a specific form of public life: the life of the street.

CHAPTER 10

A CULTURE OF RESISTANCE

The street is the place of communicative exchange beyond the primary relations of the family; it is the melting pot that creates suburban life without which it would be no more than a fragmented structure, with the excluded rigidly separated from one another. The street is a kind of mediating instance between members of the lower classes, between private and public space, extending in a certain sense into shops, the entrances of buildings, and storefronts, and even into dwellings. In the context of the immediate neighborhood, the street is the place where people come into contact with one another without being complete strangers. The street thus forms a complex balance between rights and duties, distance and connection; it is also an information system of (self-imposed) social control. It is the microcosm in which the suburb has its center of gravity. It serves the exchange of information; it is symbol and playground as well as institution for the education and socialization of suburban youth. The street is the place where primary relationships are initiated. On it and through it, the components of suburban life are manifested and brought to expression. The street is the zone of territorialization of both the public realm and its opposite. It represents both "normality" and "abnormality." The territorialization of places in fact not only means making them usable and making use of them, it also means the conquest of urban space and hence the creation of an identity that distinguishes one place from another. Street kids thus conquer back streets and squares and overlay them with a network of usable surfaces, borders, and functions that are invisible to outsiders. Adults occupy their places of amusement and in this way functionalize the city. Even criminals create "their city" of the demimonde, of dark and dangerous places the normal citizen avoids in fear. The street is thus the arena of fate, joy, and pain, as well as the place of major demonstrations and mass rallies, of massive actions of resistance and revolt:

Revolutionary events generally take place in the street. Doesn't this show that the disorder of the street engenders another kind of order? The urban space of the street is a place for talk, given over as much to the exchange of words and signs as it is to the exchange of things. A place where speech becomes writing. A place where speech can become "savage" and, by escaping rules and institutions, inscribe itself on walls.[278]

It is not just the street looked at in this way that forms a place of territorialization and resistance, but also those marginal zones between industrial plants and tenement blocks, free areas that arise in the suburbs in the wake of rebuilding and new construction, still unoccupied by urban usage. This "no man's land," whether planned or arising accidentally, is a complex social space created through the conflict between various groups with differing modes of interpretation of the city and different social status. The conflict is expressed via the contradiction between planning projects and the interest of capital on the one hand, and on the other hand the user interests of those who have to establish their concrete life in these urban zones. For this no man's land is not empty, but a surface for recreation, free time, and unregulated everyday life. It is thus a representation of control and resistance, and a place between law and disorder. Such places may take very different forms: so-called *Gstetten*, i.e. sites left undeveloped in the wake of the construction of new highways or mixed residential and factory quarters; half-finished or just finished tenement blocks; parks or, as with the Vienna Schmelz, a military exercise ground only occasionally used; fenced-off areas and gardens; finally also alehouses and spirit counters. These are what Lucius Burkhardt calls the "empty space between the urban body and the too loosely tailored suit planned for it"; thus they tend also to be a space free of domination. The lack of supervision and the paucity of possibilities for control allow these territories to become a place of primary socialization for those who naturally bear the stigma of ill-discipline: suburban adolescents.

Paradigmatic was the largest of Vienna's *Gstetten*, the Schmelz. The peripheral landscape of the Schmelz, originally some fifty hectares of heathland, stretched at the turn of the century (when a large part of it had already been built up in the form of the Neu-Ottakring grid development) from the Neubaugürtel up a gentle slope toward Breitensee, an "endless distance that was bounded by the suburban railroad."[279] This was, as Siegfried Weyr put it, a "landscape of destiny" like no other in Austria.[280] At the time of the second Turkish siege, the grand vizier Kara Mustafa had erected a gigantic tent city here; in 1809 Napoleon had reviewed his troops here; and in October 1848 it was one of the places where the end of the bourgeois revolution was proclaimed, when the Imperial forces under Prince Windischgrätz fired on the mobile guards barricaded in the Schmelz cemetery and in the adjacent Neulerchenfeld cemetery and fought hand to hand in the ensuing battle. Shortly before, in 1847, the army had acquired the Schmelz for 50,000 gulden and subsequently established an exercise and practice ground for the Vienna garrison, marked out by black and yellow wooden posts and later by cast-iron obelisks. Finally, in 1896, the Radetzky barracks was built.

Before World War I, the military again ceded a large area of the Schmelz for urban development. In 1911, on the part of the exercise ground abutting onto the cemetery, the construction of a so-called "Luegerstadt" was planned, named after the recently deceased mayor. The architectural outlines were laid down by Camillo Sitte, who championed urban planning on aesthetic principles, strictly rejecting schematic grid development and the maximal use of surface area. The idea was to build a fashionable quarter, which would among other things provide a home for the city museum and be separated from its proletarian surroundings by a wall. But this ambitious plan was only put into effect in a watered-down version and the Luegerstadt became known as the "Nibelungen Quarter" after the names of its newly erected streets and squares.[281] Also in 1911, the Vienna municipality under the Christian Social mayor Weiskirchner transferred to a society for social housing a block of land bordered by Herbststraße, Gablenzstraße, and Koppstraße (now the site of the Franz-Novy Hof). Soon thereafter a barracks settlement for homeless families was erected. Eight plain two-story buildings with wooden walls clad in asbestos and plaster sheltered a total of 128 families, most of whom had at least six children. The settlement, popularly known as "Negerdörfl," soon became a byword for social squalor, desperation, immorality, and (petty) criminality; its last remains were demolished in 1952.[282]

The broad uncultivated heathland of the Schmelz, for its part, covered with brick dust, stones, and pebbles, was regularly described in contemporary reports and memoirs as a paradise for suburban children and adolescents. In an enlightening reminiscence, Alfons Petzold even managed to see this as a natural counter-pole to the metropolitan Moloch, which—with its bare streets and ugly tenements, full of children wasting away with tuberculosis, men the worse for drink, and women at the washtub or in endless childbirth—was already eroding like a cancer the intact natural landscape of the Schmelz and threatening to eventually destroy it:

> Everything possible happened on this heathland, seemingly infinite to the mind of a child, which began almost at the front door of the row of houses where we lived, and stretched like a sea toward the hills of the Vienna woods. Clumps of trees and fantastic military entrenchments formed islands crossed with secretive ditches, in which rare weeds grew rank, and lizards, frogs, and toads abounded; on the plains there were even field mice and wild hares. For us children the heath was a measureless prairie, an African desert, the playground of Asiatic hordes, and when the rain poured down it became a sea full of all kinds of dangers. In this empty space we established a republic of children, playing out stories of the Wild West learned from Cooper and Hoffmann in the most realistic way … Tents arose on its ground, concealing adventurous youngsters disguised as Red Indian or Teutonic heroes, who smoked potato leaves and dried coltsfoot. From our heath we drew an honorable savagery, the courage for daring deeds.[283]

On fine afternoons, if the army did not lay claim to the area, the Schmelz was transformed into Vienna's largest café, as Max Winter described in a newspaper essay of 1913. In sheltered hollows, unemployed men improvised card tables from piles of bricks covered with wax cloth and played tarot:

Here was one group of players, there another, and yet again more. After six o'clock, the close of work for the lucky ones who had jobs, the whole meadow was covered with these groups, who devoted the hour that remained until sunset to the diverting distraction of tarot, as well as filling their lungs with the fresh air that blew down to the valley from the hills to the west and south.[284]

The Schmelz was the preferred rendezvous for courting couples, it was where kites were flown, and where twelve- to eighteen-year-old boys enthusiastically practiced the new game imported from England that was in the process of developing into an unparalleled passion and had, according to Winter, already conquered the Viennese youth: soccer.

Space for recreation and fresh air on the one hand, the Schmelz was also a synonym for social deviance and the raw abyss side of the suburb. To maintain their territories, sometimes precisely bordered and strictly controlled, the kids from the adjacent streets formed gangs, whose frequent and violent disputes led to regular turf wars. Petzold recalls these street kids as "desperate young good-for-nothings" who were unwilling to tolerate any kind of outsider intruding onto their territory: "Woe to him if they caught one of us! They would take everything he was wearing and practice the most frightful beastliness with him."[285] After night fell, however, their adult role models took possession of the unlit Schmelz: the rumored and feared toughs, pimps, and gang members from Fünfhaus, Sechshaus, and Neulerchenfeld.

As a multiply coded place used for recreation and free-time pleasures, for military parades and exercises, as the romanticized playground of suburban youth as well as a place of crime, the Schmelz remained a myth right through to the 1960s, as demonstrated by the following quotation from Siegfried Weyr, who describes the situation around 1900:

In the evening, after a working day of ten or eleven hours, exhausted workers came and flopped down on the dry grass. In the daytime, hordes of their barefoot children ran between the exercising companies of soldiers, bathing in the dirty water of the Fixl pond, the exercise ground of the technical forces ... The "riders," i.e. the mounted police, were always on the lookout for these desecrators of the military's sanctuary, who organized themselves in gangs just like the grown-ups. The "Fünfler" and the "Lercherln," kids from Fünfhaus and Neu-Lerchenfeld, ruled the Schmelz ...

At the end of a gentle spring evening, or a glorious summer or fine autumn one, the sad tones of a harmonica could be heard on the Schmelz, blown by dark figures that could not be made out. Glowing cigarettes punctuated the groups until night fell. If it was a starless new moon, everyone scattered in good time, for on the unlit Schmelz the "*Platten*" gangs now ruled. These fearful bands of criminals from the surrounding districts had made the Schmelz into a regular Sodom and Gomorrah. No policeman would dare to venture alone at night onto the Schmelz, they only came in patrols. The police reports of the 1880s and 1890s often contained frightful descriptions that put in the shade anything one might have read in crime novels or seen in a gangster film.[286]

Weyr's description clearly shows a certain mystification and romanticizing, but the existence of the "*Platten*" gangs, often young but not invariably so, is well attested to around the turn of the century. These gangs can be interpreted as an early expression of the deviant youth cultures of industrial society. They arose from a deficit in the life-world, or as U. Tartaruga (pseudonym for the Viennese police officer Edmund Otto Ehrenfreund) put it: "Parents in the suburban districts often have to leave their children to look after themselves, and so hunger and bad company lead them into trouble at an early age."[287] A study undertaken by the Favoriten school board, which Tartaruga cites, gave a total of 255 police prosecutions of members of these gangs, ninety-six for theft and thirty-seven for damage to property—results "that must fill anyone with dismay, especially because they are not just typical of Favoriten, but also cast a fearful spotlight on the economic and social conditions in other working-class districts."[288] Even children of compulsory school age formed gangs and began to use cigarettes and alcohol, taking part indeed in "all the amusements of adults," hiding out in sordid dives, indulging in card games, and making a living from begging and petty theft. The "Kastelspritzer" and "Fetzer-Platten," who stole from shop windows and displays, recruited especially from school-age minors, while the so-called "Randal-Platten" were composed of adolescents above school age and attacked persons rather than just private property. As they grew older, pimping was added. At the same time, according to the contemporary press, these bands of youths only made up one section of the overall gang trouble, which was a far more widespread phenomenon as a whole. Many of the gangs recruited not just youths, but adult men, many of whom were casual workers, coachmen, deserters, or ex-servicemen.

By the mid-1900s, at any rate, the gang troubles had become virulent, increasingly escaping the efforts of the police and legal authorities to discipline them.[289] The *Illustriertes Wiener Extrablatt* devoted a sensational series of articles to the problem from June to September 1905, drawing parallels with London's "hooligans," the "*apaches*" of Paris, and the "*mularia*" of Trieste, and coming to the dramatic though clearly exaggerated conclusion, since the empirical evidence was lacking, that fewer crimes were committed by such gangs in two months in Paris (likewise London, Berlin, Rome, Madrid, Budapest, and Prague) than in two nights in Vienna.[290] Regardless of the claim's veracity, the sensational press had made the problem of criminal gangs a public talking point, confronting a fearful and terrified citizenry with the horrific, deviant, and violent aspects of suburban life.

The immediate forerunner of these *Platten* gangs lay in what was called in the Viennese context the *Galerien* of the 1870s and 1880s, which specialized in organized pimping, pickpocketing, and blackmail. A number of these, such as the famous Leopoldstadt "Koreisl-Galerie," were composed of adolescents. "Coarse and violent fellows," feared in the neighborhood for their "barroom excesses," they were characterized by the public prosecutor by "boldness" and "constant violent aggression" as well as "pleasure in doing injury and unpleasantness to others":[291] In their organization the *Platten* followed a strict hierarchy along social Darwinist lines. The gangs were named for the most part after their leaders, as with the "G'stutzen Mirzl-Platte" (after the scarcely twenty-year-old receiver Marie Herold, whose "crude facial features," in contemporary descriptions, were set off by short-cropped hair), the Brigittenau "Holumek-Platte," the Ottakring "Brosch-Platte," the "Pustak-Platte" operating in the vicinity of the Währinger Gürtel, as well as the "Steinhauer-Platte" and the so-called "Wunderdoktor-Platte" (named after an unemployed quack), both of which stemmed from Lichtental. More rarely the names reflected geographical or social criteria, such as the Brigittenau "Capskutscher-Platte," the Hernals "Flohberger-Platte," the Landstraße "Fasan-Platte" (divided into a "young *Platte*" from the vicinity of the Paulus Park and an "old *Platte*," which was also known as the market porter gang after its leader, the drover Pauli, or after the occupations of most of its members), and finally the legendary "Richard-Wagner-Platte" from Neulerchenfeld, whose members were exclusively recruited from the immediate surroundings of the square named after the composer.

What brought "good and decent citizens" of the time into a state of terror and dismay, however, was less the mere existence of these gangs, whose members numbered typically between ten and twenty-five, but rather their rapid increase, which became strongly palpable at the turn of the century, as well as their intrusion into territories and zones that had up until then been spared such forms of organized petty crime. Citizens had grown accustomed, according to the *Extrablatt*, to conditions on the Laaerberg and Draschefeld, or around the Schmelz, being "scarcely believable and begging any description," but now the once splendid Praterstraße was also full every evening with gang members, prostitutes, and their pimps. Similar conditions had also spread to the Mariahilfer Gürtel, "details of which we shall spare our readers."[292]

Whatever the real substance of reports such as this and many other similar ones might be, gangs, pimping, and prostitution were certainly closely interconnected, something that had a long tradition. The police medical officer Dr. Josef Schrank dates the appearance of quantitatively significant and efficient pimping from the 1840s, a time of fermenting, pre-revolutionary social protest. These *strizzis*—also known as *Hackerbuben, Strawanzer, Strotter*, or, from an expression for prostitutes used by the "lower classes of the Viennese population," *Krameltreiber*—were generally young fellows marked out by their bold and violent behavior and by a characteristic, almost standard appearance. They wore a typical cap with turned-up brim, their hair was combed smooth with pig-fat and sugar-water, with "generous locks" on both temples; they sported strikingly stiff ties and wore a fur coat in winter and in summer a "gypsy jacket":

> When night fell, all the avenues of the Glacis, the banks of the dark and dirty Vienna river, the Prater, Brigittenau, the Danube promenade, the moats and the remote corners of the suburbs were literally covered with these vermin; they were followed by swarms of the commonest hetaeras, who often enticed passers-by simply to have them plundered by a gang of hoodlums.[293]

Prostitution formed the main source of income for the *strizzis*, supplemented by theft and petty robbery, which they carried out in collaboration with the prostitutes, with whom they generally had intimate relations—a model of behavior that remained essentially unchanged down to the turn of the century, though by then pimping was increasingly practiced by organized gangs. The prostitutes themselves generally took up their trade between the ages of twelve and fifteen, something that did not alter significantly over the decades. Every evening, according to Josef Schrank, they emerged "from the dark distant regions" of the suburbs "into the gaslit spaces of the city."[294] With them came the *strizzis* and gangsters, breaking all spatial and social barriers that the symbolic order had erected between center and suburb. The article series in the *Illustriertes Extrablatt* is also full of reports of inner-city innkeepers and café and saloon proprietors whose businesses had been adversely affected by the gang activity, some of whom were forced to give up their trade altogether.

The so-called "*Pflanzmurrer*" trick was especially notorious. Two or more gangsters, after heavy drinking and at a point when the bar in question was at its fullest, would begin a mock fight, which rapidly involved the staff and other guests. Other gang members would take advantage of this staged brawl and the general confusion to wreck the establishment and then make their getaway before the police arrived. They would subsequently ask for protection money, which the proprietors affected would generally pay up for fear of further incidents. Often the staged commotion was not even necessary; their mere appearance, their bullying and martial manner—this was particularly true for the Leopoldstadt "Beer-Platte," perhaps the most prominent and spectacular gang of the time—sufficed for the proprietor to pay up and allow the *Plattinger* free booze: "One of them drew out his pocketknife and used it to cut holes in the wallpaper. Then he stuck the point of the knife into the wall between two bricks and hung his hat and overcoat on this improvised hook. The guests took flight and the café owner suffered considerable damages."[295]

If a gang member was arrested and locked up by the police, he would generally feign an attack of maniacal rage, with the aim of being taken not to prison but to the psychiatric clinic in Steinhof, from which it was much easier to escape. The hoodlums and pimps were generally described as dealing with the authorities in a very clever, sometimes even ironic and distanced but refractory manner. This involved a certain knowledge of prevailing legal conditions. Thus, on many occasions, the granting of liquor concessions was used as an opportunity for petty blackmail; and as refuges they often used shelters for the homeless, as well as the ramified drainage system of underground Vienna, where they could easily avoid capture by the police.

Besides pimping, protection rackets, and liquor fraud, the various gangs specialized in different forms of petty crime such as theft, cardsharping, affrays, knifings, etc. Their specific intention, however, was "to spread fear and terror," for example by staging fights and commotions. Though each of the gangs had its base and territory in a different part of the city, they had certain characteristics in common. In the obvious effort to escape the pressure of poorly paid work, they sought to ensure through petty criminality and especially pimping a livelihood that went beyond bare subsistence and to copy a bourgeois lifestyle, which often led the typical *strizzis* and hoodlums to caricature the insignia of the luxury life they aspired to (gold watches with chains, swanky diamond rings, lavish and excessive consumption). "Many of them are elegantly dressed, travel frequently by cab, and attend the races, where they also practice all kinds of crooked deeds. Work is the last of these people's concerns."[296] As much as these gangs defined a counter-world, they also copied the bourgeois order in their strictly hierarchical internal organization. Nevertheless they sought in their public behavior to disrupt this order through fights, scandals, and riots. Their preferred places were inns, amusement parks, and cafés:

> They spread fear and terror among innkeepers, café owners, and their employees, practicing blackmail and violence. They drank in the cafés and refused to pay their bill, despite having the money, as the scandal was part of their amusement. They didn't always cheat on their drink. It sometimes happened that they paid in advance, if a café owner refused to take their order. But then they would throw glasses and bottles around and threaten the other guests, simply to make trouble.[297]

This collective conversion of riot, fighting, and scandal into amusement and a collective goal expresses a number of things: first the attempt to escape the misery of the suburb through an economy of petty crime, and second the attempt to turn the symbolic order of the city—the separation of periphery and center—upside down. What was involved was not just the disruption of public order, but also the appropriation of space and territory. In this way a "city within the city" was created, defined by its own quasi-autonomous system of norms and rules. This articulated the only reserve *strizzis* and petty criminals had to oppose to the power of the center, to urban rational prescription and regulation. The collective use of physical violence and the satisfaction of flouting the ruling order articulated a kind of "plebiscite" of the marginalized. Yet the public character of this protest made it easier for the police to prosecute. The apparent aimlessness and irrationality of such behavior ultimately derived from a spontaneous individual hedonism and a popular presence that lacked a political dimension. This popular presence of the gangs was not a matter of chance, for it was based on a traditionally rooted sympathy of ordinary people for gangs and robbers who stood outside the law, staging their deviance as a protest against the powers that be, or at least facilitating such an interpretation. This popular tradition, which elevated *strizzis* and gangsters to the romantic rank of urban pirates and freebooters, is indicated by Tartaruga when he writes about the gang disturbances that seemed to erupt from nowhere: "This common name of *Platten*, under which every kind of theft, robbery, begging, violence, burglary, etc., was quite incorrectly subsumed, gained public currency, was spoken and sung about on the stage, illustrated on postcards, and became in a word popular."[298]

In September 1905, at a time when the press was full of a regular hysteria about the *Platten* gangs, Turl Wiener, the much-loved and celebrated popular singer and comedian, had great success with his "gangster show" at the

Rudolfheim Colosseum. He won high praise from the critics and regular ovations every night. With his characterization of a "genuine suburban *strizzi*," wrote the *Extrablatt*, Turl Wiener had managed to bring a lively Viennese figure onto the stage. The brazen expression, typical swaggering gait, and smart appearance, together with dialogue that splendidly parodied the gang subculture, were apparently the main ingredients of a stormy public success in a city richer than any other in its strong characteristic types.[299]

In this way, the "Viennese *strizzi*" as quintessential gangster became a public figure, though this says less about the character himself than about the yearning of the declassed to oppose the ruling order and their inhuman conditions of life. The *strizzi* was as it were a substitute for a constantly fermenting collective protest, projected into popular culture in a pre-political fashion.

More than anyone else (except perhaps the Ottakring "people's tribune" Franz Schuhmeier), Johann "Schani" Breitwieser symbolized the hopes and yearnings, the latent rebellion and refractoriness, the social romanticism, and the projections of a different, better, and fairer life of the impoverished suburban population. He was a celebrated burglar, picklock, and safecracker, the "king of Meidling" and "Vienna's Robin Hood." The population saw him as "a good and just man, a hero," and Egon Erwin Kisch described him in a powerful obituary as "a man of action, of courage, of seriousness and intelligence."[300] Breitwieser was shot by the police on April 1, 1919, in the village of St. Andrä-Wördern northwest of Vienna in a house he had recently acquired through an intermediary and under a false name, where he was living with his seventeen-year-old girlfriend Anna Maxian.[301] His burial at the Meidling cemetery turned into an unusually demonstrative manifestation of the suburbs. An immense crowd followed the coffin (between 20,000 and 40,000 according to contemporary estimates), the grave was swathed by a sea of flowers and garlands, and a quartet from the Court Opera sung the funeral dirge.[302] Years later Breitwieser's final resting place was still permanently strewn with fresh floral tributes, and on All Souls' Day it was generally impossible for his family to reach the grave, as it was surrounded by a thick wall of people and hundreds of candles.

When the police, according to their report, conducted a search at Breitwieser's home, they unearthed some remarkable things. In a windowless cellar they came across a fully equipped laboratory of modern technologies. Five strong cash boxes were used for scientific experimentation as well as different kinds of iron and steel for materials testing; an autogenic welding apparatus, assembled and ready for use and capable of heating up to 3,600 degrees centigrade, was found alongside a two-meter-high container with 5,000 liters of concentrated acid. Machines, turning benches, and a field smithy completed the facilities, as well as a variety of files, skeleton keys, crowbars arranged in transportable boxes, and even electric drills, mostly of Breitwieser's own manufacture. The police also found Breitwieser's detailed coded descriptions of his research, and a technical library quite up to the standards of the time.[303]

A large number of popular myths and legends surround the figure of

Breitwieser, a consistent modernizer and technical fanatic, who revolutionized his trade and yet at the same time still acted the "social rebel" in a thoroughly pre-modern style. The Viennese journalist and editor of the *Internationale Justiz- und Kriminalzeitung Tribunal*, Hermann Kraszna, wrote Breitwieser's biography two years after his death.[304] Schani Breitwieser was born in 1891, sixth in a total of sixteen children in an "accursedly poor, dog-poor" family in the suburb of Meidling, at 13 Breitenfurterstraße. His father was a shoemaker's assistant, his mother a domestic worker and washerwoman, who despite her constant pregnancies carried on working "as patiently as a carthorse." When Schani appeared in court the first time at the age of fifteen, the defense lawyer explained the living and housing conditions of the family, who had been forced to move four times in ten years, seeking accommodation each time in a smaller apartment, further out toward the periphery and ever closer to the celebrated "robbers' woods" of Gatterhölzl behind the Meidling Tivoli. A single window brought light into a "bare, injurious poverty," the furniture consisted of one bed, straw sacks, a broken old chest of drawers, a few dishes and plates on a metal stove, and some rotten boxes. The parents slept in the bed together with four of the children, the others on the straw sacks, Schani himself in a black chest containing the "family rags," another brother in the washtub, and the smallest in the washing basket. The father supplemented his average weekly earnings of three gulden by casual work at the Meidling cemetery; he was also allowed to grow potatoes on some unused land at the cemetery, these being the family's main food. The Breitwieser children played among the graves and tombs, thus growing unaccustomed from their earliest years to a key civilizing boundary, namely, respect for the dead. The lawyer concluded that, when Schani ventured into the clean and elegant quarters of the inner city, he would have been able to feel more clearly than ever before the division of the metropolis into two entirely disparate worlds.[305]

Schani was regarded as a gifted and highly intelligent child, characterized by extraordinary physical dexterity, earning a few extra kreuzer for the family as early as age four by performing various, almost acrobatic tricks in the side streets of the neighborhood. But he soon showed his inclination to despotism, his contempt for authority of any kind, his tendency to outbreaks of rage, and his demand for unconditional obedience. He grew up as a typical street kid, more "savage than Viennese," and the ragged barefooted boy would stay away from his parents' home for night after night, no one knowing where he was or even worrying about him. Her "*Bua*" (boy), as his mother called him, was obviously "as rotten as the sausage at the grocer's next door."[306] Schani liked to spend these nights in the Gatterhölzl (in Viennese dialect known as the Räuberhölzl), a small wood at the outer limit of Meidling, which had formerly served as a retreat for a motley "daylight-shunning riffraff" and which remained the subject of the strangest and most sensational rumors. Or else he wandered round the Meidling cemetery: "He knew all the names in the old cemetery nearby, the dead were as familiar to him as the living. He hunted around between the mounds, he wondered at the miracle of death, he would lie down on a grave with his arms outstretched, looking up to heaven, and imagine he could see through the eyes of the dead."[307]

16. The criminal as dandy. Police photo of Johann Breitwieser. Source: Wiener Kriminalmuseum.

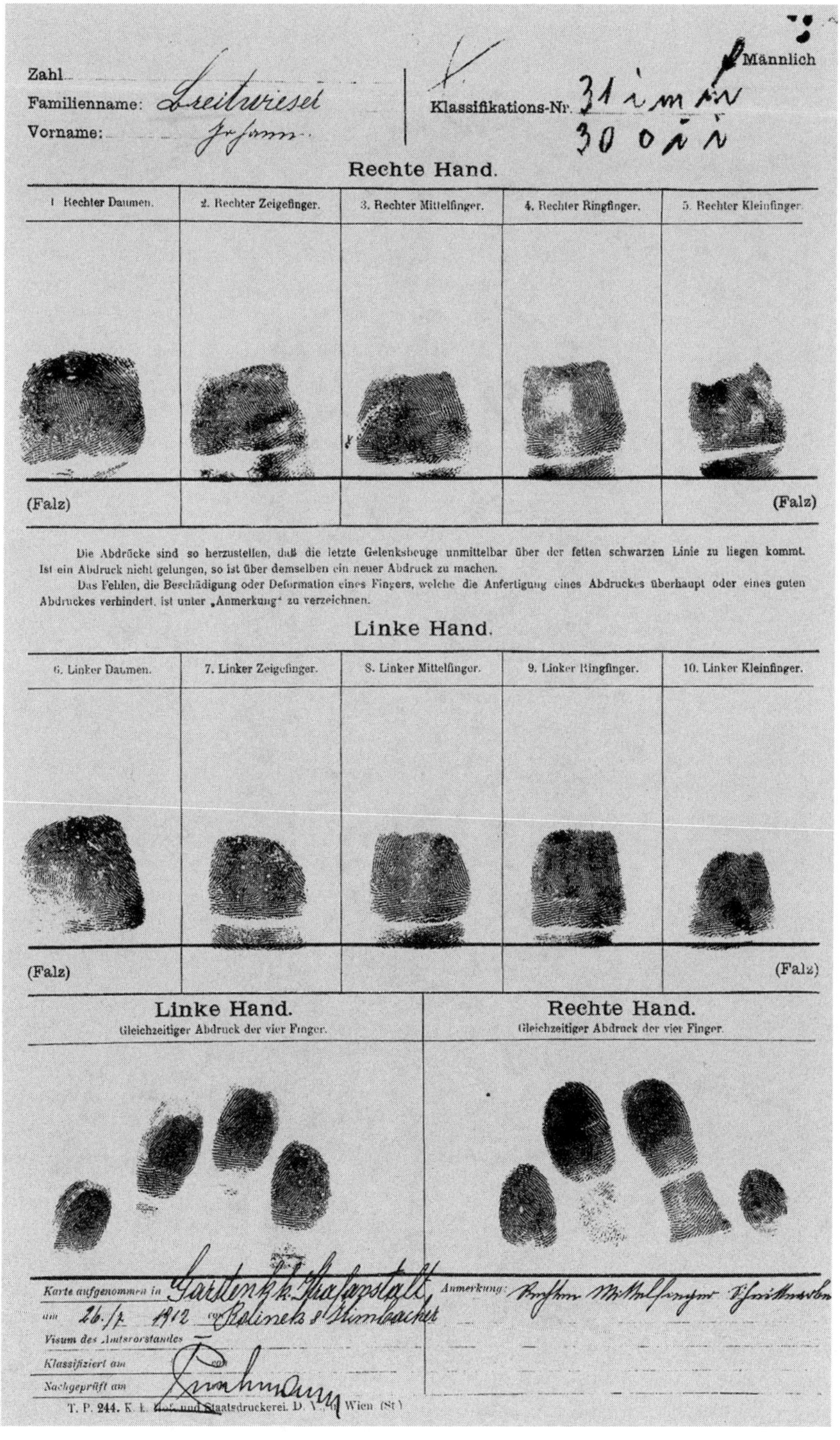

Männlich

Zahl

Familienname: Breitwieser

Vorname: Johann

Klassifikations-Nr. 31 i m ...

Rechte Hand.

1. Rechter Daumen.	2. Rechter Zeigefinger.	3. Rechter Mittelfinger.	4. Rechter Ringfinger.	5. Rechter Kleinfinger.

(Falz) (Falz)

Die Abdrücke sind so herzustellen, daß die letzte Gelenksbeuge unmittelbar über der fetten schwarzen Linie zu liegen kommt. Ist ein Abdruck nicht gelungen, so ist über demselben ein neuer Abdruck zu machen.

Das Fehlen, die Beschädigung oder Deformation eines Fingers, welche die Anfertigung eines Abdruckes überhaupt oder eines guten Abdruckes verhindert, ist unter „Anmerkung" zu verzeichnen.

Linke Hand.

6. Linker Daumen.	7. Linker Zeigefinger.	8. Linker Mittelfinger.	9. Linker Ringfinger.	10. Linker Kleinfinger.

(Falz) (Falz)

Linke Hand. Gleichzeitiger Abdruck der vier Finger.	Rechte Hand. Gleichzeitiger Abdruck der vier Finger.

Karte aufgenommen in Garsten k.k. Strafanstalt

am 26./7. 1912 *durch*

Visum des Amtsvorstandes

Klassifiziert am

Nachgeprüft am

Anmerkung:

T. P. 244. K. k. Hof- und Staatsdruckerei. D. [illegible] Wien (St)

17. The criminal as social rebel. Police photo of Johann Breitwieser. Source: Wiener Kriminalmuseum.

Influence of science

In summer, when the Imperial palace at Schönbrunn was to all intents unoccupied, he would sometimes break in and spent the night in one of the luxury apartments. But his undivided love was really for the Tiergarten, which he broke into an untold number of times to study the detailed behavior of the animals, especially the bears and apes. When a police commissioner asked him many years later about his education, he supposedly replied that "an ape was my teacher and a bear my professor."[308]

At the age of thirteen he had in a certain sense completed his education; he was familiar with all aspects of human existence, and he knew Meidling, which he liked to describe as his kingdom, better than anyone else. He displayed a kind of ironic distance toward the forces of order but had developed a deep hatred for the bottomless poverty of the people and for a social order that made such poverty possible and could calmly accept it.

Breitwieser started an apprenticeship with a stonemason but left a short time later following differences with his master, who wanted to use him for work that did not help his training. Confronted with the master's reproach that he was a "*Lumpenbua*" (good-for-nothing), but also influenced by his first great love, who had promised she would "go with" him as soon as he was "nicely dressed," he committed his first major theft and acquired a brand new outfit. He appeared in court for the first time on February 5, 1906. He was accused of breaking into a warehouse belonging to Ignaz Winter, stealing a pair of fur boots and preparing to remove twenty other pairs. Breitwieser pleaded guilty and answered the judge's question as to his motive with a curt, "Need." The plea of the defending counsel that the judge should take a quick look at the Breitwieser home was rejected, and Schani was sentenced to a month in prison.

He subsequently alternated between casual work (as an animal trainer, market assistant, worker in an umbrella factory, etc.) and casual theft, which led to further spells in prison; in 1908 he went missing when he was due to start a six months' sentence. He worked incognito as a bicycle messenger boy. When a relationship with a high-class prostitute (like him from suburban origin and a similar social milieu) ended, he also left this job and began his professional career—at first in the organized company of a gang, the "Black Mask Brotherhood." His life swung between burglary, flight, and prison, and raised him over the next few years to the romantic rank of a heroic suburban outlaw, summed up by the *Neuer Tag* as a "champion against society, freebooter leader against the state, appropriator on his own behalf, victor in his own private feud".[309] He still ran the zigzag course that led to the broad road of consummate violator of the law, but the people, in recognition of his courage, in admiration of his boldness, in respect for his honesty toward his own kind, for his unflinching Yes or No, and for the sake of his generosity, proclaimed him the king of his dark guild.[310]

Breitwieser worked in and around Vienna professionally, speedily, and restlessly. He undoubtedly had an artistic nature and had developed his own unmistakable style but was also brutal and incalculably dangerous, while at the same time humorous, ironic, and with an "original Viennese good-heartedness."[311] And he began, first in his immediate geographical and social surroundings, then in the whole district of Meidling, to distribute part of his booty—sometimes only a small part—among the impoverished population.

In 1912 Breitwieser received a sentence of four years' hard labor in the Garsten penitentiary. He was released on March 16, 1916, and transferred to the Klosterneuburg forced labor colony. He avoided internment by reporting for military service as a volunteer but then deserted on his very first day. The last two years of World War I and the following brief period of social-revolutionary unrest were his real heyday, and he developed in accord with the ever growing madness of the time. When he was captured again, he feigned a maniacal rage upon his arrest and a stupor while in jail awaiting trial, which he did so well that he was transferred for observation to the Wagner-Jauregg clinic and finally taken to the psychiatric clinic at Steinhof. A short while later, toward the end of 1917, he fled and began a new series of burglaries in grand style, not (as previously) at noble villas and upper bourgeois residences on the Ringstraße, but almost exclusively at businesses and corporations. In the eyes of the population of both Meidling and the whole of Vienna, his crimes acquired a higher significance; it was generally said that he now stole only for others. Breitwieser grew into the role of social rebel and philanthropist, and, in the imagination of a population exhausted and further impoverished by the sacrifices of the war, his image was reinforced as a figure removed from concrete reality, a symbolic hero who only stole to give to others:

> Breitwieser gradually became so well-known in the district that no one would have betrayed him. Indeed, he himself observed that even many of the police turned a blind eye and passed him by. He now enjoyed the reputation of a man ready to

18. The criminal as bourgeois. Living room of Breitwieser's villa in Sankt Andrä-Wördern. Source: Wiener Kriminalmuseum.

help, of whom all kinds of deeds were told, and he also laid down the law among his companions if quarrels broke out among them. A whole raft of legends surrounds this time, and it is impossible to determine how many of these have a truthful foundation.[312]

Breitwieser made his final and most spectacular coup with a burglary at the Hirtenberg Arms and Ammunitions Factory in January 1919, where he is supposed to have gotten away with a haul of some half a million gold crowns.[313]

The subversive potential of this culture of resistance represented by the *strizzis* and suburban desperadoes is composed of a number of elements. The first thing it expresses is a bundle of attitudes and orientations to life that relate to the persistence of the feudal-popular within the modernization process. It also reveals a phase of social transition and the dissolution of the old order, together with the renegotiation of political and cultural hegemonies. From the demimonde of the first half of the nineteenth century, from the army of urban vagabonds, outcastes, outlaws, and marginalized, there now grew a group of visible and describable outsiders, who were checked and observed by the police. For the citizenry and police they were enemies of civilization; for large sections of the impoverished suburban population, however, they were a projection screen for their own hopes and yearnings. And, if the *Platten* and suburban gangs reflected the organization culture of modernism with its hierarchies and divisions of labor, they simultaneously harked back to the pre-modern myth of brigands and social rebels with its attendant yearnings for social justice. They were a transitional phenomenon, composed of both feudal-popular traditions and the codes of modernity. Johann Breitwieser embodied this most palpably, the criminal of the Vienna suburbs with his popular Robin Hood charm and American know-how.

The culture of resistance articulates a questioning of the ruling order more than simply criminal deviance. But the organizational potential of modernity cannot be thus transformed into political action. This requires protracted learning processes, it requires the experience of the street as a site of politicization and politics, and it requires strikes and revolts if this potential is to be built up to a mass politics in the dialectic of trial and error.

CHAPTER 11

THE REVOLT OF THE STREETS

A suburban proletarian culture of insubordination should by no means be seen as a linear and schematic expression of the antagonisms of labor and capital, powerlessness and power, resistance and domination. It must rather be placed in the whole spectrum of suburban life-worlds in which developing "class consciousness" is interwoven with unconsciousness, refractoriness with indifference, morality with deviance, secularizing spirituality with anarchistic practicality, and suburban proletarian insolence with rural fearful conservatism. It expresses resistance and insubordination as a contingent formation without determinate goal, which can endure unacceptable living conditions longer than expected and which can quickly grow into a stream of sweeping violence. The forms of social protest and revolt that develop from such an internally contradictory matrix are already prefigured therein. In this sense, revolt is at the same time its opposite. It is incipient organized revolution within the anarchy of the uprising, and it is the desperate shrill voicing of articulated political rhetoric. It is anger and destruction, without being in a position to abolish the ruling order. It attacks the totality of domination and yet only affects its individual representatives. It can start out from the most apparently minor causes and end with the most minor results. Its actors are not only class-conscious workers, but also gangsters and *strizzis*, men and women, children and old people. As the "mass" that bears this revolt, it is pervaded by a division of hope and desperation, calculation and spontaneity, courage and timidity, utopia and pessimism, for in each of its individual participants these divisions are present in microcosm. Without having any overall form and strategy, individual actions can nonetheless be marked as highly precise and prepared.

The collision between the people in revolt and the forces of order is not only one of physical bodies and formations, but also of different political conceptions of urban space; for the uprising aims at dismantling the symbolic order in the city, which is why state power seeks not simply to clear the streets, but also to maintain the distance between center and periphery. The state authorities' fear of revolt is not simply that the "masses" might conquer the suburban terrain, but rather that such a circumstance would put in question the center of the symbolic order. This perspective represents the real terror of those in power, that the individuals united by misery, origin, and hopelessness might through their common experience of refusal, protest, and revolt experience themselves as undifferentiated equals and thus raise the demand for social equality. ⟶ *Result of class conciousness ?* [handwritten]

Strikes at this time became an almost daily phenomenon in (sub)urban life, counterbalancing the competitive logic of the industrial system and the urban living context with a directly experienced, so to speak self-determined "political economy" of labor; thus it always contains elements of uprising and revolt. In the refusal to work, in the moment of stoppage, the strikers become equals. The fictitious equality that arises from their common manual activity becomes an actual concrete equality: "What they do *not* do is imparted to society as a whole."[314] The work place itself becomes forbidden territory, removed from its everyday character, acquiring sacral features in its stillness and emptiness; it has to be protected and kept free from intrusion. As long as the strikers act as a unit of equals, the spontaneous organization of refusal to work remains unbroken; as long as this inscribed significance is intact, it disciplines the entire behavior of the actors. Only when the internal organization is suspended by strikebreakers or other measures from outside are "dignity," "discipline," and "respect for the law" lost, with an outbreak of "savagery" and "willful destruction" leading to "outrage" and "excess."

At Easter 1888 a majority of the employees of the Vienna Tramway Company went on strike. The first horse-drawn streetcars had started running on November 4,1865, between Dornbach and Schottenring; three years later, the city's major thoroughfares were all fitted with streetcar lines, with the profitable business operated by private companies. In the mid-1880s, the urban tramway network amounted to some sixty kilometers (or eight Austrian postal miles), and almost all stretches had double sets of rails. But the monopolization of public transport by two private companies (the second being the Vienna General Omnibus Company) prevented the establishment of an efficient modern transit system with an appropriate tariff structure.

The highly profitable Tramway Company at first employed mainly Czechs, Slovaks, and Poles, establishing a complex system of supervision, discipline, and punishment laid down in a comprehensive forty-five-page handbook.[315] These instructions and statutes, however, were only distributed to a tiny minority of the personnel, so that one of the main demands of the strike in 1888 was that every employee should receive a printed copy "containing all the regulations about working hours and wages as well as the precise cases and levels of penalty, insofar as these are even necessary."[316]

In any case, the company's system of labor relations based on compulsion, penalties, and constant reduction in wages meant a far-reaching encroachment on the accepted norms and values of the work force, these being centered on notions of honest work and fair reward, traditional rights, conscientious performance, and the maintenance of self-determination and autonomy in certain aspects of work. In 1885 the priest Father Eichhorn published a pamphlet based on detailed research, in which he described the working and living conditions of these "white tramway slaves," making frequent comparison with the rigor of medieval monastic orders and the severity of military disciplinary codes: "Such physical stress and deprivation as the Tramway Company forces on its employees was not imposed on its members by even the strictest of medieval orders … I have first-hand knowledge of both monastic and barracks life and can add that, compared with the dependence of these slaves of capital, the often denounced servitude in the monasteries is a paradise."[317]

The effective working day for drivers and conductors was between sixteen and eighteen hours, in special cases as much as twenty-one hours. The grooms and forage workers had to work at least sixteen hours during the week, and seventeen hours on Sundays and public holidays. The 300 or so stable workers were almost entirely recruited from former members of the Imperial cavalry and had 2,500 horses to look after in nine large stables, which had to be kept spotlessly clean. Each man was responsible for either ten double-span (i.e. smaller) horses or nine one-span (larger) horses, whereas in the cavalry it was exceptional for a soldier to have to look after two horses, and three was very rare. The tone and manners of the stablemen were correspondingly crude and rough, their inclination to excessive use of spirits and tobacco was notorious, and their external appearance was marked by undernourishment, exhaustion, and overwork.[318]

Conditions for the drivers and conductors were scarcely any better. From the Hernals depot in the period just before the strike, for example, fifty-six drivers made 377 trips daily. The circular trip lasted 145 minutes, the quay trip 109 minutes. Each driver thus spent a daily total of fourteen hours and thirty-eight minutes actually en route; then there was mealtime, the journey from the depot to the railhead and back, and harnessing and unharnessing, which altogether took a further two and a half hours. The average working day of a driver (and likewise a conductor) thus came to seventeen hours.[319] Every seventh day was free and supposedly paid in full. But it had become established practice that even on the most trivial grounds—such as if the streetcar returned more than one minute late—one or two extra trips could be imposed, so that it was common for a driver and conductor to have to work four to six hours even on their free day. The midday break was from twenty to forty minutes, depending on the route, and had to be taken between 10 and 12 a.m., which meant in many cases that the driver could not eat at all from then until midnight. In order to avoid accidental delay, they often had to eat while they were traveling. Eichhorn reported that many of the staff posted their wives or children at places along the route, signaling to them "either verbally, or with notes or gestures" when they would be home for the hot dinner that had been prepared for them.[320] Such a system inevitably led to repeated family conflicts. Eating and quarreling went together for the drivers and conductors, one conductor told Eichhorn, and the frequent lack of natural sleeping and eating times "easily made the unmarried man a wretch and the married man a tyrant."[321]

The Tramway Company, according to Victor Adler, had two kinds of staff. One group had a working day of sixteen to twenty-one hours and insufficient food; the other worked for four hours and was fed very well. The first group were men, the second group horses. Men were dirt-cheap, but horses cost a great deal. And, if the human staff had adapted so willingly, patiently, and silently to such conditions, this was unsurprising in view of the gigantic reserve army of unemployed and job-seekers, who could be mobilized at any moment, at a time when each year hundreds of people committed trivial crimes such as lese majesty simply so as to be sentenced to a few months' imprisonment, if not more, and enjoy at least the miserable prison food, or when the hospitals were full of malingerers who were just seeking basic shelter and nutrition.[322] But even the "most patient Czechs, Slovaks, and Poles," who made up the bulk of the employees, wrote Eichhorn, had "a sense of justice and honor": "I understand now why the Slavs, living under such conditions quite defenselessly among Germans, are accused of deviousness and revenge."[323]

When the management of the Tramway Company undertook a further reorganization of the routes in April 1888, demanding still longer working hours, the limit had been reached even for these "poor devils of tramway slaves," as they were frequently called—"slaves not only by their condition but by nature," under the whip of "slave drivers" and "tramway pashas."[324] The time to be taken for each stretch of the route was so minutely laid down that returning too soon or too late was almost inevitable, resulting in a number of penalty trips to be worked on the supposed free day. The strike organizer, Victor Adler, reckoned in detail that on just one route, in a single week, twenty-two drivers were saddled with forty-three additional trips.[325] It was then that the majority of drivers, conductors, and stablemen came out on strike.

Adler's tactic aimed at rationalizing the conflict, maintaining its legality, and underscoring its symbolic significance; this proved remarkably successful and effective in the first phases of the conflict:

> We do not remember any event arousing the sleeping conscience and consciousness of the people to such a degree for a long time, with such profound resonance, as the struggle of the streetcar workers against the Tramway Company and its managers ... Initially people were content to express their contempt for those workers who cowardly left their colleagues in the lurch and performed drivers' duties. Insults were hurled at them, and they were spat at not only in the suburbs, but even by "decently dressed persons" on the Ringstraße.[326]

The drivers held their meetings and strike assemblies in taverns they customarily frequented near the depots. They appeared in public in their uniforms and generally obeyed without further resistance the demands of the intervening authorities, much to the surprise of the administration, as the following police report illustrates:

> When we passed in an open carriage the garden of the Rieha Inn on Rosensteingasse at the corner of the Hernalser Hauptstraße, we heard cries of "Dogs!", "Off with you!", and more of the same addressed to us and to the patrol of hussars who had been sent from the depot and were just then passing. After expressing concern that the gang assembled at the aforementioned inn, who seemed to have a certain leadership, would, if I left them to their own devices,

overpower the small hussar detachment I had left at the Marktplatz, or commit another act of violence, I immediately jumped from the carriage, letting the District Officer continue by himself to the depot; I added the request for him to send foot forces and entered the building unaccompanied.

I ordered the hussar patrol to halt and block off the adjacent side streets. Then I ordered the innkeeper Rieha to close his establishment immediately, still without any cover. A few beer mugs were indeed raised in my direction, along with some insults and threats; yet the guests, over 150 of them, were intimidated by my decisive demand made at risk to my own life, and left the inn and its garden, at the gates of which I then posted hussars. When the ten foot-police I had requested from Chief Commissioner Müller later arrived from the depot, I took the same action at the Wiedermann Inn (where insults to the military were hurled as well) and at the other similar establishments from Dorotheergasse up to the depot. I allowed the guests—almost all workers and streetcar drivers—to make their departure only one at a time, and in different directions.[327]

But, as the Tramway Company increasingly brought in unskilled strikebreakers without any kind of training, and as the state deployed dragoons in Favoriten and hussars in Ottakring and Hernals (thus enforcing a regular state of siege on the suburbs affected), there were a number of violent altercations, riots, and fights. The security forces at first cleared the drivers' meeting places, seeing their appearance in uniform as a provocation, arresting any of them they found, and keeping them under arrest until they took off their uniforms or declared themselves ready to return to work again. Cavalry attacks were frequently employed against the massive and spontaneous protest meetings, which took place everywhere on the streets. It was now the hour of women and adolescent youths from the suburbs. Time and again (as had been the case, for example, with the great mass riot in the course of the strike at the Favoriten-based Wangermann company in August 1893), it was reported that it was principally "women and half-grown lads" who put up the most stubborn resistance to the forces of order.[328]

What is also striking in this connection is the forceful presence of women, children, and adolescents in the public space, whereas the workers' struggle remained chiefly confined to places of production or employment. The violence of these disturbances repeatedly reported in the newspapers harks back to the subversive potential traditionally contained in the popular. This may go together with the fact that the suburb could never be completely subordinated to the public order.

The combination of police and military force was accordingly deployed with "speed and precision." The police reports contain the following passage about the streeter drivers' strike:

So as not to be exposed for too long to the hail of stones, I commanded running pace and now began a merciless attack against anyone who attempted resistance, succeeding by way of several arrests to clear the area so energetically (Laxenburgerstraße, Quellenplatz, Erlachgasse, Eugengasse [now Pernerstorfergasse]) that no further notable incidents occurred there.[329]

Because of the large assemblies taking place, I continued at around 3 p.m. from Eugenplatz [now Viktor-Adler-Platz] into Eugengasse, where a young man hit me twice on the head with an umbrella after I had demanded from the running board of my open carriage that the crowd should disperse, whereupon I drew my sword and struck him above the chest, presumably injuring him; he escaped, as I was only accompanied by one dragoon, who was hindered from following him as he had trampled a woman.[330]

Following such attacks, the "rabble" scattered in all directions, "carrying the crowd with them, who had pelted the police and tramway officials with a veritable hail of stones."[331] Hundreds of people took refuge in stables, beneath carriages, in the hallways of buildings, in the sizable rooms of beer and liquor taverns, and in half-finished buildings. On the Keplerplatz in Favoriten women fled with their children into the adjacent church or assembled on its steps.

At the other end of the city, in Hernals, a section of the young "troublemakers" withdrew to an abandoned cemetery in Dorotheergasse (now Taubergasse):

I decided despite the dark to search the cemetery, so as finally to find the fellows who had been throwing stones from there for the last three days. The army general, from whom I requested military assistance to the tune of two companies and a squadron, was very happy to provide this to me. After the cemetery was clear from all sides ... I encircled it so that each division entered at the same time. The cavalry advanced on a given signal, forming a second circle around the cemetery wall. I had with forethought brought four lanterns from the streeter depot, and I went ahead flanked by policemen carrying these; after me the infantry division spread out around the cemetery, and we managed to apprehend a number of individuals ... As a result of this excursion, an end was put to the stone throwing from the cemetery, whereas earlier on—in the words of the gravedigger—the lads had been there, running to and fro all the time.[332]

But the scattered crowd repeatedly gathered afresh with astonishing speed in order, in the words of the report, to "proceed with indescribable roughness and brutality" against the police forces. Eugenplatz in Favoriten, in the vicinity of Himbergerstraße (now Favoritenstraße), was fenced around with strong wooden market stalls, and from this defense young boys and adolescents bombarded police and soldiers with stones, likewise hurling "missiles of every kind" from parks and storage yards and infuriating them "in an indescribable way." They were effectively supported in their efforts from the tenement blocks, from which tiles, flatirons, pots, coal, and broken glass were flung, as well as pieces of wood with nails affixed. All of these actions were accompanied by "an indescribable howling and whistling."[333]

The "excesses" in Favoriten had their origin at the so-called "red court" of the anti-Semitic agitator Hauck. They displayed overt anti-Semitic aspects, as did many other spontaneous protest actions of the suburban population. The following passage is taken from the report of District Inspector Tobias Anger:

A civilian rushed towards me (apparently the concierge of 32 Erlachgasse), hurriedly telling me that a Jew had taken refuge there after being pursued by the mob; he was afraid that the mob would storm the building and kill the Jew.

I immediately proceeded with the greatest haste to Erlachgasse, together with all the police available. Before we reached the street, we were met in Laxenburgerstraße by a howling and whistling crowd throwing stones at us, coming from the direction of Quellenplatz ... We advanced against the mob of stone-throwers with such energy that the crowd scattered in all directions, whereupon I turned around and entered Erlachgasse. There I encountered a jeering and whistling crowd, which again threw stones not badly aimed but which hurriedly fled when we reached them.

I ordered Police Inspector Antlanger from the Meidling division, assisted by several policemen, to fetch the trembling Hebrew from no. 32, took him with me to the depot, and sent him from there to the commissariat with appropriate escort.[334]

The destructive rage of the masses in revolt, however, more generally targeted buildings and objects; shops and cafés were plundered, breakables such as windowpanes, glazed street doors, gas lamps, etc., were smashed. The ease of breaking such things was certainly a basic impulse for their destruction, but not the decisive aspect. It was rather an attack on all boundaries, the forceful symbolic abolition of everything that separates.[335] In the act of destruction there is manifested for a brief moment the transgressing of borders, best symbolized in the destruction of glass or earthenware containers, which are nothing but borders (Elias Canetti). We see this, for example, in a report in the *Arbeiter-Zeitung* on an attack by adolescents on the chemistry laboratory of the secondary school in Possingergasse in the context of the Ottakring hunger revolt of September 1911:

Yes, in this secondary school they really had acted as vandals. It happened that a pack of young people found themselves in front of the school in Thalhaimergasse after they had already almost completely ripped out the railings enclosing the yard in front. This gave them material to continue their campaign of destruction. The most agile and nimble climbed into the yard, and before anyone noticed they had gotten through the high mezzanine window, the panes of which had long been broken, and entered the chemistry laboratory. Here their senseless rage found sufficient material for destruction. The tables were all covered with bottles of acids and chemicals ... Bottle after bottle was broken ... Boxes flew about, benches were overturned, and tables rattled so that retorts and bottles fell to the ground.[336]

CHAPTER 12

THE TRANSGRESSION OF THE POPULAR: KARL LUEGER AND FRANZ SCHUHMEIER

A year and a half after the Ottakring hunger revolt, the same "masses" appeared in the same streets of this district but for a different purpose, and in a different form, disciplined in an organized community of grief. This was likely the largest and most impressive mass demonstration Vienna had ever known. It took place on a clear winter Sunday, February 16, 1913. In the four brief days before the event, the Social Democratic Workers' Party made full use of its organizational apparatus, which by this time was already quite significant and covered all the suburbs, but the arrival of the masses was beyond all expectations and could scarcely be controlled by any organization. Half a million people, in other words a quarter of the Viennese population, showed up; the Ottakring district organization alone, which the deceased had called into existence in the early 1890s with a couple of dozen colleagues, provided 2,600 functionaries. As the Viennese press nearly unanimously agreed, it was an uncrowned king, a ruler, a people's tribune "elected to this high dignity by voluntary love and respect," who was buried that day:

> For in these few days that have passed since the fateful shot of the murderer at the Nordwestbahnhof, this impressive, powerful, and shattering homage could not have been arranged. These thousands upon thousands who yesterday filled the streets of Ottakring, the endless long procession following the coffin in a silent, stirring mission, had come of their own free will, without command, to fulfill a heartfelt duty ... It was not curiosity, but piety, most honest and glorious piety for a man who was loved.[337]

As early as February 13, directly after the coroner's autopsy, the body was transferred to the Ottakring Arbeiterheim and placed on view in a metal coffin with a glass cover. The large hall of this Arbeiterheim used for celebrations and theater was transformed into an impressive memorial hall under the leadership of the Reichsrat deputy Albert Sever and a professional undertaker. A black palanquin was erected over the catafalque, with palms and exotic flowers, candles and candelabras placed around. The guard of honor was recruited from local officials in their livery, party comrades from the different corporations, members of the Arbeiterheim fire department, and workers' athletic clubs. For two and a half days, the stream of people coming to pay their last respects did not diminish. Entry times had to be extended several hours, and there were frequent dramatic outbreaks of grief, rage, and desperation.

At the actual funeral at midday on February 16, leading politicians, government officials, diplomats, and military officers were present. When the coffin was sealed, the funeral march from *Götterdämmerung* sounded from the balcony, followed by Franz von Suppé's "Rest, Weary Traveler" by a band of brass players of the Court Opera and a workers' choir of four hundred. The coffin was then raised onto a splendid glass carriage decked with a towering civic crown; six richly ornamented black horses with coachmen and riders in old-Spanish costume drew the carriage. The funeral route led for a good seven kilometers from Hasnerstraße to the Gürtel and then through Thaliastraße to the Ottakring cemetery, and the procession included eighteen carriages full of flowers, four funeral hearses and innumerable flower-bearers, as well as two lantern carriers also dressed in the old-Spanish style. From the early morning, columns converged on the Ottakring Arbeiterheim from all directions, with banners, standards, and splendid floral tributes. The entire route was lined with rows of people six to ten deep, indeed dangerously

19. Vienna's largest demonstration before World War I. The burial of Franz Schuhmeier. Source: Verein für Geschichte der Arbeiterbewegung Wien.

crowded in some places, such as the Gürtel. The participants in the funeral procession itself, "this vast, endless, incredibly silent crowd," were divided into an advance and a rear section. The former filled Thaliastraße from the Lerchenfelder Gürtel to Kreitnerstraße and beyond, the latter occupied the parallel Koppstraße and only started on its way when the advance party had already reached the Ottakring cemetery. At the open graveside representatives of the party leadership and the trade union federation spoke, as well as the man who would become Vienna's first Social Democratic mayor, Jakob Reumann. The official funeral ended with the "Pilgrims' Chorus" from Wagner's *Tannhäuser*, but the line of people queuing to pay their respects continued until the evening, transforming the grave into a sea of red carnations.[338]

This fascinating and intricate funeral choreography was for Franz Schuhmeier, the most popular Viennese Social Democrat at the turn of the century, a mass politician of a new style, talented both as populist agitator and as persuasive public speaker, a child of the suburb who had risen from the poorest conditions to the highest political functions. He had succeeded like no one before him in leading the politically and socially deprived of the suburbs from their isolation into an organized and politically conscious mass movement that gave them a new identity. His burial in the form of a mass demonstration reflected the close connection between funeral ceremonies and mass popular display so typical of Vienna, formalized in the Baroque period in thanksgiving for the end of the plague. But what could this mean in the concrete historical and social context of 1913? Was it simply a stubborn persistence of feudal-popular tradition and pleasure in the public spectacle of a "schöne Leich," or was a new political dimension somehow represented? It was all these things and at the same time something more. For this funeral did not just honor a great man of the people in the established fashion rather the "people" in its new social organization gave itself this public political expression. New significances were inscribed in the popular: the coding of urban areas as political territories, the public demonstration of the political identity of a modern mass movement, and finally the latent presence of the subsequently nascent "Red Vienna." Franz Schuhmeier was not just laid in his grave; he was enshrined as a political icon of a proletarian suburban culture.

At a time when the majority of the male working class already enjoyed equal suffrage in the Reichsrat elections but was still largely excluded from the political life of the municipality, the funeral served as a screen for the display of a political counterculture. This had several functions to fulfill: the presentation of a mass social movement that demanded participation in public life, the visualizing of the working class as a future-oriented, visionary counter-society, and the self-display and self-assertion of the "other" as a political subject of social emancipation. The orderly, disciplined, and ranked mass of participants demonstrated itself as a community and a counterforce to the petit-bourgeois Vienna of Karl Lueger, thus destroying the latter's vision of a homogeneous social body. The feudal-popular as theatrical staging and self-celebration became a component of a new political narrative. In this way the popular-modern found expression as a phenomenon of social "*transgression.*"

Both Franz Schuhmeier and Karl Lueger were prototypical exponents, actors, and directors of the phase of transition and regrouping of political forces and hegemonies in Vienna that followed the end of the liberal era, a phenomenon we characterize as transgression. We mean by this a process of change and renegotiation of social, political, and economic hegemonies and a new cartography of the urban terrain. The city was both united and newly segmented, in architectural and symbolic terms. Transgression denotes a specific state of Viennese society between 1890 and 1910. The social structures were still overlaid with a feudal code of monarchy, nobility, clergy, and estates. The late arrival of capitalist modernization led to both social overdetermination and political fragmentation with the collapse of the universalistic claim of liberalism. The symbolic sphere, on the other hand, was characterized by the antagonisms of populism versus urban dignitaries, and the late Enlightenment versus the persistence of powerful Baroque traditions. The urban body of Vienna was re-formed and extended beyond its old limits; it was modernized and technicized in its infrastructure and rapidly lost its old Baroque and Biedermeier face. The incorporation of the suburbs, the massive immigration from the crown lands, and the capitalization of the urban economy not only changed social conditions, but also brought about a restructuring of social divisions and a rise in complexity—the emergence of the industrial working-class professionals as well as a further stratification of the bourgeois strata. Political hegemonies were put into question and restructured under the pressure of new actors.

Transgression in this context meant the attempt to articulate and bring into the political arena the unfinished tasks of liberalism. It was a matter of applying the principle of equality in the new urban conditions of anonymity, social division, and the reification and abstraction of the social against the background of enormous population growth and urban expansion. In the symbolic sphere, transgression was articulated in the discourses of political and cultural identity and in the drawing of boundaries. It was displayed organizationally in symbolic orientations along ethnic, economic, and ideological lines, in a multitude of associations, political clubs, and the early democratic mass parties. This contradictory amalgam of symbols and value orientations, of ideological positions, and forms of social organization, took visible form in the popular-modern, with the mass opposed to the individual, with the authentic opposed to tradition, and with the foundations of the present sought in the past.

This was a profound change in which the old still showed its power while the new had yet to find its definitive form. The feudal-popular lost its force as a foundation of identity and into its place stepped a mass politics that presented itself as a politics of authenticity. The claim of bourgeois substantiality was relativized under the influence of collective articulations of the seemingly genuine, unfalsified, and particular. The old was cited in order to give the city a new signature and novelty a context. The genuine was insisted on, to bridge over the alienation experiences and culture shock of the modern. In a crisis situation that destroyed old relationships, community was sought through imagination and construction. A "we" was constructed as separate from the "other," and the dream of a lost social harmony was articulated as the memory of an abandoned popular tradition.

Transgression was thus an eclectic mixture of transition and transformation, of persisting traditions and decisive innovations; it meant both a return and a tentative but determined advance:

> No one knew exactly what was in the making; no one could have said whether it was to be a new art, a new humanity, a new morality, or perhaps a reshuffling of society ... Talents of a kind that had previously been stifled or had never taken part in public life suddenly came to the fore. They were as different from each other as they could be, and could not have been more contradictory in their aims. There were those who loved the overman and those who loved the underman; there were health cults and sun cults and cults of consumptive maidens; there was enthusiasm for the hero worshipers and for the believers in the common man; people were devout and skeptical, naturalistic and mannered, robust and morbid. They dreamed of old tree-lined avenues in palace parks, autumnal gardens, glassy ponds, jewels, hashish, disease, and demonism, but also of prairies, immense horizons, forges, and rolling mills, of naked wrestlers, slave uprisings, early man, and the destruction of society. These were certainly opposing and widely varying battle cries, but they were uttered in the same breath.[339]

The vehemence of this process was not accidental. The period from 1890 to 1910 initiated mass politics, reacting to the undelivered universalism of liberalism and at the same time signaling its end. It represented a time of transition, renegotiation, and restructuring of political and cultural hegemonies in a phase of post-liberal and populist-oriented mass politics. Liberalism in Vienna came to grief both because of its political particularism, which excluded large sections of the population from suffrage (those on low incomes), and because of an instrumental notion of reason, which produced less enlightenment, emancipation, and freedom than new social inequalities and divisions, without ever really managing to expel the traditional powers of the nobility and the church.

The development of liberalism in the Austrian crown lands took a very particular form. As Pieter M. Judson[340] has shown in regard to the politics of liberal associations in the various provinces, these sought to maintain and reinforce their supremacy over other political currents (Social Democrat, Czech and Hungarian nationalist, Christian Social, etc.) by increasingly adopting German-national positions and solutions and by seeking to bridge social inequalities though a nationalistically tinged discourse. This transformed "ethnic universalism" corresponded to the new nationally coded context of politics in 1900, characterized by the fact that the German-speaking population of the Habsburg monarchy was more concerned with distinguishing itself from other groups of the population than it was with winning these over with an attractive political program. German-national identity, which in the 1880s had been more of a fiction than a real marker of identity, especially for the German-speaking rural population, gradually came to be seen in the 1890s as something fixed, innate, and trans-historical, subsequently forming the basis for a national liberalism consisting of "stridently defensive nationalist rhetoric and an extremely progressive, optimistic assertion of the effectiveness of education and science"[341] for the good of humanity.

Liberalism had proclaimed the "everyday utopia" of the Enlightenment without seeking to make this into the genuine "everyday experience" of the Viennese population. Its elites were trapped in a pre-1848 mentality, seeking to make up for the trauma of the failed bourgeois revolution of 1848 by ever new compromises with the feudal elites. While liberalism achieved an immense catching-up process in economic terms, socioculturally it remained exclusively confined to the propertied bourgeoisie and to assimilation-seeking Jews, who expected final social recognition in the wake of economic success. Liberalism was successful in establishing a state of law and civil rights (the constitution of 1867), but it failed on account of the excessive universalism of its ideology. Since it only delivered this in particular terms and excluded the lower classes, liberalism radicalized the petite bourgeoisie and was doomed to ruin by their anti-modernism and aggression. The one-sided proclamation of freedom and progress for the educated and prosperous led to massive political countermovements of those excluded from the glamour of the Ringstraße and the blessings of capitalism:

> During the last quarter of the nineteenth century, the program the liberals had devised against the upper classes occasioned the explosion of the lower. The liberals succeeded in releasing the political energies of the masses, but against themselves rather than against their ancient foes. Every shot aimed at the enemy above produced a hostile salvo from below. A German nationalism articulated against aristocratic cosmopolitans was answered by Slavic patriots clamoring for autonomy. When the liberals soft-pedaled their Germanism in the interest of the multinational state, they were branded as traitors to nationalism by an anti-liberal German *petite bourgeoisie*. Laissez faire, devised to free the economy from the fetters of the past, called forth the Marxist revolutionaries of the future. Catholicism, routed from the school and courthouse as the handmaiden of aristocratic oppression, returned as the ideology of peasant and artisan, for whom liberalism meant capitalism and capitalism meant Jew. By the end of the century even the Jews, to whom Austro-liberalism had offered emancipation, opportunity, and assimilation to modernity, began to turn their back on their benefactors.[342]

The years after the great stock-market crash of 1873 and the ensuing economic depression, which lasted until the mid-1880s, brought not only reduced income, poverty, and economic stagnation, but also a rationalization of production and with this an acceleration of structural change in the economy. Small firms, handicrafts, and trade were subjected to a modernization push largely propelled by finance capital, bringing with it a substantial expansion of the industrial sector and installing new leading sectors of heavy industry. Austria's belated but rapid and sudden entry into the era of capitalist modernity had massive social effects, not only on the proletariat but also on small-scale trade and handicrafts. By the 1880s at the latest, Viennese traders saw themselves threatened by the factory system, domestic industry, and new systems of distribution whose competitive pressure they could not meet.[343]

The division that consequently ran through the higher, middle, and petite bourgeoisie, and which brought the (lower) middle class into a critical economic situation between bourgeoisie and proletariat, had a surprising radicalizing effect on the conflict regulation mechanisms of the traditional political culture, to which the liberals could not offer any adequate forms of political articulation. The alienation between the liberals and the dispossessed and hard-up petite bourgeoisie thereby deepened. The conflict of interest between petite bourgeoisie and propertied bourgeoisie was not a new phenomenon; signs of it had already appeared during the bourgeois revolution of 1848. Under the new economic and social conditions, however, it grew into a divisive determinant of politics, which was only further intensified by an extremely hierarchic electoral system graded by income and the exclusion of a large swathe of the lower middle class.

It was precisely these sections of the lower middle class, however, who were addressed by the discourse of a new populist politics developed by those German-national, free democratic, and Christian Social movements that split away from the liberals and established an independent political and cultural camp in opposition to them. The liberals lacked a developed left wing, radical-democratic tradition that might have been able to establish a civic alliance of skilled workers and lower middle-class strata as an intermediate group between the bourgeoisie and the political actors excluded from civil society. Hence what developed was an ominous amalgamation of "left wing" anti-capitalist and "right wing" structural conservative and anti-modern sentiment, which found its clearest public expression in a growing hostility toward foreigners and Jews on the part of small artisans and traders. John W. Boyer has indicated how political protest movements of the commercial sector in other major cities in Western and Central Europe also grew up on a basis of anti-Semitic resentment, but it was only in Vienna that this became the specific motor and political foundation of a successful anti-liberal municipal politics. Boyer sums up: "Antisemitism in Vienna was notable not for what it was, but for what it made eventually possible—the destruction of Liberal rule in the city."[344]

Alongside the division and regrouping of political camps and movements, Vienna completed its evolution into a metropolis. Rapid industrialization altered the social structure and diversified the lower classes into traditional handicraft and proto-industrial skilled tradesmen, new industrial workers—from the unskilled casual worker up to highly skilled specialists in the mechanical and electrical industries—and the newly growing ranks of white-collar workers and managers in commerce, insurance, and banking. The increasing ethnic diversity of the population and the differentiation of enterprises and wage-earners by purchasing power, performance, and skill level sharpened tensions between individual groups and the different nationalities. For the architectural and infrastructural profile of Vienna, the rapid expansion of the city brought the requirement of a second phase of modernization beyond the *Gründerzeit* development of the Ringstraße. The communications network, the streetcars, and the public transit systems had to be renewed and expanded, as did the water, gas, and electric supply.

Liberalism, which was no longer in a position to offer the citizens identity and political autonomy, had no effective municipal politics with which to counter the double challenge of massive proletarianization on the one hand, and escalating petit-bourgeois radicalism on the other. In contrast to its original intent, the elite-oriented politics of the liberals only furthered social disintegration and the discontent of both the lower middle class and the workers. The new mass movements were articulated along both economic and ethnic vectors and opened up an explosive political spectrum of Social Democrats, Christian Socials, Czech nationalists, and pan-Germanists (Georg Ritter von Schönerer), as well as the Zionism of Theodor Herzl in reaction to growing racist anti-Semitism.

The decay of the social body was expressed both in the rapid changes of governments and in the increasing street demonstrations of workers, in the sharp ethnic conflicts on the occasion of the so-called Badeni crisis of 1897[345] and in the conflicts between German student organizations and non-German students at the University of Vienna. Political language took on a new tone, and the tone of parliamentary and local political debate, formerly marked by the values of education and decency, collapsed into insult, denunciation, and outbursts of hate. Public opinion, especially the print media, became a rhetorical battlefield where political opponents were attacked with stereotypes, insinuations, and hate campaigns. This new political tone was most clearly expressed in the person of Karl Lueger, leader of the Christian Social party, who combined anti-Semitism, anti-capitalism, and opposition to the liberals and Social Democrats into an extremely effective style of popular mass rhetoric. Lueger had a masterful way of addressing the disoriented petit bourgeois and intermediate strata, who lost ground in between the bourgeoisie and proletariat, and of presenting himself as their mouthpiece and medium. He took what they did not say, or still refrained from saying—that is, their collective resentment—and gave it public presentation and political demonstration:

> Look at the way he addresses them! The roar of their applause releases all his talent. It is almost a work of genius how he brings his arguments together … In the quick-fire attack that befits his temperament, he overruns reason and proof, stamps great meanings into the ground, and then holds up trivialities with a single word so rapidly that they appear the very pinnacle of truth … In his furious speech, when he doesn't care what he says, he is happy to adopt the insults of the street, voice the stupid phrases of old superstitions, and use clerical gestures that have long been abandoned in the pulpit—but all this only makes him more effective … His power over the Viennese people is that they all speak through his mouth: the cab driver and the cobbler's apprentice, the retired army captain and the decent lawyer, the average woman of the street and the welfare functionary. And all the popular singers as well, from Guschelbauer to Schmitter. You can hear a Viennese band in the melody of his words, its particular rhythms and instruments sound constantly in his voice.[346]

Lueger was the first self-made man in Austrian politics. The son of a housekeeper at the Imperial Polytechnic in the petit-bourgeois suburb of Wieden, he rose to become one of the most powerful mayors of Vienna, managing to force his ideas on both Emperor Franz Joseph and various

Imperial governments. As a child in the suburbs he already showed great ambition and zeal; graduating from the elite Theresianum secondary school, he then completed his law studies at the University. After an interlude as a clerk and lawyer, he went into politics in the early 1870s and was elected five years later as a liberal municipal councillor. Like both Schönerer and Herzl, Lueger soon broke with the liberals and joined the German nationalists, bringing about the fall of the liberal mayor Cajetan Felder. He supported the German-Nationalist Schönerer in his Linz program of 1882 and in the debate on the so-called Nordbahn question, in which he took an anti-capitalist position against the Rothschild Company and called for the nationalization of the railroads. The expansion of suffrage to men who paid a minimum tax of at least five gulden per year brought Lueger into the Reichsrat with the votes of Vienna's "kleiner Mann." In the 1880s and 1890s, a "lukewarm, dull, indecisive period" in which a "broad mass of petit-bourgeois ... found their way into meeting halls,"[347] Lueger built up his political following. He took the despondency and skepticism of artisans, tradesmen, small business people, carters, meat traders, and white-collar workers and turned their feelings of inferiority into a powerful popular movement. He occupied and articulated the gaps that a democracy of the elite had opened up between itself and these marginalized groups:

> Formerly they had been ignored. He praised them. They had been required to show respect. He absolved them of any respect. They had been told that only the educated were to rule. He showed how poor the educated were at ruling. He, an educated man, a doctor, a lawyer, tore the doctors to shreds, demolished the lawyers, insulted the professors, made fun of science. He exposed everything that intimidated and confined the masses, tore it all down and laughingly trampled it, and the cobblers and tailors, the coachmen, vegetable sellers, and barkeepers were excited and jubilant, believing that the time had finally come that they were promised with the words "Blessed are the poor in spirit." He confirmed the Viennese lower class in all its characteristics: its intellectual helplessness, its distrust of education, its drunkenness, its love of street brawls, its adherence to the old-fashioned, its overweening self-satisfaction. And they raved, they raved with delight when he spoke to them.[348]

In 1887 Lueger joined the anti-liberal Christian Social Union, becoming its leader in 1893 and changing its name to the Christian Social Party. When Schönerer abandoned politics in 1888, Lueger integrated the remaining German-nationals through marked anti-Semitic propaganda. His party now became a gathering place for Catholics and anti-liberals of all sorts. Lueger's greatest political achievement, however, was the creation of an anti-liberal citizens' bloc, which joined the groups of petit bourgeois on the one hand and well-to-do proprietors on the other, who had been divided in the wake of 1848, into a clerical, anti-socialist, and anti-Semitic combination:

> Lueger gathered all those people together who strove for freedom beneath the upper bourgeoisie and above the proletariat; they seemed ready to consider him their liberator. These disparate strata without any common economic or cultural interests—the oppressed artisans and small traders, the petty officials and shop

assistants—he fused together in his party, organized and disciplined them, and made these "little men" despised by the liberal snobs the masters of the city. His negative program was anti-Semitism, his positive one clericalism. Both were originally just reflex actions to a particularly tinged liberalism that he sought to dethrone. He freed Vienna from "Jewish rule" and delivered us to the rule of the priests.[349]

Lueger was elected mayor in 1895 but only confirmed in the office two years later, after serious conflict with the Emperor. In this post he showed himself a master of political historicizing. He made his own tradition of what was properly Viennese into a new horizon of political action, thus giving the city a new signature of his own making. He insinuated the supposedly true and genuine Vienna of the petit bourgeois against the alienation experience and culture and work shock of modernity. Friedrich Austerlitz, editor-in-chief of the Social Democratic *Arbeiter-Zeitung* (and thus a leading figure in the competing mass movement that was Lueger's main political opponent after the defeat of the liberals), ascribed him with unique capabilities of populism and mass suggestion:

> Lueger was neither distinguished nor significant, but his success owed much to the fact that he was an interesting man, a real Viennese in politics who completely embodied the mental physiognomy of the city, inspired by love as well as anger, so that every Viennese could recognize in his mentality a part of himself. He could be generous in a kind of live-and-let-live way that is possible only in this city, but he could also be vindictive and spiteful ...
>
> He was completely at home in the Viennese dialect like no one before him, which is why his words were so effective. If you didn't like it, you were at least riled by it. This made him the great celebrity of our city, eventually even a sight that visitors to Vienna had to see. He was more popular than any actor, more famous than any scholar; he was a phenomenon and a force in politics such as no other great city has displayed, something that is only possible in Vienna and that only arose in the form of Lueger.[350]

Lueger created an image of the city that united the various petit-bourgeois and middle-class segments of Viennese society. He created Vienna as a paternalistic, a fatherly city so to speak, as imagined by the petite bourgeoisie. This presented an idea of Vienna as quintessentially a city of pre-industrial burghers—Christian, patriarchal, and ordered by traditional rank, resting on authority, paternalism, inheritance, and Catholic values. Lueger's urban vision and imaginary had many characteristics of what Benedict Anderson has conceived as an "imagined community."[351] Like Anderson's interpretation of the nation, it was defined as sovereign (a quasi-state within the state), exclusive (German-national and anti-Semitic), egalitarian, and communitarian. Lueger's urban vision constructed and addressed a community that existed as such only in the minds of its subjects and could not be experienced as real. He brought them together via a secessionist code of populism that made anonymous individuals into an "us" against a "them." Lueger's community of underprivileged petit bourgeois was formed in a situation of cultural alienation that no longer offered face-to-face social relationships and produced a tie of community only by social exclusion and inclusion. This image of the city, however, was more than merely a reaction to industrialization and anonymity in a rapidly expanding metropolis; it also mourned the loss of a supposedly existent totality. Since the present was experienced as chaotic and unfathomable, threatening and fearful, Lueger could speak of the pre-1848 era as the golden age of Vienna with its characteristic *Gemütlichkeit*, while at the same time evoking the civic unity of 1848 as a moment of community. What had started out in the early 1880s as a movement of petty traders and small taxpayers developed a decade later into a broad flood of middle-class protest, which Lueger instrumentalized in the name of traditional bourgeois values of respectability and virtue. If the liberals of 1848 had evoked civic unity only to divide and fragment it in subsequent years, Lueger now embarked on a revision that would mobilize those who had lost out in the modernization of the post-revolutionary era, first against the liberals themselves and later against the Social Democrats. By 1900 his political machine represented not only the small traders, but also both politically and culturally the imagined ideal of civic unity on a pre-industrial and early industrial basis.[352]

20. Tribune, populist, and anti-Semite. Mayor Karl Lueger.
Source: Historisches Museum der Stadt Wien.

Lueger simultaneously used the crisis conditions of the Habsburg monarchy (feudalistic conservatism, belated modernization, and the "economics of backwardness"[353]) and the segmentation of the social brought about by capitalism (embryonic German nationalism and the decline of a would-be supranational liberalism) in order to create a new and distinct political style. He combined populism (the aggregation of different social segments into an "imagined community" as the mass basis for his politics), personalism (he presented himself as both party leader and father figure), anti-Semitism (he made a contingent cultural formation of the feudal-popular into a tactical political metaphor serving as an identity narrative for the masses), and collectivism ("Christian Socialism" as counter-strategy to both the secular socialism of the Social Democrats and the particularistic universalism of the liberals) into a characteristic mixture of modern styles and backward contents. His personality and politics displayed both the technical imperatives of modernity (municipal socialism and the creation of a "Fordist" urban structure) and regressive, authoritarian, and paternalistic visions of society as a "community." He went with the time in order to confiscate its radical-democratic agenda. What mattered for him was not political content but personal power; he aimed not to put a program into practice, but to direct an authoritarian politics as the theater of emotion and resentment. He built up his power base by a ramified client system among officials and dependants. He derived his claim to power not from ideology, but from constant recourse to the "Vienneseness" of which he saw himself as spokesman and director:

> He was in fact, however, not at all a man of convictions. He loved a disordered mixture of opinions and views, from the jumble of which he could extract whatever principle was suitable at the particular moment. The container in which Karl Lueger stored his ever controversial ideas was labeled "Viennese *Gemütlichkeit*." There was room for everything in this pot: democracy and servitude, generosity to proprietors and workers, anti-Semitism and friendship with Jews, German nationalism and clericalism, and a welter of other incompatible contradictions.354

When Lueger died on March 10, 1910, it was not just the end of a successful political career. Vienna's petite bourgeoisie and lower middle class lost not only a popular political figure, they lost their own mouthpiece and medium of political articulation. He had been, as Friedrich Austerlitz emphasized, "the first bourgeois politician who reckoned with the masses, moved the masses, and sunk the roots of his power deep in the earth."[355]

Lueger's funeral[356] was a major social event. Hundreds of thousands lined the route to the Central Cemetery, where the burial took place with the public excluded. The funeral procession crossed the whole city—from the City Hall along the Ring to St. Stephan's Cathedral, where a memorial service was held in the presence of the Emperor, the high nobility, urban and rural dignitaries, ministers, cardinals, archbishops, and officers. A countless number of carriages stood ready on the Aspernplatz to carry those invited to the cemetery. Extra streetcars were deployed on the route to the cemetery, and uniformed ranks of soldiers, policemen, city officials, and shooting-club members occupied the streets through which the procession moved. The whole of Vienna put out black flags, concession stands offered food and drink, and most businesses were closed to honor the deceased. "Vienna" stood still to pay respect to its great politician and to celebrate a great popular feast at the same time.

Lueger's populism had destroyed liberalism and brought Vienna's petite bourgeoisie to political power. Franz Schuhmeier, like Lueger a politician of transgression and a child of the suburbs, and like him also the embodiment of an "authentic Vienneseness," had been his great opponent. Schuhmeier also recruited his following in the wake of liberalism's demise, but in a completely different form. The issue for him was not the destruction of liberalism but the redemption of its unfulfilled political agenda. The great promises of the Enlightenment and modernity—education, equality, progress, and welfare—should not be reserved for a narrow elite, but should become a real universalism of the "people." In Schuhmeier the contradictions of the outgoing nineteenth century are found in exemplary form: on the one hand belief in progress, commitment to the Enlightenment, and belief in the uplifting of the masses by way of education and knowledge, on the other the persistence of oral culture and popular tradition. He stood, as the *Arbeiter-Zeitung* put it in an obituary written under the immediate impact of his murder, "for the bright, the joyous, the resolute, the decisive," which made up the characteristic strength of the Viennese proletariat and which anyone could trace "if they came into intimate contact with it"—in short, he was "a true proletarian and a true Viennese."[357] Like no one else, Schuhmeier as a typical figure of social and cultural transgression did not merely represent the suburb, he was the suburb, and at the same time something more. A pronounced anticlerical, professed freethinker and Freemason, he had also become a symbolic figure of identification for the liberal-minded Viennese bourgeoisie, who would fondly remember him, so the *Neue Freie Presse* wrote in a posthumous commemoration, as "a fearless opponent of clericalism and a firm-rooted Viennese character."[358] And the liberal paper *Der Morgen* concluded its own assessment of Schuhmeier as politician with the following words:

> This is why the liberal-minded citizens of Vienna should also stand in mourning at this grave in which a Social Democratic leader is laid to eternal rest. For every true and genuine man of the people shares the common fight of all liberal-minded men, all whose outlook on life rejects the police spirit that seeks to keep us on a leash and under custody. [359]

The forty-nine-year-old Schuhmeier was shot down in the late evening of February 11, 1913, in the arrivals hall of the Nordwestbahnhof station, on his return from a propaganda tour in Stockerau, where he had spoken in his capacity as member of the provincial Social Democratic party executive of Lower Austria. The assassin Paul Kunschak (brother of the leading Christian Social workers' official Leopold Kunschak) had the reputation of a quarrelsome person and political muddlehead. He had gotten to know Schuhmeier as his stenography teacher at the Ottakring Arbeiterheim, and his first contact with him went back even earlier, in connection with the disturbances during the streetcar drivers' strike of 1888, when he was still a Social Democratic sympathizer and in the course of which he had been imprisoned. He gave as his motive that he wanted to hurt one of the most popular and prominent representatives of the Social Democrats, by whose Free Trade Unions he felt persecuted and kept on reins.[360]

Franz Schuhmeier was born the eldest of five children of the frequently unemployed bookbinder and alcoholic Eduard Schuhmeier and his wife Theresia, housekeeper and washerwoman, in the Margareten district of Vienna.[361] While at school he already had experience of hard labor on a cab, and he had to break off his apprenticeship as an engraver following an eye injury. After two years on the road, he joined the colored-paper factory of Goppold and Schmiedl in 1882, which at that time had the reputation of being a center for socialists, social revolutionaries, and world-improvers of all kinds.

Within a short time, Schuhmeier became a member of a revolutionary sect and attended meetings and assemblies in the back rooms of various suburban taverns and cellar dives. His start in politics came in the era of anarchism and radical-democratic rhetoric, his basic political socialization being anticlericalism, which, inspired by a marked desire for education, he wanted to understand "on a scientific level." When a state of emergency was proclaimed on June 30, 1884, he became the representative of an illegal and marginalized workers' movement, itself split into different factions. Under the influence of Albert Sever, who was likewise employed at Goppold and Schmiedl, and the young editor of Victor Adler's *Gleichheit*, Franz Bretschneider, he took up increasingly "reformist" positions. Schuhmeier became a convinced supporter of party unity, which however, did not prevent him from continuing to maintain regular contact with the left.

In 1887, under the cover name of "Shakespeare," Schuhmeier joined a political workers' association in Ottakring disguised as a smoking club (a common form of organization for the workers' movement in this period of illegality) and soon became its leader.[362] After a police roundup he served a seven-week jail term, and later he was sentenced to a twenty-four-hour arrest for violating a ban on assembly (altogether he was arrested nearly a dozen times for political offenses). In the wake of the smoking club's dissolution, the workers' educational association "Apollo" was founded under his aegis, which had a membership of 2,300 at the end of 1891 and which held its sessions in such legendary Neulerchenfeld inns as the Rote Bretzen, the Schwarzer Adler, and the Weißer Engel. He gave his first major public speech at a May Day celebration in 1890 held at the Goldene Luchs.

A year earlier, Schuhmeier had been involved briefly with the administration of the *Arbeiter-Zeitung*, and here began his meteoric rise. At twenty-five he was still an unskilled worker, but by thirty he headed the General Workers' Sickness Fund and was national party secretary and editor-in-chief (later publisher) of the *Volkstribüne*, which within a short time reached a circulation of 60,000, and subscription to which in Vienna and Lower Austria was seen as equivalent to membership in the Social Democratic Workers' Party. In 1894 a confidential memorandum of the Viennese police described him as one of the "most active leaders" and "most radical agitators" of the party, who was known especially for his "immoderate attacks on the existing social order, against the government, the authorities, the propertied classes and entrepreneurs, etc."[363] Schuhmeier's ever direct temperament, his impulsiveness, and his ability to translate the emotions of the masses into political rhetoric frequently brought him into heated conflict with the uncontested leader of his party, Victor Adler, even if these conflicts were

21. Working-class agitator and suburban patriarch Franz Schuhmeier. Source: Verein für Geschichte der Arbeiterbewegung Wien.

concealed from public view. Adler's own political conception and strategy hinged on a strictly rationally led social and cultural modernization. In a letter to Karl Kautsky of November 18, 1901, for example, Adler subjected Schuhmeier's often overflowing populism to devastating critique: "Then there's Schuhmeier, who has brewed up a kind of noisy opportunism, which would be impossible outside of the Wild West" (Adler means here the western suburbs of Vienna), "a tremendously talented demagogue, but who lacks the sense even to understand our problems."[364]

But Schuhmeier outgrew the role of suburban populist. One of his greatest achievements was the establishment and construction of the Ottakring Arbeiterheim in collaboration with the university historian Ludo Hartmann, a people's college in the best sense of the word, which offered courses not just in general education and vocational specializations, but also in folk dancing and languages (including German for Czechs and Czech for Germans). Between 1895 and 1905 no fewer than 100,000 people attended popular science classes at the Volksheim, a third of whom were working men and women.[365]

In the municipal elections of May 31, 1900, two Social Democrats were elected for the first time in the fourth curia (winning a total of 43 percent of the votes): Jakob Reumann for Favoriten and Franz Schuhmeier for Ottakring. On January 3, 1901, Schuhmeier went on to enter the Reichsrat, where he remained a member until his death and where as a passionate hunter he soon made a name as his party's armaments expert. On the Vienna municipal council, he became the outstanding opponent of the ruling Christian Social party and its foremost leaders, Hermann Bilohlawek and Karl Lueger. Already in the first year of his membership on the council, Reumann and Schuhmeier voted for the Christian Social municipal budget, thus breaking a taboo of the Social Democratic movement. This consensus politics came to an end, however, when Lueger broke his promise to democratize municipal suffrage. The fundamental opposition that Schuhmeier championed was subsequently suspended only in particular cases, such as the municipalization projects. Schuhmeier identified Bilohlawek (known for such remarks as "I gobble a book up as soon as I see it" and "Science is when one Jew copies another") as the classic Viennese philistine and despised above all his "political folk singer" nature. Lueger, however, he recognized as a worthy opponent who shared his congenial popular character. Their arguments in the council chamber became legend; the quick wit, humor, and mocking sense of fun that they shared could collapse into profound hostility, but their shouting matches and wild insults just as often ended in theatrical gestures of reconciliation, and Lueger in particular harked back time and again to the original "Vienneseness" they both shared. The relationship between these non-identical and yet similar twins of the popular, marked by all kinds of ambivalence and ambiguity and running the whole gamut from massive coarseness and biting scorn to mutual respect right through to an almost loving honor, was thus also a central theme of press commentary after Schuhmeier's assassination. Attention was drawn in particular to the similarity of their popular rhetoric, their diction, but also their unreserved style of debating, and the fact that they could never suppress their mutual sympathy. This was summed up by *Die Zeit* as follows:

> Schuhmeier's popularity in Vienna in the last few years was probably matched only by Lueger, with whose character he had a great deal in common, despite the bitterest political enmity. Both were typical representatives of the Viennese popular classes—Dr. Lueger, the Vienna burgher, and Schuhmeier, a son of the people. Starting from humble beginnings, Schuhmeier acquired a prominent position in political life, and just as Lueger became the particular leader of the Viennese middle class, so Schuhmeier was leader of the broad masses of organized labor.[366]

Schuhmeier was neither a theorist nor an organizer, and even less a political tactician. He avoided petty organizational work if he could, and he also disliked petty work in thought and action. His specialty was agitation, and above all rhetoric. As a speaker in debates and meetings he showed an unparalleled brilliance, and it was in this domain that his most genuine successes were achieved. He could make masterful use of his irreplaceable Viennese dialect, and let himself be swept along by his impulses. A master of quick repartee, full of humor and force, he could match his words to the immediate perception of his audience. At such moments, it is reported, he completely got into the feelings of the masses. This may well have been a fundamental reason for the devotion he enjoyed, above all from "his own" people of Ottakring, but it also was responsible for his frequent and rather unconsidered coquetting with anti-Semitism—what Wilhelm Ellenbogen called an "Ottakring atavism" that he had long since overcome within himself. Indeed, "his most passionate admirers had always been Jews."[367]

This genuine figure of the popular contained contrasts, antagonisms, and contradictions. A deliberately cultivated sharpness and resolve, in a certain sense the nature of a Viennese "grumbler," contrasted with a "real Viennese softness" always attested to by his close personal acquaintances, an unbounded zest for life, a light and careless existence, a love of music, and an almost naive enthusiasm for theater.[368] Schuhmeier always laid great value on simplicity and plainness in outward behavior, but, when he became a member of parliament, he exchanged his tenement apartment on Kaiserstraße for a Secessionist villa in Wilhelminenberg. The *Arbeiter-Zeitung* columnist Hugo Schulz saw his character as giving living expression to "the genius of Schubert's music and Raimund's poetry."[369] It was no surprise, therefore, that Max Eitelberg should draw concrete parallels, in a special issue of the satirical weekly *Glühlichter*, to Girardi, the most well-known and best-loved popular actor of the time, and identify Schuhmeier very pertinently as a genuinely Viennese character in the intermediate zone between "timeless-popular" and high-culture or bourgeois-theatrical performance: "The tension around his mouth and furrows ploughed very likely by sorrow gave him a similarity with Girardi. He certainly shared something of Girardi's character, and it was part of the power that won him boundless affection."[370]

Schuhmeier's self-fashioning as the quintessential popular hero embodying all the idealized virtues of the genuine Viennese and the genuine worker had a solid historical background. In a certain sense Schuhmeier was the continuation, even the exaggeration, of the essentially good-humored and convivial Viennese worker who in the October days of 1848 had suddenly emerged as a historical player:

> He was like the good-natured Schottenfeld silk workers and Lichtental coppersmiths, who gave free rein to their quick tongues harmlessly enough at their festivities in Neulerchenfeld and Altottakring until 1848, when it was their quick fists that came into play ... These Viennese workers then grew tough and sharp and edgy and stubborn, and a race of men grew up in Schottenfeld that engaged in proletarian class struggle and that found in Franz Schuhmeier its truest and most quintessential embodiment.[371]

Schuhmeier, who rose from an unskilled worker who had only attended elementary school to a brilliant municipal politician, parliamentary expert on defense matters, and acclaimed journalist, served in this sense as a concrete symbol for the social and cultural ability of the suburban working class, a man in whom many could see the fulfillment of their hopes for the future. And in this sense what "the people" loved in Franz Schuhmeier was themselves; they were proud of themselves.[372]

Schuhmeier's rhetoric and politics created a notion of the Viennese suburb as *chrono-topos*, in other words, the suburb was defined as a terrain of politics. From a chaotic conglomeration of anonymous social connections, urban arrangements, and fragments of space and life, from hopelessness and lack of perspective, experiences of poverty, and petty everyday escapes, from an existence confined to the here and now in which the next day was always uncertain, it became a territory of transition to something possibly different. Schuhmeier and the Social Democrats made the political utopia of this "possibly different" into a perspective of everyday life. The suburb was not seen as a present without history, but constructed as a place of transition toward a better life. In this light the changes in the Vienna suburbs before and after the turn of the century can be understood not just in terms of architectural expansion, migration from the provinces, and the development of new technical infrastructures, communications systems, and new forms of consumption, etc., but also as changes in space-time experience. This involved a new politics of identity. Workers were no longer simply workers, proletarians no longer simply proletarians, but rather a new entity, a "working class" endowed with expectations and hopes for the future. Those without power or rights thus experienced themselves no longer as impotent objects of industrial and political processes that went on above their heads, but as proper subjects, part of a project for the future, so that their present suffering could be seen simply as a transitional stage.

The suburb thus appears not only as the site of an endless duration of poverty and wretched living conditions, but as a place of social and political transformation. The powerfulness of this construction lies in its mixture of political progress narrative, concretely conceived future, and comprehensive organization. It was precisely this politics of anticipation that allowed the

Social Democrats to build out of the nothing of suburban social relations with their contingency and aimlessness a powerful and efficient organizational structure beyond comparison. Even simple organizational initiatives, such as collecting membership dues and selling the party newspaper, became part of a quasi-religious ritual when placed in an overall context in which ideals of the bourgeois revolution were combined with vague notions of a classless society into a utopian civic religion. How pervasive and extensive the organizational strength of the Social Democrats was in the suburbs, already at the time of the first free elections held on universal male suffrage in 1907, is shown by the results for the districts of Ottakring, Floridsdorf, Favoriten, and Brigittenau, where the number of Social Democratic votes was only an average of 9.3 percent less than the total number of working-class electors (5 percent in Neulerchenfeld, 13.5 percent in Brigittenau).[373] The Social Democrats were in a position to make use of the face-to-face social relations formed in the rural village and convert these into the cell and section structures of their party organization. As early as 1896, a confidential report of the Lower Austrian provincial government concluded that the Social Democratic sectional and local organization in the Vienna suburbs was set up in such a way as to have a representative for virtually every building who was responsible for agitation by way of the distribution of leaflets, personal influence, etc. The re-territorialization of the city was thus accomplished, and the creation of a political cartography of the urban found expression in a system of local representatives numbering in the thousands, who, as the Ottakring Reichsrat deputy Albert Sever put it, were more familiar with the tenement buildings than the proprietor or his agent.[374] This micro-politics of the social, contrasting a dense network of communication with the anonymity of the metropolis, conditioned a discourse of the local that became the coauthor of a new politics of the public sphere.

What did this mean, then, for the traditional cultures of the oral and popular? First of all, it did not mean the inscription and thus abstract modernization of suburban life-worlds, but rather the constitution of the suburb as primarily an object of educational discourse. A new proletarian culture was founded by recourse to oral tradition and reference to pre-modern social structures. This did not mean the banal imitation of a "village in the city," but rather the ongoing refoundation of urban life forms in the process of transgression. Village and pre-industrial biographies and family traditions were overlaid with new attributions of identity and horizons of expectation. Those without trace or history were given an orientation and an anticipatory political action—the amorphous "other" organized itself into a historical subject. The traceless modernity of the suburbs began, by way of mass politics and organization, to determine and shape the public sphere. The Social Democratic progress narrative occupied the empty place in urban life that liberalism had never occupied, despite addressing this in universalistic terms. In this double process through which the terrain was politicized and the amorphous "other" became a subject, the masses arose as a political factor. At a time and in a city when, according to Robert Musil, the constitution was liberal but the government clerical, though despite this life went on in a freethinking fashion, when all citizens were equal before the law but not everyone was a citizen,[375] a counter-society antagonistic to the bourgeois world took shape in the suburbs. There was a parallel movement of center and periphery, in the sense that at the periphery a transformation of the subject from alterity and indifference to political identity took place, while at the same time the subjects of the center, the bourgeois elites faced with decline and the crisis of liberalism, underwent a painful transformation from political identity toward cultural difference. In the inner city there developed on the one hand an abstract capitalism detached from its subjects, and on the other hand a highly complex culture of pluralism and subjectivism. The bourgeois ego split into modernity's irreducible experiences of difference:

> Time was on the move. People not yet born in those days will find it hard to believe, but even then time was racing along like a cavalry camel, just like today. But nobody knew where time was headed. And it was not always clear what was up or down, what was going forward or backward. "No matter what you do," the man without qualities thought with a shrug, "within this mare's nest of forces at work, it doesn't make the slightest difference!"[376]

The "ego" became the object of a cultural discourse of difference, and the "masses" a discursive field of political identity. At the end of this transgression, there resided at the center the nervous and fragmented ego of the fin de siècle,[377] thematized as the "irredeemable ego" in the philosophy of Ernst Mach and related in Musil's *Man Without Qualities* as the fragment text of the individual. The "masses" of the suburbs on the other hand were newly constructed as group identities—both as the political collective subject of Social Democracy and as the object of social resentment for Karl Lueger's populism.

The transgression phase of Viennese society in the two decades before World War I created and completed the double convolution of the city and in this way effected both the decisive marginalizing of feudal traditions and hegemony and the constitution of a plateau of democratic mass politics. An irony fraught with consequences was contained in this process: the birth of democracy not as a logical consequence of liberalism, but rather as the division of the urban body both spatially and socially into the Social Democratic working masses of the suburbs and the Christian Social camp of petit bourgeois, civil servants, and middle class. Democracy did not develop out of a homogeneous polis, but rather from the concentric power and social gradient of the Ringstraße era, in which liberal consciousness of power and self combined with the residual core of feudal power into a hegemonic amalgam. The new democratic mass politics appeared less as the abolition of the diachronic concentric power gradient of the urban body that liberalism had created in the Ringstraße era than as its reinforcement. Social Democracy successfully addressed the unredeemed universalistic political message of liberalism by its creation of a modern and organized mass party, but it could not touch the legacy of liberalism in the form of an architectonic of power, since on the basis of a municipal suffrage by curia, which lasted until 1919, it was to a large extent excluded from real political influence on the city. Lueger and the Christian Socials, on the other hand, destroyed the political power of the liberals chiefly by their projects of municipalization and by the construction of a loyal power base in the urban bureaucracy. The concentric convolutions of the urban body, however, they left untouched. Lueger enthroned the petit bourgeois as the new political hegemon at the municipal level, and in place of liberal ideology he put his own person as politics and program. Social Democracy as a mass movement was limited to configuring the urban body symbolically as the possible topos of a different politics, a different society and culture, thus creating an egalitarian cultural code that after World War I was determinant for "Red Vienna."

Lueger, for his part, developed a secessionist and xenophobic cultural code, addressing not the city as a whole, but rather its divisions. His politics was one of "evangelizing" the poor and excluding the "other." Leaving to a large extent untouched the underlying social and cultural segregation of the city, he needed to thematize the explosive tensions it contained in a different form. The suburb became for him a territory that in its petit-bourgeois aspect was to be managed in a clientelist fashion, and that in its proletarian aspect was to be satisfied by a politics of symbols (church building, charitable initiatives for the poor and orphans). The social and economic tensions of the city as a whole, however, he addressed with a discourse of alterity, that is, not just culturally marking foreigners and others, but declaring them the root cause of political evil and social misery. This politics was functionalist more than essentialist. Lueger's anti-Semitism was not racist, but casuistic and populist: "His anti-Semitic sentiments were not very deep. Lueger became an anti-Semite on political grounds, as a pretext, never with his heart ... If he met a Jew in private life who tried to reproach him for his hostility, this really upset Lueger. Politics and human feeling for him were always two strictly separate departments."[378]

Lueger's anti-Semitism can be understood as a symbolic act of sacrifice, that is, the fantasized killing of Jews and foreigners, escaping the internal perpetrator/victim dynamic present in the unredeemed tensions of the city. The "other" was stereotyped as outsider so as to evoke the fantasy of an internally identical society in general and awaken this in the sense of an "imagined community" of civic Vienna. Thus what appeared as a hindrance to the full self-identity of the community was in actual fact the condition for its existence. Only by imposing on Jews and foreigners the role of outsiders and "parasites," who supposedly brought dissolution and paralysis of the urban body, was the fantasy of society as a harmonious community made politically possible and functional in populist terms.

Lueger's instrumental anti-Semitism was not invented from nothing. He was able in fact to draw on a long-standing tradition of anti-Jewish resentment, fueled ideologically and at a micro-political and municipal level by a Catholic anti-Semitism that was more a function of popular myths about the supposed ritual murder of Christian children than of official church doctrine.[379] This Catholic Judeophobia had developed over centuries, reinforced and legitimized time and again by countless pogroms, and deeply embedded especially in the popular culture of the Alpine lands. More economically based forms of anti-Jewish feeling developed with early industrialism in the first half of the nineteenth century, in Bohemia and Prague as well as Vienna, identifying Jewish industrialists (such as the Mauthner, Wertheimstein, Epstein, and Pribam families) as the cause of working-class poverty in the textile and clothing trades, even though the actual share of Jewish industrialists was extremely low.[380] As economic forms of anti-Semitism merged with those of Catholic provenance, a role was also played by the fact that the overwhelmingly illiterate lower classes employed in this sector viewed with hostility the "cultural capital" of Jewish entrepreneurs and business people, who were not only literate, but conducted their businesses on the basis of calculation, bookkeeping, and rational strategy.

These contingent articulations of anti-Semitism, which did not amount to a systematic political narrative, and which Arthur Schnitzler characterized as "an emotion in numerous hearts so inclined and an idea with great possibilities of development," though "it did not play an important role politically or socially,"[381] only changed in the wake of the stock-market crash of 1873. The revolutionary year of 1848 had brought real progress in emancipation for the Viennese Jews, and—with the exception of what were at first only isolated attacks on Jewish entrepreneurs—it had not led to any acts of anti-Jewish violence, unlike the situation in other parts of the monarchy, for example Bratislava and Hungary. The personal involvement of Jewish intellectuals in the revolutionary events (Adolf Fischhof, Karl Tausenau, Avram Chajzes, and Hermann Jellineck)[382] rather led to an almost philo-Semitic attitude among the Viennese population, an example of this being the funeral for Rabbi Isak Noe Mannheimer, a victim of the March uprising, which was joined by a Catholic priest and Christian dignitaries. With the abolition of the restrictions set by the toleration decree of Joseph II, the full civic emancipation of the Viennese Jews in the wake of 1848 led to a material and cultural blossoming of Viennese Jewry and a rapid increase in number from between 6,000 and 7,000 thousand before 1848 to around 40,000 in 1869.[383] This Jewish population comprised a relatively large core of middle-class families (many of them born in Vienna) as well as new immigrants from Hungary, Slovakia, Bohemia, and Moravia. After the 1867 constitutional settlement, migration of Jews from Galicia increased, and in the following decades these formed a large and publicly visible section of the Viennese Jewish community, also marking its culture significantly.[384] By 1910 around 200,000 Jews lived in Vienna, and many of the new arrivals settled in the Leopoldstadt district, where they made up 34 percent of the population.[385]

The stock-market crash of 1873 and the ensuing recession not only led to a traumatic break in the assimilation and modernization efforts of Viennese Jews, but also divided them politically. The crash created the foundations for a modern anti-Semitism that not only made Jews an "accidental scapegoat" for economic crisis and stagnation in the pre-modern pattern, but formed the nucleus for economic conspiracy theories that identified Jews with the evils of laissez-faire capitalism[386] and made them the target of anti-liberal politics after the collapse of political liberalism. The overblown expectations of the stock-exchange miracle machine, which had infected not just the middle class but also many artisans and small traders as well, were vented on the Jews, and the crash was interpreted as a "Jewish betrayal" of the "Christian people."

Jewish reactions to this rise of a new kind of anti-Semitism, which mobilized large sections of the urban population, were mixed. One section, which included the leaders of the community and a large part of the assimilated bourgeoisie, sought to ignore the hostile mood and intensified their integration into the educated German-speaking world or into a professional middle-class culture.[387] Another section of bourgeois and middle-class Jews turned to politics and sought to reform the liberal party (Heinrich Friedjung) or in the wake of the liberals' defeat adhered to new post-liberal movements of the late Enlightenment (Victor Adler). Others, such as Dr. Josef Bloch, a rabbi who hailed from Galicia, espoused a variant of reformed liberal politics with a Jewish stamp and opposed both anti-Semitism and assimilated reformers such as Adler and Friedjung. Max Nordau, however, and above all Theodor Herzl countered the anti-Semitic project of Lueger's "Viennese homeland" with their own project of an "imagined community," designed to win for nationless Jews their own state as the context for emancipation and a bulwark against anti-Semitism.

Viennese Jewry at the turn of the century was divided socially, politically, and culturally and characterized by two extreme poles. On the one hand, those Jews who were assimilated or ready for assimilation, overwhelmingly from the upper bourgeoisie, saw themselves as a central part of the "modern" project inherent to civil society based on universalistic principles and committed to the ideas of the late Enlightenment. Their cosmopolitan orientation, however, still went together with a strong internal group coherence and distinct cultural identity.[388] On the other hand were the large number of Jewish immigrants from Galicia, who created an independent ghetto culture in the metropolitan context, still closely tied to orthodoxy and tradition, which in its foreignness, strangeness, and seclusion became the target of massive racist resentment. In contrast to the already long-established Jewish (upper) bourgeoisie, who had undergone a lengthy assimilation process and who as part of the way of the *haskala*, or Jewish Enlightenment, cultivated a Hebrew culture without particular external markings, the new immigrants were distinguished by their lifestyle and outwardly apparent religious customs, and were thus all the more readily subject to caricature, discrimination, and racist stereotyping.[389]

If Franz Schuhmeier had latched onto anti-Semitic resentment (which was already deeply diffused in Viennese society by the turn of the century, forming a political axis cutting right across different social groupings)[390] as a strategic device of the popular-modern, Lueger's anti-Semitism was something fundamentally different. Lueger's demarcation and defamation of Jews was designed to cover over the traumatic legacy of liberalism and use the new social divisions as the foundation for a policy of exclusion. Anti-Semitism represented in his political strategy not only an instrument of mass mobilization, but also an integral component of a new kind of political culture, rousing the masses against the (old) elites and the "integrated" against the "outsiders." Schuhmeier and the Social Democrats, for their part, took these social divisions onto their political agenda and prepared the entire city for a cultural program of inclusion. Against Lueger's politics of alterity they proposed a politics of anticipation and emancipation. Both Lueger and the Social Democrats certainly used the popular as a medium for their political mobilization, but in different constellations. Lueger sought to unite the disparate interests of the petite bourgeoisie by means of historicization and stereotyping; the Social Democrats imagined the future ennoblement of the proletariat as the social and cultural bearer of a new homogeneous city. Lueger instrumentalized the others—Jews and foreigners—as outsiders to keep his hold on power, while the Social Democrats integrated these in order to come to power. Their politics of anticipation ascribed the proletariat a function of creative destruction in the here and now in order to create a social order together with a freethinking, assimilated intellectual Jewry, in which both would be citizens and neither outsiders, both center and neither periphery.

Modernity as social text inscribed the transgression of Viennese society onto the city. This process drew on the oral and pre-modern cultures at the same time as it abolished them. It brought those aspects into modernity which could be made objects of inscription, scientific rationalization, education, and planning. It marginalized the rest in a dual way: on the one hand as a contingent and arbitrary past, to be excluded from the canon of memory, and on the other as an exotic construct lamented as "typically Viennese." This exotic construct was evoked as the mythological dimension of popular and populist politics and constituted the foundation of both Lueger's historicization of the city and the Social Democratic ennoblement of the proletariat. This last can be understood as an experiment to make the "other" marginalized by modernity, with its tracelessness and sense of loss, into a central reference point for politics and identity. In this way it compensates for the shock ensemble of the modern. However differently the intentions and interests of "democratic mass politics" might be constructed, they exhibit in their collective aspect the "same breath" that Robert Musil noted. The traceless "other" of modernity thus returns as a mythological moment of mass politics, it returns as a dream of social wholeness, cultural identity, and authenticity. It is articulated as a utopia originally stipulated by modernity. The traceless "other" is thus one of the essential foundations of this "short" twentieth century.

NOTES

1. Carl E. Schorske, *Fin-de-Siècle Vienna. Politics and Culture*, New York 1981.
2. Robert Musil, *The Man Without Qualities*, London 1995, p. 3.
3. Ibid., p. 4.
4. Georg Simmel, "Soziologie des Raumes" (1903), in G. Simmel, *Schriften zur Soziologie*, ed. H.-J. Dahme and O. Rammstedt, Frankfurt am Main 1983, p. 229.
5. See Richard Saage, "Otto Bauer," in Walter Euchner (ed.), *Klassiker des Sozialismus*, vol. 2, Munich 1991.
6. Otto Bauer, "Die Teuerungsrevolte in Wien," *Die Neue Zeit*, 29th year, September 1911, pp. 913–17. On the demonstration against price hikes and the subsequent wave of mass trials, see Wolfgang Maderthaner and Siegfried Mattl, "'… den Strassenexzessen ein Ende machen.' Septemberunruhen und Arbeitermassenprozeß 1911,' in Karl R. Stadler (ed.), *Sozialistenprozesse. Politische Justiz in Österreich 1870–1936*, Vienna/Munich/Zurich 1986, pp. 117–50.
7. *Arbeiter-Zeitung* (AZ), September 19, 1911, p. 1.
8. *Neue Freie Presse* (NFP), September 19, 1911, p. 1.
9. Peter Feldbauer, *Stadtwachstum und Wohnungsnot, Determinanten unzureichender Wohnunsversorgung in Wien 1848 bis 1914*, Vienna 1977, pp. 191ff.
10. Ibid., p. 193.
11. Bauer, "Die Teuerungsrevolte in Wien,' p. 914. The quantitative extent of homelessness is illustrated by a 1912 report of the Vienna police authority on the homeless shelter in Triesterstraße. According to this report, 29,522 individuals took refuge there in the first three months of that year, making a daily average of 324. The police commissioner for Favoriten reported a decline in the number of individuals reporting homeless from 367 in the first quarter of 1911 to 135 in the same period of 1912. A total of 4,574 homeless is given for the entire district. (Bundepolizeidirektion Wien, Archiv 1912/Scha V/1, "Obdachlose," GZ 227/4 of June 30, 1912.)
12. See Gerhard Melinz and Susan Zimmermann, "Stadtgeschichte und Modernisierung in der Habsburger Monarchie," in G. Melinz and S. Zimmermann (eds.), *Wien/Prag/Budapest. Urbanisierung, Kommunalpolitik, gesellschaftliche Konflikte*, Vienna 1996, p. 24.
13. Ministerium des Inneren (MdI), Präsidium (Präs), 9251, Tagesrapport 253 ex 1911.
14. Bauer, "Die Teuerungsrevolte in Wien," p. 916.
15. MdI, Präs, 9951, Pr.Z 2761/18, September 26, 1911.
16. MdI, Präs, 9069, Pr.Z. 2334/3, September 6, 1911.
17. MdI, Präs 9798, September 19, 1911 (copy of a note by the royal and imperial police authority to the royal and imperial Lower Austrian Stadthalterei on the matter of the measures taken by the police authority on September 17, 1911).

18. AZ, September 18, 1911, p. 3.
19. Ibid., p. 2.
20. Ibid.
21. MdI, Präs, ad 9951 Pr.Z. 2761/7, September 18, 1911.
22. AZ, September 18, 1911, pp. 2ff.
23. MdI, Präs, 9951, September 21, 1911.
24. NFP, September 18, 1911, p. 4.
25. MdI, Präs, 9951, Pr.Z.2761/6 and 2761/7, September 18, 1911.
26. AZ, September 18, 1911, p. 4.
27. NFP, September 18, 1911, p. 4.
28. MdI, Präs, ad 9951, Pr.Z. 2761/18, September 26, 1911.
29. MdI, Präs, ad 9951, Pr.Z. 2761/6, September 17, 1911.
30. MdI, Präs, ad 9951, Pr.Z. 2901/1, October 3, 1911.
31. AZ, September 18, 1911, p. 4.
32. NFP, September 18, 1911, pp. 1ff.
33. MdI, Präs, 9798, September 19, 1911.
34. MdI, Präs, 9951, Pr.Z. 2761/18, September 26, 1911.
35. NFP, September 18, 1911.
36. MdI, Präs, 9798, September 19, 1911.
37. AZ, September 19, 1911.
38. MdI, Präs, ad 9951, reports of Captains Eisenkolb and Holy.
39. Ibid.
40. MdI, Präs, ad 9951, Pr.Z. 2761/6, September 17, 1911.
41. MdI, Präs, 9798, September 19, 1911.
42. AZ, September 19, 1911.
43. The view that the events of September 17 represented principally a revolt of Ottakring street youth from the lowest social class is supported by a list that the police compiled of arrested persons by age. The value of this list, however, is reduced by the fact that the arrests were mostly made quite arbitrarily, and necessarily so. According to this list, out of a total of 263 arrested, 152 were under 25 and 111 over 25, 197 were single and 66 married or widowed. Of those arrested for criminal offences, 104 were younger than 25 and 47 older, 116 were single and 35 married. In the convictions for felony, the figure is more balanced with 11 younger than 25 and 11 older (17 single, 5 married), in those for misdemeanors individuals over 25 are in the majority with 21 compared with 16 (29 single, 8 married), and likewise in those sentenced by police courts, with 32 as opposed to 21 (35 single, 18 married or widowed). (MdI, Präs, ad 9951, Pr.Z. 2901/33.) The Social Democratic parliamentary group maintained in any case that there were only a handful of organized workers among the arrested and accused, and not a single member of the Social Democratic youth organizations. (Interjection by MPs David, Reumann, and comrades, House of Representatives, Stenographische Protokolle, addendum, 9th sitting of the 21st session on October 5, 1911.)
44. This is so-called *Rotwelsch*, a slang heavily saturated by Yiddish, and used by marginal social groups such as vagabonds, hawkers, beggars, (petty) criminals, etc., constantly changing with the social context.
45. Here and below, Bericht der Polizeidirektion, BPoldion Archiv, "Demonstrations, Teuerungsrevolte 1911."
46. AZ, September 18, 1911, p. 5.
47. MdI, Präs, 9951, Pr.Z. 2971/8, October 9, 1911.
48. AZ, September 18, 1911, p. 5.
49. See Wolfgang Slapansky and Uli Fuchs, "'Die G'stetten und der Ziegelteich'. Über die Grauzonen im Alltag und die Freiräume vor der Vorstadt" (unpublished manuscript), Vienna 1991.
50. Peter Heumos, *Agrarische Interessen und nationale Politik in Böhmen 1848–1889. Sozialökonomische und organisatorische Entstehungsbedingungen der tschechischen Bauernbewegung*, Wiesbaden 1979, pp. 70ff.
51. Jan Havranek, "Die ökonomische und politische Lage der Bauernschaft in den böhmischen Ländern," *Jahrbuch für Wirtschaftsgeschichte*, part II/1966, pp. 96–136, esp. p. 123.

52. Karl Renner, *An der Wende zweier Zeiten. Lebenserinnerungen,* Vienna 1946, p. 65.
53. Ibid., p. 59.
54. Ibid, pp. 59ff.
55. Michael John, "Zuwanderung in Österreich 1848–1914. Zu ökonomisch und psychologisch bedingten Faktoren der Zuwanderung in Österreich," in *Archiv. Jahrbuch des Vereins für Geschichte der Arbeiterbewegung,* Vienna 1988, pp. 102–32. The Jewish migration to Vienna, significant in both quantity and quality, represents a special case, and will be treated in more detail below in the chapter on the "transgression of the popular." In this context see the following secondary literature: John Bunzl, *Klassenkampf in der Diaspora. Zur Geschichte der jüdischen Arbeiterbewegung,* Vienna 1975; Anson Rabinbach, "The Migration of Galician Jews to Vienna," in *Austrian History Yearbook* 11/1976, pp. 44–54; Ruth Beckermann (ed.), *Die Mazzesinsel. Juden in der Wiener Leopoldstadt 1918–1938,* Vienna 1984; Klaus Hödl, *Als Bettler in die Leopoldstadt. Galizische Juden auf dem Weg nach Wien,* Vienna/Cologne/Weimar 1994; Marsha L. Rozenblit, *The Jews of Vienna, 1867–1914: Assimilation and Identity,* Albany 1983; Robert S. Wistrich, *The Jews of Vienna in the Age of Franz Joseph,* Oxford 1989; Pierre Genée, *Wiener Synagogen 1825–1938,* Vienna 1987; Pierre Genée, *Synagogen in Österreich,* Vienna 1992; and Steven Beller, *Wien und die Juden 1867–1938. Eine Kulturgeschichte,* Vienna 1993.
56. Otto Bauer, "Die Bedingungen der nationalen Assimilation," in *Der Kampf,* 5th year, March 1912, pp. 246–63, esp. p. 253.
57. See Monika Glettler, "The Acculturation of the Czechs in Vienna," in Dirk Hoerder (ed.), *Labor Migration in the Atlantic Economies. The European and North American Working Classes During the Period of Industrialization,* Westwood/London 1986, pp. 297–320. By the turn of the century at the latest, Vienna had become the largest Czech city in the world. The Czech share of the population was fairly constant in the second half of the nineteenth century, at between 16 and 18 percent, even if in the official censuses only between a quarter and a third of the population gave their origin, this signifying their arrival in the last six to eight years. With the reorientation of the center of gravity of production from the suburbs and outlying districts to the southern and eastern quarters of the city, and the corresponding rise of heavy industry, the settlement patterns of the immigrants also diversified. The most favored area of settlement was still Favoriten (with the Wienerberg brick works), where Czechs made up nearly a quarter of the population. Then came Brigittenau with around 15 percent, while Landstraße, Ottakring, Hernals, Leopoldstadt, and Rudolfsheim each also had a significant Czech population. In no fewer than eleven of the city's twenty districts at the turn of the century the Czech minority was above 5 percent, with a strikingly high proportion of female domestic servants in the residential and business quarters of the inner city as well as in the villa districts on the western periphery. In the outer districts, on the other hand, male workers were in the majority, mostly unskilled, with many branches such as building and brick-making undergoing higher than average fluctuations. See Gerhard Koller, "Die Zuwanderung nach Wien und Budapest," *Beiträge zur historischen Sozialkunde,* 1/1986, pp. 19ff, and Michael John and Albert Lichtblau, "Ceská Viden: Von der tschechichen Großstadt zum tschechischen Dor," in *Archiv. Jahrbuch des Vereins für Geschichte der Arbeiterbewegung,* Vienna 1987, pp. 34–55.
58. Renate Banik-Schweitzer, "Die Großstädte im gesellschaftlichen Entwicklungsprozeß in der zweiten Hälfte des 19. Jahrhundert," in Melinz and Zimmermann *Wien/Prag/Budapest,* pp. 40ff.
59. See "Restructuring the Rural," in John Urry, *Consuming Places,* London/New York 1995, pp. 77–89.
60. Wolfgang Maderthaner, "Das Entstehen einer demokratischen Massenpartei: Socialdemokratische Organisation von 1889 bis 1918," in W. Maderthaner and W.C. Müller (eds.), *Die Organisation der österreichischen Sozialdemokratie,* Vienna 1996, pp. 21–92, esp. pp. 72ff.
61. See in particular Raymond Williams, *The Country and the City,* London 1985.
62. Heidrun Suhr, "Die fremde Stadt. Über Geschichten vom Aufstieg und Untergang in der Metropole," in Thomas Steinfeld and Heidrun Suhr (eds.), *In der großen Stadt. Die Metropole als kulturtheoretische Kategorie,* Frankfurt am Main 1990, p. 25.

63. Henri Lefebvre, *The Urban Revolution*, London 2003, p. 33.
64. Ibid., pp. 118–19.
65. Richard Sennett, *Flesh and Stone: The Body and the City in Western Civilization*, London/Boston 1994, p. 21.
66. Ferdinand Hanusch, *Aus meinen Wanderjahren. Erinnerungen eines Walzbruders*, Reichenberg n.d. [1904], pp. 9ff.
67. Lucius Burckhardt, *Die Kinder fressen ihre Revolution*, Cologne 1985, p. 97.
68. Simmel, "Soziologie des Raumes," p. 234.
69. Gustav Haberman, *Aus meinem Leben. Erinnerungen aus den Jahren 1876–1877–1884–1896*, Vienna 1919, pp. 55ff.
70. Michael John and Albert Lichtblau, *Schmelztiegel Wien – einst und jetzt. Zur Geschichte und Gegenwart von Zuwanderung und Minderheiten*, Vienna/Cologne 1990, pp. 244ff.
71. Renner, *An der Wende zweier Zeiten*, p. 187.
72. Felix Salten, *Der Wurstelprater*, Vienna [1912] 1993, p. 76.
73. Ibid., p. 75.
74. Ibid., pp. 77ff.
75. Ibid., p. 81.
76. Schorske, *Fin-de-Siècle Vienna*, pp. 24ff.
77. Renate Banik-Schweitzer, *Zur sozialräumlichen Gliederung Wiens 1869–1934*, Vienna 1982, p. 88.
78. Elisabeth Lichtenberger, *Wien – Prag. Metropolenforschung*, Vienna/Cologne/Weimar 1993, pp. 62ff.
79. Walter Kieß, *Urbanismus im Industriezeitalter. Von der klassizistischen Stadt zur Garden City*, Berlin 1991, p. 184.
80. Ibid., p. 183.
81. Schorske, *Fin-de-Siècle Vienna*, p. 27.
82. Ibid., pp. 30ff.
83. These quarters were also interposed with homogeneous and self-contained proletarian housing estates. An example of this was Weinhaus in the "civil servants' town" of Währing, a gathering point for the rural proletariat, or the "Krim" (Crimea) proletarian settlement established by the firms Bensdorp, Danubia, and Gräf & Stift in Döbling, which was otherwise an exclusive district with its villas around the Hohe Warte and in Grinzing. Krim, located between Obkirchergasse, Arbesbachstraße, and Krottenbachstraße, was a typical case of a proletarian district laid out on a drawing board, with a comparatively high rate of petty crime and a generally bad reputation. Whenever there were break-ins, thefts, assaults, etc., in Döbling or Währing, the police regularly focused their investigations almost exclusively on this quarter. (Christine Klusacek and Kurt Stimmer, *Döbling. Vom Gürtel zu den Weinbergen*, Vienna 1988, p. 120.)
84. Gerhard Meißl, "Im Spannungsfeld von Kundenhandwerk, Verlagswesen und Fabrik. Der Herausbildung der industriellen Marktproduktion und deren Standortbedingungen in Wien vom Vormärz bis zum Ersten Weltkrieg," in Renate Banik-Schweitzer and Gerhard Meißl, *Industriestadt Wien. Die Durchsetzung der industriellen Marktproduktion in der Habsburgerresidenz*, Vienna 1983, pp. 99–151.
85. *Denkschrift der Vororte Wiens über die Folgen einer eventuellen Hinausrückung der Verzehrungssteuer-Linie*, Vienna 1884, p. 40.
86. Ibid., p. 47. The suburban communities in question were Hernals, Neulerchenfeld, Ottakring, Währing, Fünfhaus, Untermeidling, Rudolfsheim, and Sechshaus.
87. Max Winter, "Ein Tag in Ottakring. Wie das Volk lebt," in AZ, October 16, 1901.
88. Renate Banik-Schweitzer, "Production and Reduction of Social Segregation in Vienna Through the Inter-War Period', in Susan Zimmermann (ed.), *Urban Space and Identity in the European City 1890–1930s*, Budapest 1995, pp. 25–34.
89. Kieß, *Urbanismus im Industriezeitalter*, p. 188.
90. Chessboard-type grid quarters arose in the upper Donaustadt around Engerthstraße—a kind of disposal site for both architecture and the unwanted—in Völkert in Leopoldstadt, on the Landstraße in the Fasangassenviertel and on the site of the former Liechtensteinscher Garten, on the meadows in the "Blechernes Turmfeld," in Fünfhaus around

Henriettenplatz on the former country seat of Baron Arnstein, in Ottakring in the factory quarter around the brewery, as well as in Brigittenau, where Förster's regulation plan, however, was only partly combined with a correspondingly organized construction activity.

91. Wilhelm Kainrath, Friedl Kubelka-Bondy, and Franz Kuzmich, *Die alltägliche Stadterneuerung. Drei Jahrhunderte Bauen und Planen in einem Wiener Außenbezirk*, Vienna/Munich 1984, p. 45.
92. Christine Klusacek and Kurt Stimmer, *Ottakring. Vom Brunnenmarkt zum Liebhartstal*, Vienna 1983, pp. 70ff.
93. Hans Bobek and Elisabeth Lichtenberger, *Wien. Bauliche Gestalt und Entwicklung seit der Mitte des 19. Jahrhunderts*, Graz/Cologne 1966, p. 100.
94. Hans Tietze, *Wien. Kultur – Kunst – Geschichte*, Vienna/Leipzig 1931, p. 388.
95. Max Winter, *Meidlinger Bilder*, Vienna 1908, pp. 2ff.
96. Banik-Schweitzer, *Zur sozialräumlichen Gliederung*, p. 22.
97. "Fahrt nach Simmering," *Neues Wiener Tagblatt*, November 1, 1918, p. 3.
98. Ibid., pp. 4ff.
99. Ernst Eigner (in collaboration with Peter Pokay), "Die wirtschaftliche und siedlungsmäßige Entwicklung des Wiener Vorstadt- und Vorortebereichs," in *Wiener Wirtschaftschronik*, Vienna n.d. [1989], pp. 176–235, esp. p. 203.
100. See Heinrich Berg and Gerhard Meißl, "Floridsdorf, 1894–1904–1954–1994' (*Wiener Geschichtsblätter*, supplement 3/1994); Raimund Hinkel, *Wien XXI. Floridsdorf. Das Heimatbuch*, Vienna 1994.
101. Renate Schweitzer, "Die Entwicklung Favoritens zum Industriebezirk," *Wiener Geschichtsblätter* 4/1974, pp. 253–63.
102. Bobek and Lichtenberger, *Wien*, p. 299.
103. Max Winter,"Rund um Favoriten. Eine Skizze aus dem Leben der Enterbten," AZ, December 14, 1901.
104. Kainrath et al., *Stadterneuerung*, p. 121.
105. Sennett, *Flesh and Stone*, p. 359.
106. Lefebvre, *The Urban Revolution*, p. 28.
107. Sennett, *Flesh and Stone*, p. 359.
108. Kainrath et al., *Stadterneuerung*, p. 126.
109. See "Vienna and Paris, 1850–1930: The Development of the Modern City," in Merry E. Wiesner, Julius R. Ruff, and William B. Wheeler, *Discovering the Western Past. A Look at the Evidence*, Boston/Toronto 1993, pp. 201–39.
110. Lichtenberger, *Wien – Prag*, p. 71. In 1830 the "suburbs" within the customs barrier comprised two-thirds of the Viennese population. Although they experienced a high growth, especially in the mid nineteenth century and again around 1900, they reached a maximum of 900,000 by 1910, at which point the districts within the Gürtel now made up only 43 percent of the total, as against 52 percent in the former suburbs and 2.6 percent in the inner city. In 1870 the corresponding figures had been 63.7 percent, 28.7 percent and 7.6 percent, and in 1890, 50.4 percent, 44.6 percent and 5 percent. Favoriten, which was adopted as the tenth district in 1874 and was the only region outside the "Line" that formed part of the municipality, grew at an annual rate of 27.5 percent between 1870 and 1890, with a similar economic and social structure to the outlying suburbs. In Neulerchenfeld, until the end of the nineteenth century a settlement of workers, artisans, and casual laborers that was closely linked with the commercial suburbs, the population grew by 150 percent in the 1870's (the number of buildings rising by 110 percent and of households by 137 percent), followed by a further 75 percent the following decade. The mainly agricultural area to the east experienced a similar development in the 1860's. Floridsdorf, Groß-Jedlersdorf, and Donaufeld, the industrial bridgeheads on the far side of the Danube, grew at an annual rate of between 10 and 20 percent, and the twenty-first district as a whole by a further 50 percent in the first decade of the twentieth century.
111. Ibid., p. 71.
112. Ibid., p. 45.
113. Karl Ziak, *Von der Schmelz auf den Gallitzinberg. Gang durch die Gassen meiner Kindheit und die Geschichte Ottakrings*, Vienna/Munich 1987, p. 66.

114. The study by Feldbauer, *Stadtwachstum und Wohnungsnot* (details in note 9), is still the standard work on this subject.

115. See the pertinent references in Peter Feldbauer and Gottfried Pirhofer, "Wohnungsreform und Wohnungspolitik im liberal Wien?" in Felix Czeike (ed.), *Wien in der liberalen Ära*, Vienna 1978, pp. 148–90.

116. Ibid., p. 186.

117. Feldbauer, *Stadtwachstum und Wohnungsnot*, p. 161; see also Eda Sagarra, "Vienna and its Population in the Late Nineteenth Century. Social and Demographic Change 1870–1910," in G.J. Carr and Eda Sagarra (eds.), *Fin de Siècle Vienna*, Dublin 1985, pp. 178–207, esp. p. 186.

118. Feldbauer, *Stadtwachstum und Wohnungsnot*, p. 183.

119. Bruno Frei, *Wiener Wohnungs-Elend*, Vienna 1919, pp. 29ff.

120. Arthur Schnitzler, *Dream Story*, Copenhagen/Los Angeles 2003, p. 61.

121. Hilde Spiel, *Glanz und Untergang. Wien 1866 bis 1938*, Munich 1994, pp. 34ff.

122. Stefan Zweig, *The World of Yesterday*, London 1944, p. 22.

123. Schnitzler, *Dream Story*, p. 34.

124. Arthur Schnitzler, *My Youth in Vienna*, New York 1971, p. 92.

125. Emil Kläger, *Durch die Quartiere der Not und des Verbrechens. Wien und die Jahrhundertwende*, Vienna 1908.

126. Ibid., p. 13.

127. Winter, "Rund um Favoriten. "

128. Winter, *Meidlinger Bilder*, pp. 12ff.

129. AZ, December 14, 1901.

130. Ibid.

131. Kläger, *Durch die Quartiere der Not*, p. 72.

132. Ibid., pp. 55ff.

133. The young Adolf Hitler stayed for several months in the men's hostel on Meldemannstraße. See Brigitte Hamann, *Hitler's Vienna*, New York/Oxford 1999, pp. 158ff.

134. Kläger, *Durch die Quartiere der Not*, p. 140.

135. Ivan Cankar, *Vor dem Ziel. Literarische Skizzen aus Wien*, Klagenfurt/Celovec 1994, pp. 84ff.

136. Ibid., pp. 69ff.

137. Ibid., pp. 71ff.

138. Ibid., p. 59.

139. Ivan Cankar, *Pavliceks Krone. Literarische Skizzen aus Wien*, Klagenfurt 1995, pp. 7ff. (original mimeograph, 1900).

140. *Bericht des Wiener Stadtphysikats über seine Amtsthätigkeit und über die Gesundheitsverhältnisse der kk. Reichshaupt- und Residenzstadt Wien in den Jahen 1897–1899*, Vienna 1901, p. 425.

141. Ibid., p. 426.

142. Cited in Peter Haiko and Hannes Stekl, "Architektur in der industriellen Gesellschaft," in H. Stekl (ed.), *Architektur und Gesellschaft von der Antike bis zur Gegenwart*, Salzburg 1980, p. 289.

143. F. von Radler, "Die Volkszüge nach den Vororten in den Abendstunden," in *Wienerstadt. Lebensbilder aus der Gegenwart*, Prague/Vienna/Leipzig n.d., p. 105.

144. See note 144.

145. Max Winter, "Streifzüge durch die Brigittenau. Eine Studie aus dem Leben des Proletariats," in AZ, November 12, 1901.

146. Kieß, *Urbanismus*, p. 192.

147. It is in this connection that Donald Olson writes of:
the exuberant use of historical forms by suburban architects, for whom the façade was the kind of decoration to be chosen by the owner, with no necessary organic relationship to the building that lay behind. Architectural forms which in the hands of serious designers in the sixties had intellectual content by the eighties became frivolous disguises, intended to flatter the socia ambitions of modest suburban flat-dwellers. (Donald J. Olsen, *The City as Work of Art: London, Paris, Vienna*, New Haven/London 1986, p. 272.)

148. Tietze, *Wien*, p. 359.
149. Haiko and Stekl, "Architektur in der industriellen Gesellschaft," p. 288.
150. For a detailed description of the underlying demographic data, see Andreas Weigel, *Wien im demographischen Übergang. Bevölkerungsentwicklung einer Metropole im Modernisierungsprozeß*, Vienna 1998.
151. Michel de Certeau, *Das Schreiben der Geschichte*, Frankfurt am Main 1991, pp. 137ff.
152. Fred Heller, "Ottakring, Die Kleinstadt," *Der Tag*, September 16, 1923.
153. *Neues Wiener Tagblatt*, November 1, 1918.
154. "Der Wurstelprater," in AZ, July 17, 1910.
155. Olson, *The City as Work of Art*, p. 151.
156. Josef Schrank, *Die Prostitution in Wien in Historischer, Administrativer und Hygienischer Beziehung*, Vienna 1886, vol. 1, p. 310.
157. Simmel, "Soziologie des Raumes," p. 229.
158. Schrank, *Die Prostitution*, pp. 308ff.
159. Peter Stallybrass and Allon White, *The Politics and Poetics of Transgression*, Ithaca/New York 1986.
160. Ibid., p. 191.
161. Fredric Jameson, *The Political Unconscious: Narrative as a Socially Symbolic Act*, Ithaca 1986.
162. Stallybrass and White, *The Politics and Poetics of Transgression*, p. 5.
163. See Leonardo Benevolo, *Die Stadt in der europäischen Geschichte*, Munich 1993, p. 196.
164. NFP, May 1, 1890.
165. Friedrich Schlögel, *Gesammelte Schriften* (vol. 2, *Wiener Luft*), Vienna/Leipzig 1893, p. 151.
166. R. Eichhorn, "Ein Nachtrag zur Darlegung der materiellen Lage des Arbeiterstandes in Oesterreich. Floridsdorf und Umgebung, ein sociales Bild," in *Österr. Monatschrift für Christliche Socialreform, Gesellschaftwissenschaft, volkswirtschaftliche und verwandte Fragen*, vol. 6, Vienna 1884, p. 480.
167. Ibid., pp. 481ff.
168. "It was above all around the figure of the prostitute that the gaze and touch, the desires and contaminations, of the bourgeois male were articulated" (Stallybrass and White, *The Politics and Poetics of Transgression*, p. 137).
169. Salten, Der Wurstelprater, pp. 76ff.
170. Zweig, *The World of Yesterday*, p. 74.
171. Ibid.
172. Karin Jusek, *Auf der Suche nach der Verlorenen. Die Prostitutionsdebatten im Wien der Jahrhundertwende*, Vienna 1994.
173. Josefine Mutzenbacher, *Die Lebensgeschichte einer wienerischen Dirne, von ihr selbst erzählt*, Reinbek bei Hamburg 1978.
174. Ibid., p. 108.
175. Max Pollak, "Ein Monstreprozess gegen Jugendliche," in *Archiv für Kriminalanthropologie und Kriminalistik* (ed. Prof. Dr. Hans Gross), vol. 32, Leipzig 1909, pp. 1–28.
176. Ibid., p. 18.
177. Ibid., p. 16.
178. Ibid., pp. 24ff.
179. Cited after Hamann, *Hitler's Vienna*, p. 365.
180. Simmel, "Soziologie des Raums," p. 242.
181. Karl Renner, "Soziale Demonstrationen," in *Der Kampf*, 5th year, October 1911, pp. 2ff.
182. Gilles Deleuze and Félix Guatarri, *Anti-Oedipus. Capitalism and Schizophrenia*, London 1984.
183. Ivan Cankar, "Das Fräulein," in *Vor dem Ziel*, pp. 158ff.
184. *Wiener Bilder*, October 24, 1897, p. 8.
185. *Constitutionelle Vorstadt-Zeitung*, April 30, 1884.
186. *Wiener Bilder*, October 24, 1894, p. 8.
187. For more detail on the history and development of this site, see Wolfgang Slapansky, *Das kleine Vergnügen an der Peripherie. Der Böhmische Prater in Wien*, Vienna 1992, pp. 52–97.

188. *Illustriertes Wiener Extrablatt*, May 22, 1884.
189. Slapansky, *Das kleine Vergnügen*, pp. 82ff.
190. Alfons Petzold, *Das rauhe Leben. Roman eines Menschen*, Graz 1970, p. 385.
191. Felix Salten, *Das österreichische Antlitz. Essays*, Berlin 1910, pp. 57ff.
192. Schrank, *Die Prostitution*, p. 367.
193. Salten, *Der Wurstelprater*, pp. 75ff.
194. Petzold, *Das rauhe Leben*, p. 178.
195. Ibid., pp. 470ff.
196. Walter Benjamin, *Charles Baudelaire: A Lyric Poet in the Era of High Capitalism*, London 1973, pp. 35ff.
197. See Simmel:
     Small town life in antiquity as well as in the Middle Ages imposed such limits upon the movements of the individual in his relationships with the outside world and on his inner independence and differentiation that the modern person could not even breathe under such conditions. Even today the city dweller who is placed in a small town feels a type of narrowness which is similar. ("The Metropolis and Mental Life" [1903], in Georg Simmel, *On Individuality and Social Forms*, Chicago/London 1971, p. 33.)
198. Hanusch, *Aus meinen Wanderjahren*, pp. 11ff.
199. *Wiener Bilder*, October 20, 1897.
200. For a comprehensive discussion of mass and popular culture, see among others James Naremore and Patrick Branntlinger (eds.), *Modernity and Mass Culture*, Bloomington/Indianapolis 1991; also Dominic Strinati, *An Introduction to Theories of Popular Culture*, London/New York 1995.
201. Georg Simmel, *Das Individuum und die Freiheit. Essais*, Frankfurt am Main 1993, p. 195.
202. See Kaspar Maase, *Grenzenloses Vergnügen. Der Aufstieg der Massenkultur 1850–1870*, Frankfurt am Main 1997, pp. 38ff.
203. See Peter Laslett, *The World We Have Lost*, London 1965.
204. Schlögl, *Wiener Blut*, pp. 137ff.
205. Ibid., p. 138.
206. Schrank, *Die Prostitution*, p. 380..
207. See Friedrich Reischl, *Wien zur Biedermeierzeit. Volksleben in Wiens Vorstädten nach zeitgenössischen Schilderungen*, Vienna 1921, pp. 206ff.
208. Ibid., p. 207.
209. Franz Grillparzer, "Der arme Spielmann," in *Grillparzers sämtliche Werke in zwanzig Bänden*, ed. August Sauer, vol. 13, Stuttgart n.d., p. 226.
210. Ibid., p. 225.
211. Ibid., p. 227.
212. Mikhail Bakhtin, *Rabelais and His World*, Bloomington 1984.
213. Ibid.
214. F. Reischl, *Wien zur Biedermeierzeit*, p. 97.
215. M. Alland, *Licht- und Schattenbilder aus dem Wiener Leben*, Leipzig n.d., p. 29.
216. Ibid., p. 38.
217. Adolf Glaßbrenner, *Bilder und Träume aus Wien*, vol. 1, Leipzig 1836, p. 86.
218. Reischl, *Wien zur Biedermeierzeit*, p. 138. The *Engelmacherinnen* were readily available to carry out abortions in case of unwanted pregnancy. There were also occasional cases of deliberate killing of foster children.
219. Cited in Ferry Kovarik, *100 Jahre Ottakring bei Wien*, Vienna n.d. [1992], pp. 7–10.
220. Schrank, *Die Prostitution*, p. 278.
221. Ibid., pp. 288ff.
222. Karl Ziak, *Des heiligen Römischen Reiches größtes Wirtshaus. Der Wiener Vorort Neulerchenfeld*, Vienna/Munich 1979, p. 44.
223. Franz de Paula Gaheis, *Wanderungen und Spazierfahrten in die Gegenden um Wien*, vol. 7, Vienna 1804, pp. 96 and 117.
224. Ibid., p. 96.
225. Cited in Reischl, *Wien zur Biedemeierzeit*, p. 140.
226. Adolf Schmidl, *Die Kaiserstadt und ihre nächsten Umgebungen*, Vienna 1843, p. 337.

227. Glaßbrenner, *Bilder und Träume aus Wien*, vol. 2, p. 146.

228. Schrank, *Die Prostitution*, p. 280.

229. Ibid., p. 401.

230. Ibid., p. 403.

231. Cited in Ziak, *Von der Schmelz auf den Gallitzinberg*, p. 44.

232. Julius Rodenberg, *Wiener Sommertage*, Leipzig 1873, pp. 238ff.

233. The only case in which an inn with rich traditions was first converted into a cinema, then back into a dance and concert hall—an instance of popular culture referring to the old in a new form in the postwar era—was that of the Blaue Flasche.

234. On the history and development of the most important Viennese inns and places of entertainment, see the detailed and informative manuscript by Hans Pemmer in the Wiener Stadt- und Landesarchiv, "Alt-Wiener Gast- und Vergnügungsstätten" (in 3 vols), vol. 2, pp. 212–367.

235. Ingrid Ganster and Helmut Kretschmer, *Allweil lustig, fesch und munter* (*Wiener Geschichtsblätter*, supplement 2/1996).

236. The popular singers directly linked up with the tradition of the pre-1848 harpists: "In the Wurstelprater and Lerchenfeld a father, son, and daughter would sit around, all laughing heartily at the vilest dirty jokes from the mouths of so-called harpists, sugared by charming melodies and accompanied by characteristic expressions and gestures to heighten their effect." (Glaßbrenner, *Bilder und Träume aus Wien*, pp. 52ff.)

237. Schrank, *Die Prostitution*, vol. 1, p. 422.

238. Pemmer, *Alt-Wiener Gast- und Vergnügungsstätten*, vol. 2, pp. 226ff.

239. Schlögl, *Wiener Blut*, p. 147.

240. See Ziak, *Des heiligen Römischen Reiches größtes Wirtshaus*, pp. 105ff, and Kovarik, *Ottakring*, pp. 2–9.

241. See Stallybrass and White, *Transgression*, pp. 191ff.

242. The developed mass culture of postmodernism is not of course fully anticipated here, but its archaeology and structural apparatus are.

243. Norbert Rubey and Peter Schoenwald, *Venedig in Wien. Theater- und Vergnügungsstadt der Jahrhundertwende*, Vienna 1996.

244. In 1890 and 1894 artificial Venices had already been established in London and Berlin respectively; both, however, were aesthetically less unified, more "corridor-like" in their construction and built with less technical application.

245. Rubey and Schoenwald, *Venedig in Wien*, p. 70.

246. *Illustrierte Wochenpost*, December 26, 1930.

247. *Illustrierte Wochenpost*, January 2, 1931.

248. *Die Fackel*, no. 14, August 1899.

249. Rubey and Schoenwald, *Venedig in Wien*, p. 65.

250. See here Moritz Csáky, *Ideologie der Operette und Wiener Moderne. Ein kulturhistorischer Essay zur österreichischen Identität*, Vienna 1996.

251. Rubey and Schoenwald, *Venedig in Wien*, pp. 117ff.

252. On the function of the cinema in the specific Viennese popular context, see Helmut Gruber, *Red Vienna. Experiment in Working Class Culture*, New York/Oxford 1992, pp. 126ff.

253. See Dick Hebdige, *Hiding in the Light. On Images and Things*, London/New York 1988.

254. Werner Michael Schwarz, *Kino und Kinos in Wien. Eine Entwicklungsgeschichte bis 1934*, Vienna 1992, pp. 179ff.

255. Ibid., pp. 68 and 102ff.

256. See Monika Bernold, "Kino(t)raum. Über den Zusammenhang von Familie, Freizeit und Konsum," in *Familie: Arbeitsplatz oder Ort des Glücks*, Monika Bernold, Andrea Ellmeier, et al. Vienna 1989.

257. Schwarz, *Kino und Kinos in Wien*, p. 156.

258. Anna Staudacher, *Sozialrevolutionäre und Anarchisten. Die andere Arbeiterbewegung vor Hainfeld*, Vienna 1988; Michael John, ""Straßenkrawalle und Exzesse." Formen des sozialen Protests der Unterschichten in Wien 1880 bis 1918," in Melinz and Zimmermann, *Stadtgeschichte und Modernisierung*, Wien/Prag/Budapest, pp. 230–44.

259. Maderthaner, ",Das Entstehen einer demokratischen Massenpartei."

260. Renner, "Soziale Demonstrationen," pp. 1ff. (emphasis in the original).
261. On the development of the Mühlschüttel see Christiane Breznik, "Das Mühlschüttel in Floridsdorf. Ideologien und Instrumente der Stadtplanung verändern ein Quartier," Dipl.Arbeit, Vienna 1992.
262. Max Winter, "Alt- und Neu-Floridsdorf," AZ, December 6, 1903, p. 7; in a special supplement, Winter described the work and fate of the women scavengers in some detail: Going around a bend we almost collided with one of the scavengers. A wizened old woman stood before us, the traces of her work written all over her. Dirt was ingrained in the wrinkles of her face, almost encrusted with sweat ... Only now did I understand the relationship of the scavengers to the tenant of the place, who in this way acquires a host of unpaid workers, allowing them to keep the least valuable pickings for themselves. Even the dirt of the metropolis has its owner ... When I peered through the rain at the field in front of me, a fashionable lady suddenly appeared out of the dirt. A slender apparition in long evening gown, her hair under a protective cloth, she was outlined against the background of rain—a modern Venus on the rubbish heap. She was a young scavenger, and the evening gown was a finding from the metropolitan rubbish. ("Bilder aus dem XXI. Bezirk," AZ, July 15, 1902, p. 5.)
263. Ibid., p. 7.
264. Eichhorn, "Ein Nachtrag zur Darlegung der materiellen Lage des Arbeiterstandes in Oesterreich', p. 580.
265. Lefebvre, *The Urban Revolution*, p. 83.
266. Ibid.
267. Rudolf Eichhorn, *Die weißen Sklaven der Wiener Tramway-Gesellschaft*, Vienna 1885, p. 8.
268. Eugen Phillipovich, cited in Feldbauer and Pirhofer, "Wohnungsreform und Wohnungspolitik', p. 185.
269. Petzold, *Das rauhe Leben*, pp. 300ff.
270. Max Winter, "Liechtentaler Kinderelend," AZ, May 11, 1913.
271. Ibid.
272. Victor Adler, *Aufsätze, Reden und Briefe*, vol. 4, Vienna 1925, pp. 11–35.
273. See Wolfgang Maderthaner, "Die korporative Arbeitsverweigerung. Zur Entwicklung des industriellen Interessenkonflikts in Österreich 1890–1914," in *Archiv. Jahrbuch des Vereins für Geschichte der Arbeiterbewegung*, Vienna 1995, pp. 8–55, esp. 29 ff.
274. Women were the dominant and driving force in the strike. In the repeated riots and struggles with police and military, in which one person was killed in Brunn am Gebirge, women took the initiative as they did throughout the strike movement. "On the morning of April 18, a thousand or so brick-workers gathered on the loading site of the no. III and IV works and showered the loaders with bricks, while some women actually attacked the police. " Eight of the eleven people imprisoned as a result of these incidents were women (BPoldion, Archiv, Statistiken allgemein, 1895). The uprising ended with a great victory for the strikers and the recognition of their union organization.
275. NFP, April 25, 1895, pp. 5ff.
276. Cited from *Die Arbeitseinstellungen und Aussperrungen in Österreich während des Jahres 1895*, Vienna 1896, p. 260.
277. NFP, April 25, 1895, p. 6.
278. Lefebvre, *The Urban Revolution*, p. 19.
279. Ziak, *Von der Schmelz auf den Gallitzinberg*, p. 9.
280. Siegfried Weyr, *Von Lampelbrunn bis Hohenwarth. Durch Wiener Vorstädte und Vororte*, Vienna n.d., p. 83.
281. Felix Czeike, *Historisches Lexikon Wien*, vol. 5, Vienna 1997, p. 105.
282. See Klusacek and Stimmer, *Ottakring*, p. 85.
283. See Petzold, *Das rauhe Leben*, pp. 66ff.
284. Max Winter, "Schmelzbummel," AZ, September 25, 1913, p. 1.
285. Petzold, *Das rauhe Leben*, p. 72.
286. Weyr, *Von Lampelbrunn bis Hohenwart*, pp. 84ff.
287. U. Tartaruga, *Aus der Mappe eines Wiener Polizeibeamten. Kriminalistische Streifzüge*, Vienna/Leipzig 1919, p. 18.

288. Ibid., p. 23.

289. On the function and organization of adolescent street gangs, see the urban ethnographic works of Rolf Lindner, "Straße – Straßenjunge – Straßenbande. Eine zivilisationstheoretischer Streifzug', *Zeitschrift für Volkskinde*, vol. 79/1983, pp. 192–208, as well as his "Die wilden Cliquen zu Berlin. Ein Beitrag zur historischen Kulturanalyse," *Zeitschrift für historische Anthropologie*, vol. 3/1993, pp. 451–67.

290. *Illustriertes Wiener Extrablatt* (IWE), July 18, 1905, p. 5.

291. Public prosecutor Kleeborn in a court hearing, IWE, June 29, 1905, p. 11.

292. IWE, June 14, 1905, p. 6; June 15, 1905, p. 11; June 19, 1905, p. 6.

293. Schrank, *Prostitution*, vol. 1, p. 280.

294. Ibid., p. 279.

295. IWE, June 7, 1905, p. 4.

296. IWE, June 16, 1905, p. 4.

297. Ibid.

298. Tartaruga, *Aus der Mappe eines Wiener Polizeibeamten*, p. 20.

299. IWE, September 10, 1905, p. 17.

300. Egon Erwin Kisch, "Wie der Einbrecher Breitwieser erschossen wurde," in *Gesammelte Werke in Einzelausgaben*, vol. 6 (*Der rasande Reporter*), Berlin/Weimar 1993, p. 23.

301. "Der Bourgeois von St. Andrä," *Der Neue Tag* (NT), April 2, 1919, p. 1.

302. Report of the Vienna college correspondent, NT, April 6, 1919, p. 7.

303. Kisch, "Wie der Einbrecher Breitwieser erschossen wurde', p. 23.

304. Hermann Kraszna, *Johann Breitwieser. Ein Lebensbild*, 2 vols, Vienna n.d. [1921]; we thank the director of the Wiener Kriminalmuseum, Mag. Harald Seyerl, for the reference to this biography.

305. Ibid., vol. 1, pp. 110ff.

306. Ibid., p. 14.

307. Ibid., p. 13.

308. Christine Klusacek, "Der Einbrecherkönig aus Meidling," *Wien aktuell*, 5/1989, p. 16.

309. NT, April 2, 1919, p. 1.

310. Kraszna, *Johann Breitwieser*, vol. 1, p. 155.

311. Ibid., vol. 2, p. 21.

312. Ibid., pp. 147ff.

313. Reinhard Pohanka, "Johann Breitwieser 1919," in R. Pohanka, *Räuber, Mörder, Kindsverderber. Ein Kriminalgeschichte Wien*, Vienna 1991, p. 111.

314. Elias Canetti, *Crowds and Power*, London 2000, p. 56.

315. Eichhorn, *Die weißen Sklaven*, pp. 13ff.

316. Adler, *Aufsätze, Reden und Briefe*, vol. 4, p. 48.

317. Eichhorn, *Die weißen Sklaven*, pp. 46, 48.

318. Ibid., pp. 23ff.

319. Adler, *Aufsätze, Reden und Briefe*, vol. 4, p. 4.

320. Eichhorn, *Die weißen Sklaven*, p. 21.

321. Ibid.

322. Adler, *Aufsätze, Reden und Briefe*, vol. 4, p. 4.

323. Eichhorn, *Die weißen Sklaven*, p. 26.

324. Adler, *Aufsätze, Reden und Briefe*, vol. 4, p. 50.

325. Ibid., p. 37.

326. Ibid., pp. 50ff.

327. Bundespolizeidirektion (BPolulion), Archiv, 1888/St4, Streik der Tramwaybediensteten, Bericht des k.k. Bez.-Inspektors Tobias Anger.

328. BPoldion Wien, Archiv, 1893/St 5, 22"Straßenexzesse in Favoriten."

329. BPoldion Wien, Archiv, 1888/St 4, "Streik der Tramwaybediensteten," Bericht des k.k. Bez.Inspektors Tobias Anger.

330. Ibid., Bericht des k.k. Polizeidirektionconcipisten Roman Fuchs.

331. Ibid., Bericht des k.k. Polizei-Inspectors Camillo Windt.

332. Ibid.

333. Ibid., Bericht des k.k. Polizeidirektionconcipisten Roman Fuchs.

334. Ibid., Bericht des k.k. Bez.Inspektors Tobias Anger. he will deal elsewhere with anti-Semitism as a constitutive moment of popular context in the Viennese context.
335. Canetti, *Crowds and Power*, p. 20.
336. AZ, September 19, 1911.
337. *Der Morgen. Wiener Montagblatt*, February 17, 1913.
338. On the events of the funeral see the *Arbeiter-Zeitung, Volkstribüne, Neue Freie Presse, Neues Wiener Tagblatt, Der Morgen, Neues Wiener Journal* and *Illustriertes Wiener Extrablatt*, issues of February 17, 1913.
339. Musil, *The Man Without Qualities*, p. 53.
340. Pieter M. Judson, *Exclusive Revolutionaries. Liberal Politics, Social Experience, and National Identity in the Austrian Empire, 1848–1914*, Ann Arbor 1996.
341. Pieter M. Judson, *Wien brennt! Die Revolution von 1848 und ihre liberales Erbe*, Vienna 1998, p. 150.
342. Schorske, *Fin-de-Siècle Vienna*, pp. 117ff.
343. See John W. Boyer, *Political Radicalism in Late Imperial Vienna. Origins of the Christian Social Movement, 1848–1897*, Chicago/London 1981, pp. 44ff.
344. Ibid., p. 70.
345. Prime minister Kasimir, Count Badeni, of Polish origin, presented a language law that would require all government officials in Bohemia to show within four years proof of competence in Czech and German, including those in exclusively German- or Czech-speaking provinces. As this was interpreted as an arbitrary concession to the Czech nationalists, the German National party tried to hinder the progress of the law by obstructing the Reichstag, unleashing the greatest state crisis since 1848, leading to public unrest in Prague, Vienna, and northern Bohemia, and the decree of a state of emergency.
346. Felix Salten, *Das österreichische Antlitz. Essays*, Berlin 1910, pp. 133ff.
347. Ibid., pp. 131ff.
348. Ibid., pp. 132ff.
349. AZ, March 11, 1910.
350. Ibid.
351. Benedict R. Anderson, *Imagined Communities. Reflections on the Origin and Spread of Nationalism*, revised and extended version, London 1991.
352. See Boyer, *Political Radicalism in Late Imperial Vienna*, p. 419.
353. See Alexander Gerschenkron, *Economic Backwardness in Historical Perspective*, New York 1965.
354. Stephan Grossman, "Leger," in AZ, March 11, 1910.
355. Ibid., p. 2.
356. See Hamann, *Hitler's Vienna*, p. 300.
357. AZ, February 13, 1913.
358. NFP, February 12, 1913.
359. *Der Morgen*, February 17, 1913.
360. Leopold Spira, *Attentate, die Österreich erschütterten*, Vienna 1981, pp. 35–46. Paul Kunschak was condemned by a jury to be hanged. Following an appeal for mercy, which was basically directed against the death penalty, and a petition by the victim's widow, Cilly Schuhmeier, the verdict was commuted to life imprisonment. Kunschak was released during the revolution of November 1918.
361. For biographical details, see Wolfgang Maderthaner "Franz Schuhmeier," in *Österreichisches Biographisches Lexikon 1815–1950*, Vienna 1998, pp. 311ff.
362. Ludwig Wagner, "Der Volkstribun von Ottakring. Zum 20. Todestag Franz Schuhmeiers am 11. Februar," in *Kuckuck*, 7/1933, pp. 5ff.
363. Verein für Geschichte der Arbeiterbewegung (VGA), Altes Parteiarchiv, Mappe 69.
364. Victor Adler, *Briefwechsel mit August Bebel und Karl Kautsky*, Vienna 1954, p. 378.
365. Wolfgang Maderthaner and Siegfried Mattl, "Integration wider Willen? Die sozialdemokratische Arbeiterbewegung in Österreich um 1900," in *Traum und Wirklichkeit. Wien 1870–1930*, Vienna 1985, pp. 194–210.
366. *Die Zeit*, February 17, 1913.

367. Wilhelm Ellenbogen, Franz Shuhmeier, in: Der Kampf, Jg. 6, März 1913, 241–243.

368. Ibid., p. 241.

369. Hugo Schulz, "Ein Prachtkerl," in AZ, February 13, 1913.

370. Schuhmeier issue of *Glühlichter*, February 25, 1913.

371. Schulz, "Ein Prachtkerl."

372. Ellenbogen, Schuhmeier, p. 243.

373. Maderthaner, "Das Entstehen einer demokratischen Massenpartei," p. 75.

374. Ibid., p. 46.

375. Musil, *The Man Without Qualities*, p. 29.

376. Ibid., p. 7.

377. See here Michael Pollak, *Wien 1900. Eine verletzte Identität*, Constance 1997.

378. Grossmann, "Lueger," p. 1.

379. A particularly notorious case was that of "Anderl von Rinn," which persisted through to recent times and whose "commemoration" was banned by the Tyrol bishop Reinhold Stecher only a few years ago.

380. William O. McCagg Jr., *A History of the Habsburg Jews, 1670–1918*, Bloomington/Indianapolis 1989, pp. 84ff.

381. Schnitzler, *My Youth in Vienna*, p. 63.

382. Siegfried Mattl, *1848 – Die fatale Revolution*, exhibition catalog, Vienna 1998.

383. McCagg, *A History of the Habsburg Jews*, p. 145.

384. Klaus Hödl, *Als Bettler in die Leopoldstadt, Galizische Juden auf dem Weg nach Wien*, Vienna/Cologne/Weimar 1994.

385. John Bunzl, "Arbeiterbewegung, Judenfrage und Antisemitismus am Beispiel des Wiener Bezirks Leopoldstadt," in G. Botz, et al. (eds.) *Bewegung und Klasse, Studien zur österreichischen Arbeitergechichte*, Vienna 1978.

386. Peter Pulzer, *The Rise of Political Anti-Semitism in Germany and Austria*, Cambridge, Mass. 1988, p. 140.

387. Rozenblit, *The Jews of Vienna, 1867–1914,*, pp. 147ff.

388. Ibid.

389. See here Klaus Hödl, *Die Pathologisierung des jüdischen Körpers. Antisemitismus, Geschlecht und Medizin im Fin de Siècle*, Vienna 1997.

390. Pulzer, *Political Anti-Semitism*, p. 182.

BIBLIOGRAPHY

Adler, Victor. *Aufsätze, Reden und Briefe. Herausgegeben vom Parteivorstand der Sozialdemokratischen Arbeiterpartei Deutschösterreichs*, vol. 4, Vienna 1925.

Adler, V. *Briefwechsel mit August Bebel und Karl Kautsky. Gesammelt und erläutert von Friedrich Adler*, Vienna 1954.

Alland, M. *Licht- und Schattenbilder aus dem Wiener Leben*, Leipzig n.d.

Anderson, Benedict R. *Imagined Communities. Reflections on the Origin and Spread of Nationalism*, London 1991.

Bakhtin, Mikhail. *Rabelais and His World*, Bloomington 1984.

Banik-Schweitzer, Renate. *Zur sozialräumlichen Gliederung Wiens 1869–1934*, Vienna 1982.

Banik-Schweitzer, Renate. "Berlin-Wien-Budapest. Zur sozialräumlichen Entwicklung der drei Hauptstädte in der zweiten Hälfte des 19. Jahrhunderts," in Wilhelm Rausch, (eds.). *Die Städte Mitteleuropas im 19. Jahrhundert*, Linz 1983.

Banik-Schweitzer, Renate. "Production and Reduction of Social Segregation in Vienna through the Inter-War Period," in Susan Zimmermann, (eds.). *Urban Space and Identity in the European City 1890-1930s*, Budapest 1995.

Banik-Schweitzer, Renate. "Die Großstädte im gesellschaftlichen Entwicklungsprozeß in der zweiten Hälfte des 19. Jahrhundert," in: Melinz, Gerhard & Zimmermann, Susan (eds.). *Wien/Prag/Budapest. Urbanisierung, Kommunalpolitik, gesellschaftliche Konflikte*, Vienna 1996.

Bauer, Otto. "Die Teuerungsrevolte in Wien," *Die Neue Zeit*, 29th year, vol. 2, September 1911.

Bauer, O. "Die Bedingungen der nationalen Assimilation," *Der Kampf*, 5th year, March 1912.

Beckermann, Ruth (ed.). *Die Mazzesinsel. Juden in der Wiener Leopoldstadt 1918-1938*, Vienna 1984.

Beller, Steven. *Wien und die Juden 1867-1938. Eine Kulturgeschichte*, Vienna 1993.

Bender, Thomas and Carl E. Schorske (eds.). *Budapest and New York: Studies in Metropolitan Transformation, 1870-1930*, New York 1994.

Benevolo, Leonardo. *Die Stadt in der europäischen Geschichte*, Munich 1993.

Benjamin, Walter. *Charles Baudelaire. A Lyric Poet in the Era of High Capitalism*, London 1973.

Berg, Heinrich and Gerhard Meissl. "Floridsdorf, 1894–1904–1954–1994" (*Wiener Geschichtsblätter*, supplement 3/1994).

Bernold, Monika. "Kino(t)raum. Über den Zusammenhang von Familie, Freizeit und Konsum," in Monika Bernold, Andrea Eilmeier, et al. (eds.), *Familie: Arbeitsplatz oder Ort des Glücks*, Vienna 1989.

Bobek, Hans and Elisabeth Lichtenberger. *Wien. Bauliche Gestalt und Entwicklung seit der Mitte des 19. Jahrhunderts*, Graz/Cologne 1966.

Boyer, John W. *Political Radicalism in Late Imperial Vienna, Origins of the Christian Social Movement, 1848-1897*, Chicago/London 1981.

Boyer, Joh. *Culture and Political Crisis in Vienna. Christian Socialism in Power, 1897–1918*, Chicago/London 1995.

Boyer, M. Christine: *The City of Collective Memory: Its Historical Imagery and Architectural Entertainments*, Cambridge, Mass. 1996.

Breznik, Christiane. "Das Mühlschüttel in Floridsdorf. Ideologien und Instrumente der Stadtplanung verändern ein Quartier," Dipl.Arbeit, Vienna 1992.

Bunzl, John. *Klassenkampf in der Diaspora. Zur Geschichte der jüdischen Arbeiterbewegung*, Viennna 1975.

Bunzl, J. "Arbeiterbewegung, Judenfrage und Antisemitismus am Beispiel des Wiener Bezirks Leopoldstadt," in Gerhard Botz et al. (eds.), *Bewegung und Klasse, Studien zur österreichischen Arbeitergeschichte*, Vienna 1978.

Burckhardt, Lucius. *Die Kinder fressen ihre Revolution*, Cologne 1985.

Canetti, Elias. *Crowds and Power*, London 2000.

Cankar, Ivan. *Vor dem Ziel. Literarische Skizzen aus Wien*, Klagenfurt 1994.

Cankar, I. *Pavliceks Krone, Literarische Skizzen aus Wien*, Klagenfurt/Celovec 1995.

Cohen, Gary B. "Society and Culture in Prague, Vienna and Budapest in the Late Nineteenth Century," *East European Quarterly* 20/1986.

Csáky, Moritz. *Ideologie der Operette und Wiener Moderne. Ein kulturhistorischer Essay zur österreichischen Identität*, Vienna 1996.

Czeike, Felix. *Historisches Lexikon Wien*, vol. 5, Vienna 1997.

Danneberg, Robert. "Wer Sind die Wiener Wähler," *Der Kampf*, 6th year, June 1913.

De Certeau, Michel. *Das Schreiben der Geschichte*, Frankfurt am Main 1991.

Deleuze, Gilles and Félix Guattari. *Anti-Oedipus. Capitalism and Schizophrenia*, London 1984.

Eichhorn, Rudolf. "Ein Nachtrag zur Darlegung der Materiellen Lage des Arbeiterstandes in Oesterreich. Floridsdorf und Umgebung, ein sociales Bild," in *Österr. Monatsschrift für Christliche Socialreform, Gesellschaftswissenschaft, Volkswirtschaftliche und verwandte Fragen*, vol. 6, Vienna 1884.

Eichhorn, R. *Die weißen Sklaven der Wiener Tramway-Gesellschaft*, Vienna 1885.

Eigner, Ernst (with Peter Pokay). "Die wirtschaftliche und siedlungsmäßige Entwicklung des Wiener Vorstadt- und Vorortebereichs," in *Wiener Wirtschaftschronik*, Vienna n.d. [1989].

Feldbauer, Peter. *Stadtwachstum und Wohnungsnot. Determinanten unzureichender Wohnungsversorgung in Wien 1848 bis 1914*, Vienna 1977.

Feldbauer Peter and Gottfried Pirhofer. "Wohnungsreform und Wohnungspolitik im liberalen Wien?" in Felix Czeike, (ed.), *Wien in der liberalen Ära*, Vienna 1978.

Fischer, Gerhard. *Die Blumen des Bösen. Eine Geschichte der Armut in Wien, Prag, Budapest und Triest in den Jahren 1693 bis 1873*, Vienna 1994.

Frei, Bruno. *Wiener Wohnungs-Elend*, Vienna 1919.

Frisby, David. *Fragments of Modernity*, Cambridge, Mass. 1986.

Fuess, Jo Ann Mitchell. *The Crisis of Lower Middle Class Vienna, 1848–1892. A Study of the Works of Friedrich Schlögl*, New York 1997.

Gaheis, Franz de Paula. *Wanderungen und Spazierfahrten in die Gegenden um Wien*, vol. 7, Vienna 1804.

Genée, Pierre. *Wiener Synagogen 1825–1938*, Vienna 1987.

Genée, P. *Synagogen in Österreich*, Vienna 1992.

Gerschenkron, Alexander. *Economic Backwardness in Historical Perspective*, New York 1965.

Glaßbrenner, Adolf. *Bilder und Träume aus Wien*, vol. 1, Leipzig 1836.

Glettler, Monika. "The Acculturation of the Czechs in Vienna," in Dirk Hoerder (ed.), *Labor Migration in the Atlantic Economies. The European and North American Working Classes During the Period of Industrialization*, Westwood/London 1986.

Grillparzer, Franz. "Der arme Spielmann," in *Grillparzers sämtliche Werke in zwanzig Bänden*, ed. August Sauer, vol. 13, Stuttgart n.d.

Gruber, Helmut. *Red Vienna. Experiment in Working Class Culture*, New York/Oxford 1992.

Gulick, Charles A. *Österreich von Habsburg zu Hitler*, 5 vols. Vienna 1948.

Haberman, Gustav. *Aus meinem Leben. Erinnerungen aus den Jahren 1876–1877-1884–1896*, Vienna 1919.

Haiko, Peter and Hannes Stekl. "Architektur in der industriellen Gesellschaft," in Hannes Stekl (ed.), *Architektur und Gesellschaft von der Antike bis zur Gegenwart*, Salzburg 1980.

Hamann, Brigitte. *Hitler's Vienna*, New York/Oxford 1999.

Hanusch, Ferdinand. *Aus meinen Wanderjahren. Erinnerungen eines Walzbruders*, Reichenberg n.d. (1904).

Havranek, Jan. "Die ökonomische und politische Lage der Bauernschaft in den böhmischen Ländern," *Jahrbuch für Wirtschaftsgeschichte*, part II/1966.

Hebdige, Dick. *Hiding in the Light. On Images and Things*, London/New York 1988.

Heumos, Peter. *Agrarische Interessen und nationale Politik in Böhmen 1848–1889. Sozialökonomische und organisatorische Entstehungsbedingungen der tschechischen Bauernbewegung*, Wiesbaden 1979.

Hinkel, Raimund. *Wien XXI. Floridsdorf. Das Heimatbuch*, Vienna 1994.

Hödl, Klaus. *Als Bettler in die Leopoldstadt. Galizische Juden auf dem Weg nach Wien*, Vienna/Cologne/Weimar 1994.

Hödl, K. *Die Pathologisierung des jüdischen Körpers. Antisemitismus, Geschlecht und Medizin im Fin de Siècle*, Vienna 1997.

Horak, Roman and Wolfgang Maderthaner. *Mehr als ein Spiel. Fußball und populare Kulturen im Wien der Moderne*, Vienna 1997.

Jameson, Fredric. *The Political Unconscious: Narrative as a Socially Symbolic Act*, Ithaca 1986.

John, Michael. "Zuwanderung in Österreich 1848–1914. Zu ökonomisch und psychologisch bedingten Faktoren der Zuwanderung in Österreich," in: *Archiv. Jahrbuch des Vereins für Geschichte der Arbeiterbewegung*, Vienna 1988.

John, M. "Straßenkrawalle und Exzesse. Formen des sozialen Protests der Unterschichten in Wien 1880 bis 1918," in Gerhard Melinz and Susan Zimmermann (eds.), *Wien/Prag/Budapest. Urbanisierung, Kommunalpolitik, Gesellschaftliche Konflikte*, Vienna 1996.

John, Michael and Albert Lichtblau. "Ceská Viden: Von der tschechischen Großstadt zum tschechischen Dorf," in *Archiv. Jahrbuch des Vereins für Geschichte der Arbeiterbewegung*, Vienna 1987.

John, Michael and Albert Lichtblau. *Schmelztiegel Wien—einst und jetzt. Zur Geschichte und Gegenwart von Zuwanderung und Minderheiten*, Vienna/Cologne 1990.

Johnson, Lonnie R. *Central Europe. Enemies, Neighbors, Friends*, Oxford 1996.

Judson, Pieter M. *Exclusive Revolutionaries. Liberal Politics, Social Experience, and National Identity in The Austrian Empire, 1848–1914*, Ann Arbor 1996.

Judson, P. *Wien brennt! Die Revolution von 1848 und ihre liberales Erbe*, Vienna 1998.

Jusek, Karin. *Auf der Suche nach der Verlorenen. Die Prostitutionsdebatten Wien der Jahrhundertwende*, Vienna 1994.

Kainrath, Wilhelm, Friedl Kubelka-Bondy, and Franz Kuzmich. *Die alltägliche Stadterneuerung. Drei Jahrhunderte Bauen und Planen in einem Wiener Außenbezirk*, Vienna/Munich 1984.

Kann, Robert A. *A History of the Habsburg Empire 1526–1918*, Los Angeles 1974.

Kern, Stephen. *The Culture of Time and Space 1880–1918*, Cambridge, Mass. 1983.

Kieß, Walter. *Urbanismus im Industriezeitalter. Von der klassizistischen Stadt zur Garden City*, Berlin 1991.

Kisch, Egon Erwin. "Wie der Einbrecher Breitwieser erschossen wurde," in *Gesammelte Werke in Einzelausgaben*, vol. 6 (*Der rasende Reporter*), Berlin/Weimar 1993.

Kläger, Emil. *Durch die Quartiere der Not und des Verbrechens. Wien und die Jahrhundertwende*, Vienna 1908.

Klusacek, Christine. "Der Einbrecherkönig aus Meidling," *Wien aktuell*, 5/1989.

Klusacek, Christine and Kurt Stimmer. *Döbling. Vom Gürtel zu den Weinbergen*, Vienna 1988.

Klusacek, Christine and Kurt Stimmer. *Ottakring. Vom Brunnenmarkt zum Liebhartstal*, Vienna 1983.

Koller, Gerhard. "Die Zuwanderung nach Wien und Budapest," *Beiträge zur historischen Sozialkunde* 1/1986.

Kovarik, Ferry. *100 Jahre Ottakring bei Wien*, Vienna n.d. [1992].

Kraszna, Hermann. *Johann Breitwieser. Ein Lebensbild*, 2 vols., Vienna n.d. [1921].

Laslett, Peter. *The World We Have Lost*, London 1965.

Lefebvre, Henri. *The Urban Revolution*, London 2003.

Legates, Richard T. and Frederic Stout (eds.). *The City Reader*, London/New York 1996. Lichtenberger, Elisabeth. *Wien—Prag. Metropolenforschung*, Vienna/Cologne/Weimar 1993.

Lindner, Rolf. "Straße — Straßenjunge — Straßenbande. Ein zivilisationstheoretischer Streifzug," *Zeitschrift für Volkskunde*, 79/1983.

Lindner, R. "Die wilden Cliquen zu Berlin. Ein Beitrag zur historischen Kulturanalyse," *Zeitschrift für historische Anthropologie*, 3/1993.

Lindner, R. *The Reportage of Urban Culture. Robert Park and the Chicago School*, Cambridge 1996.

Maase, Kaspar. *Grenzenloses Vergnügen. Der Aufstieg der Massenkultur 1850–1970*, Frankfurt am Main 1997.

McCagg Jr. William O.: *A History of the Habsburg Jews, 1670–1918*, Bloomington/Indianapolis 1989.

Maderthaner, Wolfgang. "Die korporative Arbeitsverweigerung. Zur Entwicklung des industriellen Interessenkonflikts in Österreich 1890-1914," in *Archiv. Jahrbuch des Vereins für Geschichte der Arbeiterbewegung*, Vienna 1995.

Maderthaner, Wolfgang "Das Entstehen einer demokratischen Massenpartei: Sozialdemokratische Organisation von 1889 bis 1918," in W. Maderthaner and Wolfgang C. Müller (eds.), *Die Organisation der österreichischen Sozialdemokratie*, Vienna 1996.

Maderthaner, Wolfgang "Franz Schuhmeier," in *Österreichisches Biographisches Lexikon 1815–1950*, Vienna 1998.

Maderthaner, Wolfgang and Siegfried Mattl. "Integration wider Willen? Die sozialdemokratische Arbeiterbewegung in Österreich um 1900," in *Traum und Wirklichkeit. Wien 1870–1930*, Vienna 1985.

Maderthaner, Wolfgang and Siegfried Mattl. "'... den Straßenexzessen ein Ende machen.' Septemberunruhen und Arbeitermassenprozeß 1911," in Karl R. Stadler (ed.), *Sozialistenprozesse. Politische Justiz in Österreich 1870–1936*, Vienna/Munich/Zurich 1986.

Maderthaner, Wolfgang and Lutz Musner. "Vorstadt—die entern Gründ' der Moderne," in: Ferdinand Opll and Karl Fischer (eds.). *Studien zur Wiener Geschichte (Jahrbuch des Vereins für Geschichte der Stadt Wien*, vols 52/53), Vienna 1996/1997.

Marinelli-König, Gertraud (ed.). *Wien als Magnet? Schriftsteller aus Ost-, Ostmittel- und Südeuropa über die Stadt*, Vienna 1996.

Matsuda, Matt K. *The Memory of the Modern*, Oxford 1996.

Mattl, Siegfried. *1848—Die fatale Revolution*, Vienna 1998.

Meißl, Gerhard. "Im Spannungsfeld von Kundenhandwerk, Verlagswesen und Fabrik. Die Herausbildung der industriellen Marktproduktion und deren Standortbedingungen in Wien vom Vormärz bis zum Ersten Weltkrieg," in Renate Banik-Schweitzer and Gerhard Meißl, *Industriestadt Wien. Die Durchsetzung der industriellen Marktproduktion in der Habsburgerresidenz*, Vienna 1983.

Melinz, Gerhard and Susan Zimmermann. "Stadtgeschichte und Modernisierung in der Habsburger Monarchie," in: G. Melinz and S. Zimmermann (eds.), *Wien/Prag/Budapest. Urbanisierung, Kommunalpolitik, gesellschaftliche Konflikte*, Vienna 1996.

Musil, Robert. *The Man Without Qualities*, London 1995.

Mutzenbacher, Josefine. *Die Lebensgeschichte einer wienerischen Dirne, von ihr selbst erzählt*, Reinbek bei Hamburg, 1978.

Naremore, James and Patrick Branntlinger (eds.). *Modernity and Mass Culture*, Bloomington/Indianapolis 1991.

Olson, Donald J. *The City as Work of Art. London, Paris, Vienna*, New Haven/London 1986.

Pemmer, Hans. *Alt-Wiener Gast- und Vergnügungsstätten*, 3 vols, Vienna n.d. manuscpript.

Petzold, Alfons. *Das rauhe Leben. Roman eines Menschen*, Graz 1970.

Pollak, Max. "Ein Monstreprozess gegen Jugendliche," in *Archiv für Kriminalanthropologie und Kriminalistik* (ed. Prof. Dr. Hans Gross), vol. 32, Leipzig 1909.

Pollak, Michael. *Wien 1900. Eine verletzte Identität*, Constance 1997.

Pulzer, Peter. *The Rise of Political Anti-Semitism in Germany and Austria*, Cambridge, Mass. 1988.

Rabinbach, Anson. "The Migration of Galician Jews to Vienna," in *Austrian History Yearbook* 11/1976.

Radler, F. von. "Die Volkszüge nach den Vororten in den Abendstunden," in *Wienerstadt. Lebensbilder aus der Gegenwart*, Prague/Vienna/Leipzig n.d.

Reischl, Friedrich. *Wien zur Biedermeierzeit. Volksleben in Wiens Vorstädten nach zeitgenössischen Schilderungen*, Vienna 1921.

Renner, Karl. "Soziale Demonstrationen," *Der Kampf*, 5th year, October 1911.

Renner, K. *An der Wende zweier Zeiten. Lebenserinnerungen*, Vienna 1946.

Rodenberg, Julius. *Wiener Sommertage*, Leipzig 1873.

Rozenblit, Marsha L. *The Jews of Vienna, 1867–1914: Assimilation and Identity*, Albany 1983.

Rubey, Norbert and Peter Schoenwald. *Venedig in Wien. Theater- und Vergnügungsstadt der Jahrhundertwende*, Vienna 1996.

Saage, Richard. "Otto Bauer," in: Walter Euchner (ed.), *Klassiker des Sozialismus*, vol. 2, Munich 1991.

Sagarra, Eda. "Vienna and its Population in the Late Nineteenth Century. Social and Demographic Change 1870–1910," in G.J. Carr and Eda Sagarra (eds.), *Fin-de-Siècle Vienna*, Dublin 1985.

Salten, Felix. *Das österreichische Antlitz. Essays*, Berlin 1910.

Salten, Felix. *Der Wurstelprater*, Vienna 1993. (Vienna/Leipzig 1912).

Schlögl, Friedrich: *Gesammelte Schriften*, Vienna/Leipzig 1893.

Schlör, Joachim. *Nights in the Big City. Paris —Berlin —London 1840–1930*, London 1998.

Schmidl, Adolf. *Die Kaiserstadt und ihre nächsten Umgebungen*, Vienna 1843.

Schnitzler, Arthur. *My Youth in Vienna*, New York 1971.

Schnitzler, A. *Dream Story*, Copenhagen/Los Angeles 2003.

Schorske, Carl E. *Fin-de-Siècle Vienna. Politics and Culture*, New York 1981.

Schrank, Josef. *Die Prostitution in Wien in Historischer, Administrativer und Hygienischer Beziehung*, Vienna 1886.

Schwarz, Werner Michael. *Kino und Kinos in Wien. Eine Entwicklungsgeschichte bis 1934*, Vienna 1992.

Schweitzer, Renate. "Die Entwicklung Favoritens zum Industriebezirk," *Wiener Geschichtsblätter* 4/1974.

Sennett, Richard. *Flesh and Stone: The Body and the City in Western Civilization*, London/Boston 1994.

Simmel, Georg. *On Individuality and Social Forms*, Chicago/London 1971.

Simmel, Georg: "Soziologie des Raumes," in G. Simmel, *Schriften zur Soziologie*, ed. H.-J. Dahme and O. Rammstedt, Frankfurt am Main 1983.

Slapansky, Wolfgang. *Das kleine Vergnügen an der Peripherie. Der Böhmische Prater in Wien*, Vienna 1992.

Slapansky, Wolfgang and Uli Fuchs. "'Die Gstetten und der Ziegelteich'. Über die Grauzonen im Alltag und die Freiräume vor der Vorstadt" (unpublished manuscript) Vienna 1991.

Spiel, Hilde. *Glanz und Untergang. Wien 1866 bis 1938*, Munich 1994.

Spira, Leopold. *Attentate, die Österreich erschütterten*, Vienna 1981.

Stallybrass, Peter and Allon White. *The Politics and Poetics of Transgression*, Ithaca/New York 1986.

Staudacher, Anna. *Sozialrevolutionäre und Anarchisten. Die andere Arbeiterbewegung vor Hainfeld*, Vienna 1988.

Strinati, Dominic. *An Introduction to Theories of Popular Culture*, London/New York 1995.

Suhr, Heidrun. "Die fremde Stadt. Über Geschichten vom Aufstieg und Untergang in der Metropole," in: Thomas Steinfeld and Heidrun Suhr (eds.), *In der großen Stadt. Die Metropole als kulturtheoretische Kategorie*, Frankfurt am Main 1990.

Tartaruga, U. *Aus der Mappe eines Wiener Polizeibeamten. Kriminalistische Streifzüge*, Vienna/Leipzig 1919.

Tietze, Hans. *Wien. Kultur—Kunst—Geschichte*, Vienna/Leipzig 1931.

Urry, John. *Consuming Places*, London/New York 1995.

Weyr, Siegfried. *Von Lampelbrunn bis Hohenwarth. Durch Wiener Vorstädte und Vororte*, Vienna n.d.

Wiesner, Merry E., Julius R. Ruff, and William B. Wheeler. *Discovering the Western Past. A Look at the Evidence*, Boston/Toronto 1993.

Williams, Raymond. *The Country and the City*, London 1985.

Winter, Max. "Ein Tag in Ottakring. Wie das Volk lebt," AZ, October 16, 1901.

Winter, M. "Streifzüge durch die Brigittenau. Eine Studie aus dem Leben des Proletariats," AZ, November 12, 1901.

Winter, M. "Rund um Favoriten. Eine Skizze aus dem Leben der Enterbten," AZ, December 14, 1901.

Winter, M. "Alt- und Neu-Floridsdorf," AZ, December 6, 1903.

Winter, M. *Meidlinger Bilder*, Vienna 1908.

Winter, M. "Liechtentaler Kinderelend," *Arbeiter-Zeitung* (AZ), May 11, 1913.

Winter, M. "Schmelzbummel," AZ, September 25, 1913.

Wistrich, Robert S. *The Jews of Vienna in the Age of Franz Joseph*, Oxford 1989.

Ziak, Karl. *Des heiligen Römischen Reiches größtes Wirtshaus. Der Wiener Vorort Neulerchenfeld*, Vienna/Munich 1979.

Ziak, K. *Von der Schmelz auf den Gallitzinberg. Gang durch die Gassen meiner Kindheit und die Geschichte Ottakrings*, Vienna/Munich 1987.

Zimmermann, Susan (ed.). *Urban Space and Identity in the European City 1890–1930s*, Budapest 1995.

Zweig, Stefan. *The World of Yesterday*, London 1944.

Newspapers and Periodicals

Arbeiter-Zeitung (AZ): 1901, 1902, 1910, 1911, 1913.

Constitutionelle Vorstadt-Zeitung: 1884.

Die Fackel: 1899.

Glühlichter: 1913.

Illustriertes Wiener Extrablatt (IWE): 1884, 1905.

Illustrierte Wochenpost: 1930, 1931.

Der Morgen. Wiener Montagblatt: 1913.

Neue Freie Presse (NFP): 1890, 1895, 1911, 1913.

Neues Wiener Tagblatt: 1918.

Der Neue Tag (NT): 1919.

Volkstribüne: 1913.

Wiener Bilder: 1894, 1897.

Primary Sources

Die Arbeitseinstellungen und Aussperrungen in Österreich während des Jahres 1895, Vienna 1896.

Bericht des Wiener Stadtphysikats über seine Amtstätigkeit und über die Gesundheitsverhältnisse der kk. Reichshaupt- und Residenzstadt Wien in den Jahren 1897-1899, Vienna 1901.

Denkschrift der Vororte Wiens über die Folgen einer eventuellen Hinausrückung der Verzehrungssteuer-Linie, Vienna 1884.

Österreichisches Staatsarchiv

Ministerium des Inneren (MdI), Präsidium (Präs), 9251, Tagesrapport 253 ex 1911.

MdI, Präs, 9069, Pr.Z. 2334/3, September 6, 1911.

MdI, Präs 9798, September 19, 1911 (copy of a note by the royal and imperial police authority to the royal and imperial Lower Austrian Stadthalterei on the matter of measures taken by the police authority on September 17, 1911).

MdI, Präs, ad 9951 Pr.Z. 2761/7, September 18, 1911.

MdI, Präs, 9951, September 21, 1911.

MdI, Präs, 9951, Pr.Z. 2761/6 and 2761/7, September 18, 1911.

MdI, Präs, ad 9951, Pr.Z. 2761/18, September 26, 1911.

MdI, Präs, ad. 9951, Pr.Z. 2761/6, September 17, 1911.

MdI, Präs, ad 9951, Pr.Z. 2901/1, October 3, 1911.

MdI, Präs, 9798, September 19, 1911.

MdI, Präs, 9951, Pr.Z. 2761/18, September 26, 1911.

MdI, Präs, ad 9951, reports of Captains Eisenkolb and Holy

MdI, Präs 9951, Pr.Z. 2971/8, October 9, 1911.

Archiv der Bundespolizeidirektion Wien

Bericht der Polizeidirektion, BPoldion Archiv, "Demonstrationen, Teuerungsrevolte 1911."

BPoldion Wien, Archiv 1893/St 5, "Straßenexzesse in Favoriten."

Bundespolizeidirektion Wien (BPoldion), Archiv, 1888/St 4, "Streik der Tramway bediensteten."

Verein für Geschichte der Arbeiterbewegung (VGA).

Altes Parteiarchiv, Mappe 69.

Index